The European Union: How Does It Work?

The New European Union Series

Series Editors: John Peterson and Helen Wallace

The European Union is both the most successful modern experiment in international cooperation and a daunting analytical challenge to students of politics, economics, history, law, and the social sciences. The EU of the twenty-first century will be fundamentally different from its earlier permutations, as monetary union, eastern enlargement, a new defence role, and globalization all create pressures for a more complex, differentiated, and truly new European Union.

The New European Union series brings together the expertise of leading scholars writing on major aspects of EU politics for an international readership.

The series offers lively, accessible, reader-friendly, research-based textbooks on:

Policy-Making in the European Union

The Institutions of the European Union

The History of European Integration

Theorizing Europe

The EU's Member States

The International Relations of the European Union

The European Union: How Does it Work?

The European Union: How Does It Work?

Edited by

Elizabeth Bomberg
and
Alexander Stubb

OXFORD
UNIVERSITY PRESS

OXFORD

UNIVERSITY PRESS

Great Clarendon Street, Oxford OX2 6DP

Oxford University Press is a department of the University of Oxford.
It furthers the University's objective of excellence in research, scholarship,
and education by publishing worldwide in

Oxford New York

Auckland Bangkok Buenos Aires Cape Town Chennai
Dar es Salaam Delhi Hong Kong Istanbul Karachi Kolkata
Kuala Lumpur Madrid Melbourne Mexico City Mumbai Nairobi
São Paulo Shanghai Taipei Tokyo Toronto

Oxford is a registered trade mark of Oxford University Press
in the UK and in certain other countries

Published in the United States
by Oxford University Press Inc., New York

© Elizabeth Bomberg and Alexander Stubb, 2003

The moral rights of the authors have been asserted

Database right Oxford University Press (maker)

First published 2003

British Library Cataloguing in Publication Data
Data available

Library of Congress Cataloging in Publication Data
Data available

ISBN 0-19-924766-8

1 3 5 7 9 10 8 6 4 2

Typeset in Adobe Minion
by RefineCatch Limited, Bungay, Suffolk
Printed in Great Britain by
T.J. International Ltd, Padstow, Cornwall

Outline contents

Part I Background

Part II Major Actors

Part III Policies and Policy-Making

Part IV Current Issues and Trends

Detailed contents

Preface and Acknowledgements

We are delighted to offer the third book in the New European Union series published by Oxford University Press. The first two offered rich analyses for the advanced student of the EU policy-making system (Wallace and Wallace 2000) and its institutions (Peterson and Shackleton 2002). The primary mission of this book is to *introduce* the European Union to students and the curious general reader. We want to explain how the EU *really* works, how to understand it, and why it is worth the effort.

The idea of the book was easy to conceive. Both we and the series editors wanted to fill a gap in the market by producing an accessible, authoritative, clear, and lively textbook on the EU. The trick, we believed, was to bring together contributors with academic expertise, teaching experience, *and* hands-on knowledge of the EU and how it worked. Of course, actually producing a lively and coherent edited text on the EU is not as easy as recognizing the need for one. Pulling it off requires a dedicated and hard-working team of contributors, editors, assistants, readers, reviewers, and production staff. We lucked out on all counts.

Our team of contributors is top rate. It includes academics with expertise in key areas of EU politics and policy, lecturers with years of experience teaching students about the EU and its mysteries, and practitioners with first-hand knowledge. Several of the authors work or have worked in one of the EU's institutions, or in a member state's administration, or for a non-governmental organization, or in Brussels-based journalism. We thank our cast of contributors for sharing their expertise, but also for showing tremendous patience. All endured very active editing from our end; all were willing to provide yet another draft, make yet another change, and respond to yet another request.

We wish to acknowledge in particular the extraordinarily help offered by the series editors, John Peterson and Helen Wallace. Their unflagging support, often in difficult circumstances, extended well beyond the call of editorial duty.

The team also included the production staff of Oxford University Press whose professionalism is second to none. We extend special thanks to Angela Griffin for launching the project, and Sue Dempsey for seeing it through. We are grateful also to Ned Staples (University of Edinburgh) for his extremely able editorial assistance, especially on the glossary, bibliography, and tables.

More generally, the book has benefited enormously from the comments and suggestions received from students, reviewers, and colleagues. Any introductory text worth its muster will reflect the issues, concerns, and questions raised by its intended audience—students. We have thus gratefully received the comments and suggestions offered by students at Stirling, Edinburgh, and the College of Europe (Bruges) especially those who were brave enough to read draft chapters.

Three anonymous reviewers provided exceptionally useful comments on the draft, and the final product is much better because of their guidance. Specific chapters or boxes were read and helpfully commented on by Simon Bulmer (University of Manchester), Lynn Dobson, John Ravenhill, Richard McAllister, Andrew Scott, and Ned Staple (all of University of Edinburgh). For additional commentary and fact-finding, we wish to thank Torben Runge Johansen, Lars Mitek Pedersen, Sylvie Goulard, Mario Nava, Peter Sandler, Owen Sloman, Carola Bouton, and Vera Kotrschal from the Commission, and Chris Reynolds from the College of Europe. The end result—we hope—of this intensely collaborative project is an animated and comprehensible introduction to the EU and how it works.

Finally we extend a last, truly non-academic note of gratitude to our families for their extraordinary patience and unconditional support. We could not have made it without you.

Elizabeth Bomberg and Alexander Stubb

Edinburgh and Brussels
July 2002

Figures

Boxes

Tables

List of Abbreviations and Acronyms

ACP	African, Caribbean, and Pacific countries
APEC	Asia Pacific Economic Cooperation forum
ASEAN	Association of South-East Asian Nations
BEUC	Bureau Européen des Union de Consommateurs (European Consumers Organization)
CAP	Common Agricultural Policy
CCP	Common Commercial Policy
CFSP	Common Foreign and Security Policy
CIs	Community Initiatives
COPA	Committee of Professional Agriculture Organizations
CoR	Committee of the Regions and Local Authorities
Coreper	Committee of Permanent Representatives
DG	Directorate-General (European Commission)
EC	European Community
ECB	European Central Bank
ECHO	European Community Humanitarian Office
ECJ	European Court of Justice
ECOFIN	(Council of) Economic and Finance Ministers
ECSC	European Coal and Steel Community
EDC	European Defence Community
EDF	European Development Fund
EEC	European Economic Community
EFPIA	European Federation of Pharmaceutical Industry Associations
EFTA	European Free Trade Association
EMU	Economic and Monetary Union
EP	European Parliament
EPC	European Political Cooperation
ESC	Economic and Social Committee
ESDP	European Security and Defence Policy
ETUC	European Trades Union Congress
EU	European Union

FTA	free trade area
GATT	General Agreement on Tariffs and Trade
GDP	Gross Domestic Product
GMOs	genetically modified organisms
GNP	Gross National Product
IGC	Intergovernmental Conference
IR	international relations
JHA	Justice and Home Affairs
MEP	Member of the European Parliament
NAFTA	North American Free Trade Agreement
NATO	North Atlantic Treaty Organization
NGO	non-governmental organization
OECD	Organization for Economic Cooperation and Development
OSCE	Organization for Security and Cooperation in Europe (formerly CSCE)
PAPG	Public Affairs Practitioners Group
PHARE	Poland and Hungary: Aid for the Restructuring of Economies
QMV	qualified majority voting
SEA	Single European Act
SEAP	Society of European Affairs Practitioners
TACIS	Technical Assistance to the Commonwealth of Independent States
TEC	Treaty establishing the European Community
TEU	Treaty on European Union
UK	United Kingdom
UN	United Nations
UNICE	Union of Industrial and Employers' Confederations of Europe
US	United States
WEU	Western European Union
WTO	World Trade Organization

List of Contributors

ELIZABETH BOMBERG	*University of Edinburgh*
LAURA CRAM	*Strathclyde University*
DESMOND DINAN	*George Mason University*
LYNN DOBSON	*University of Edinburgh*
LYKKE FRIIS	*Danish Institute of International Affairs*
BRIGID LAFFAN	*University College Dublin*
DAVID MARTIN	*Member European Parliament*
JOHN PETERSON	*University of Glasgow*
ALBERTA SBRAGIA	*University of Pittsburgh*
MICHAEL SHACKLETON	*Secretariat, European Parliament*
MICHAEL E. SMITH	*Georgia State University*
ALEXANDER STUBB	*European Commission/College of Europe*
RORY WATSON	*Freelance journalist, Brussels*
HELEN WALLACE	*European University Institute*
ALBERT WEALE	*University of Essex*

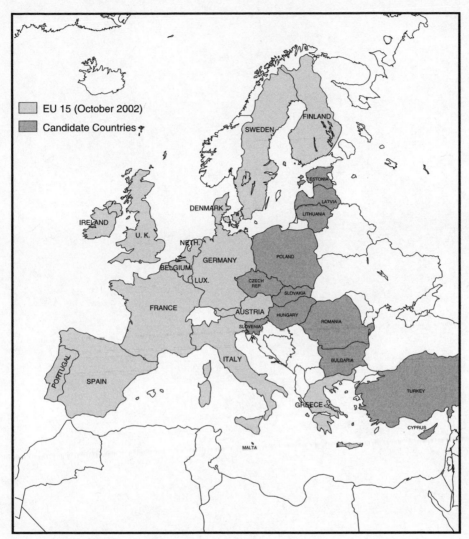

EU 15 (October 2002)
Candidate Countries

FINLAND
SWEDEN
ESTONIA
LATVIA
LITHUANIA
DENMARK
IRELAND
U. K.
NETH.
GERMANY
POLAND
BELGIUM
LUX.
CZECH REP.
SLOVAKIA
FRANCE
AUSTRIA
HUNGARY
ROMANIA
SLOVENIA
ITALY
BULGARIA
PORTUGAL
SPAIN
TURKEY
GREECE
CYPRUS
MALTA

The expanding European Union

Part I

Background

Chapter 1
Introduction

Elizabeth Bomberg and Alexander Stubb

Contents

Overview

The European Union (EU) is a challenge to study, but a challenge well worth taking on. This introductory chapter sets out the reasons—both practical and analytical— for studying the European Union. It introduces some of main conceptual approaches to understanding this unique institution, how it functions and why. Finally the chapter sets forth three broad themes which will tie together our analysis of the European Union and how it works.

Studying the EU

The European Union is not easy to understand. To the uninitiated, its institutions seem remote, its remit unclear, its operation complex, and its outputs perplexing. Such perplexity is understandable. To begin with, the EU defies simple categorization: it combines attributes of a state with those of an international organization, yet it closely resembles neither (see Box 1.1). Its development is shaped by an increasing number of players: fifteen (soon to be more) member governments,

Box 1.1 What's in a name?

Even the question of what to call the EU can cause confusion. The European Union was originally established as the **European Economic Community** (EEC, colloquially known as the Common Market) by the 1957 Treaty of Rome. The name was later shortened to **European Community** (EC). The 1992 Maastricht Treaty created the **European Union**, which is made up of the EC as well as two other 'pillars' of cooperation in the areas of foreign policy and justice and home affairs. We use the term European Community to refer to the period pre-Maastricht (see especially Chapter 2), but use the term European Union to refer to all periods—and the activities of all pillars—thereafter. Legal purists may blanch (formally, for instance, there is no such thing as 'EU law' or an 'EU budget', only Community law or Community budget) but for simplicity's sake we use the broad term 'EU'.

multiple common EU institutions, clusters of experts, private interests, and citizen groups all converge to influence what the EU is and what it does. And 'what the EU does' has also expanded enormously since its origins in the 1950s. Originally concerned narrowly with free trade in coal and steel, its policy remit has expanded to cover agricultural, monetary, regional, environmental, social, immigration, and foreign and security policy, and the list does not stop there (see Box 1.2).

This task expansion—especially into areas traditionally seen as the responsibility of elected national governments—has meant that debates about the EU are increasingly wrapped up in larger debates about sovereignty, democracy, and the future of the nation-state. Studying European integration therefore means studying a lot more than a single organization. Adding to the challenge is the fact that the EU simply will not stay still. It is always in motion, constantly changing and expanding (see Chronology in Appendix I).

Understanding the EU is thus a challenge, but one well worth taking on. First, on a purely practical level, no student of politics can make sense of European politics without knowing something about an organization which has daily and powerful effects on European (and non-European) governments, markets, and citizens. The EU and its policies have a significant impact on prosperity, jobs, social and environmental conditions, consumer habits and health, and freedom of movement for those living in Europe and beyond (see Box 1.3).

Secondly, students of politics, economics, law, and international relations are interested in the EU not just because of its practical relevance, but also because of its analytical significance: it represents the most advanced experiment in multilateral cooperation and *integration* (see Box 1.4)—the 'process whereby political actors in several distinct national settings are persuaded to shift their loyalties, expectations and political activities toward a new center' (Haas 1958: 16). Thus,

Box 1.2 The three pillars of the European Union

The activities of the EU are divided into three areas or 'pillars' created by the 1992 Maastricht Treaty.

The European Union

Pillar 1 European Community	Pillar 2 Common Foreign and Security Policy	Pillar 3 Justice and Home Affairs [formally, Police and Judicial Cooperation in Police Matters]
Policy Responsibilities internal market (including competition and external trade);	Policy Responsibilities common action to strengthen security of EU;	Policy Responsibilities cross-border crime;
related policies (environ- mental, cohesion, social);	preserve peace;	criminal law;
agriculture;	promote international cooperation	police cooperation
economic and monetary union;		
immigration, asylum, visas		
Decision-making style supranational	Decision-making style primarily intergovernmental	Decision-making style usually intergovernmental

Pillar 1: European Communities

The first pillar is the busiest, incorporating the existing European Community and including the vast majority of EU responsibilities. It covers internal market policies as well as agriculture and competition policy. It also covers immigration, asylum, and economic and monetary union.

Pillar 2: Common Foreign and Security Policy

In the second pillar, member states attempt to forge common positions and take joint action on foreign and security affairs. Decision-making is primarily intergovernmental and neither the Parliament nor Court have much direct influence.

Box 1.2 *Continued . . .*

Pillar 3: Justice and Home Affairs (now formally called Police and Judicial Cooperation in Criminal Matters)

The objective of the third pillar is to increase cooperation in the areas of 'internal security' such as the fight against international crime and the drug trade. As in Pillar 2, decision-making in Pillar 3 is highly intergovernmental. Common action is loose and unanimity required for virtually all important decisions.

Sometimes Treaty reform can shift policy responsibility from one pillar to another. When this occurs the nature of decision-making power can also shift significantly. For instance, when the 1997 Amsterdam Treaty moved policy on visas, immigration, and asylum from the third to first pillar, it signalled a shift towards more supranational decision-making in this area (see Chapter 6).

Box 1.3 The practical significance of the EU

The EU's practical impact is felt in several areas including:

- **Legislation**: it is estimated that over 50 per cent of domestic legislation of the Union's member states originates in or is linked to EU legislation (see Chapter 6).
- **Currency**: In 2002, twelve national currencies—some dating back 600 years—ceased to be legal tender and were replaced by the euro. Over 300 million consumers now use this single currency.
- **Wealth**: The EU's collective wealth (Gross Domestic Product) accounts for 28 per cent of the world's total.
- **Trade**: Not counting intra-EU trade, the EU's share of world trade (imports and exports) is about equal to that of the United States, accounting for over 20 per cent of all global trade.
- **Aid**: The EU and its member states are the world's largest donors of development aid, accounting for over 50 per cent. They are also the world's largest importer of goods from less developed countries (see Chapter 10).

While the wisdom or desirability of EU policies and actions are hotly contested, few would deny their practical importance.

Sources: Figures available from the websites of Commission, DG Trade, (http://europa.eu.int/comm/trade/pdf/wto_sharewt.pdf; and http://europa.eu.int/comm/trade/pdf/dev_ff_en.pdf); and from the World Trade Organization (http:// www.wto.org).

understanding the EU helps us frame questions about the future of the nation-state, about the prospects of international cooperation, the effects of *globalization* (see Box 1.4), and the proper role of governments in advanced industrial societies. Put another way, much of what makes the EU most challenging to study—its dynamic character and processes, its unique scope and complexity—also makes it fascinating. Rather than avoid these challenging attributes we use them as themes to glue together our analysis (see below).

Finally, the EU fascinates because it represents a political puzzle. On one hand it has been enormously successful. EU governments and institutions have transformed it from a common market of six countries into a Union of fifteen with a population of over 375 million. It is the world's largest trading block, accounting for over 20 per cent of global trade with a combined Gross Domestic Product well ahead that of the United States (see Box 1.3). It has its own currency and a fledgling common foreign policy. The queue of applicants keen to join it is longer than ever.

Yet a growing number of citizens express disillusionment with the EU, and not just in the traditionally more 'sceptical' states like the United Kingdom (UK) or Denmark. 'Brussels bureaucrats' make easy targets for almost every ill, while populist parties often gain popular success through EU-bashing. Voter turnout in European Parliament elections has fallen with each election. National referenda held on EU membership, the single currency, or treaty ratification garner only a low proportion of public support in several countries. EU institutions—the European Commission, the Council of Ministers (representing national governments), and even the directly elected Parliament—are viewed as increasingly remote and shrouded in secrecy, or just not worth bothering about. The EU certainly is not a well understood body, and it is difficult for students to see just how (or if) the EU works.

In this book we address the practical question: 'How does it work?' Who are the main actors, what are the main processes, dynamics, and explanations for what the EU does and how it does it? But we also want to address the more rhetorical question: 'How (in the world) does it work?!' Why have fifteen sovereign states agreed to relinquish part of their *sovereignty* (see Box 1.4)? With what implications? Why do policies emerge looking as they do? Why did the EU develop the way it did and where is it likely to go from here? Why does it elicit such strong demonstrations of support and antipathy? Our main goal is to address these questions in a lively and comprehensible way.

We employ several means to help us achieve that goal. The chapters are written by experts with either research, teaching, or policy-making experience (some with all three). Many of the chapters are co-authored by an academic and practitioner to illustrate both how the EU works and how to make sense of it. Students need to understand both the formal 'textbook' rules of EU practice (what do the Treaties say; what does the legislation stipulate) but also how it 'really' works (how are the Treaties interpreted; what informal rules guide action). We capture this dual dynamic through a series of boxes (entitled '*How it Really Works*') which illustrate how a particular actor, policy, or process actually works regardless of what the formal rules are. These exhibits will help the reader move from the general to the specific: the chapter narrative provides a general understanding of how the EU works; these boxed exhibits offer specific knowledge of how the EU operates 'on the ground'.

Finally, the book seeks to make the EU more comprehensible by placing its institutions, structures, or policies in a comparative perspective. Most chapters include a '*Compared to What?*' box which compares EU institutions, practices, or processes with their counterparts inside the member states or outside the EU. The intent is to help students better understand the EU by underlining how it is like other systems of *governance* (see Box 1.4), and in what ways it is unique. More generally, the book is seasoned throughout with vignettes or other boxes which draw students into the substance of the chapter through 'real life' examples or illustrations. Finally, each chapter offers 'Concept boxes' defining key terms, as well as guides to further reading and useful internet sites. All these features are designed to achieve our overall aim: to bring the EU to life for our readers.

Understanding the EU: theory and conceptual tools

When studying something as complex as the European Union we need conceptual tools to guide us. A theory or model simplifies reality and allows us to see relationships between the things we observe. There are different families or kinds of theory, and the two types presented in this book are explanatory theory and normative theory. The social sciences mostly use explanatory theories which aim to explain social and political behaviour and perhaps predict it too. Sometimes, however, it is important to evaluate rather than explain, and to improve rather than predict. For these purposes, scholars use normative theories. Chapter 8, which deals with the more philosophical issues of EU integration, draws on normative political theory.

The other chapters employ different explanatory theories developed in the study of international relations, comparative politics, and public policy. Each theory seeks to explain different developments, episodes, and dynamics of EU politics and European integration. Just as there is no single explanation for events, so there is no one explanatory theory of EU politics. We offer here a brief synopsis of four main theoretical frameworks—neofunctionalism, liberal intergovernmentalism, new institutionalism, and policy networks. Our aim is not to present or apply these theories, with all their nuances, nor to privilege one over the others. Rather, in this section we pull out for the reader the key assumptions and insights offered

Box 1.4 Key concepts and terms (listed alphabetically)

globalization is the idea that the world is becoming increasingly interconnected and interdependent because of increasing flows of trade, ideas, people, and capital. Globalization is usually presented as reducing the autonomy of individual states, although whether its impact is essentially positive or negative, inevitable or controllable, remains intensely debated.

governance means 'established patterns of rule without an overall ruler'. Even though there is no government, the EU undertakes the sort of activity that governments traditionally have done. The EU is thus said to be a system of governance without a government (or an opposition).

integration is the process whereby sovereign states relinquish (surrender or pool) national sovereignty to maximize their collective power and interests.

intergovernmentalism is a process or condition whereby decisions are reached by specifically defined cooperation between or among governments. Formally, at least, sovereignty is not relinquished. The term intergovernmentalism is usually contrasted with *supranationalism*.

multilevel governance is often used to describe the EU. It means a system in which power is shared between the supranational, national, and subnational levels. The term also suggests there is a fair bit of interaction and coordination of political actors across those levels. How they interact, and with what effects helps determine the shape of European integration (see Hooghe and Marks 2001).

sovereignty refers to the ultimate authority over people and territory. It is sometimes broken down into internal (law-making authority within a territory) and external (international recognition). Opinions vary as to whether state sovereignty is 'surrendered' or merely 'shared' in the context of the EU.

supranationalism means above states or nations. That is, decisions are made by a process or institution which is independent of national governments. The subject governments (in the case of the EU, the member state governments) are then obliged to accept these decisions. The European Court of Justice (Chapter 3) is a supranational institution. The term supranationalism is usually contrasted with *intergovernmentalism*.

subsidiarity is a principle originally derived from catholic theology. It has been developed in the EU to help determine how different public policy goals can be best pursued, by whom, and at what level of governance. The Treaties require the EU to take action only if 'the objective of the proposed action cannot be sufficiently achieved by the member states' and can 'by reason of its scale or effects be better achieved by the Community'.

by each. The following chapters will then use these insights to elaborate and explain their particular topic.

International relations approaches

The first two approaches—*neofunctionalism* and *liberal intergovernmentalism*—draw from international relations theory. They are concerned primarily with explaining the broad development of European integration: that is, how and why nations choose to form European institutions, and who or what determines the shape and speed of the integration process. One of the earliest theories of European integration was *neofunctionalism* which was developed primarily by Ernst Haas in the 1960s to explain the development of the European Coal and Steel Community (ECSC) and the European Economic Community (EEC), the predecessors of the EU. Haas and others were concerned with explaining how a merger of economic activity in particular economic sectors (say, coal and steel) across borders could 'spill over' and provoke wider economic integration in related areas (say agriculture) (Haas 1958; 1964; Lindberg and Scheingold 1970). More ambitiously, neofunctionalists believed this economic integration would produce political integration and the creation of common, integrated, supranational institutions to accelerate this process (Rosamond 1999: 2). 'Supranational' here means transcending national borders, interests, and powers (see Box 1.2). More recent analysts, inspired by neofunctionalist thinking, work under the banner of 'supranational governance' emphasizing the creation of supranational rules and society (see Sandholtz and Stone Sweet 1998). In either case, neofunctionalism challenges the assumed primacy of the nation-state, and the notion that international institutions are incapable of autonomous decisions and action.

Early neofunctionalist theory seemed to explain well the initial successes of European integration, especially the development of a European Economic Community from a modest coal and steel community, or the strengthening of the European Commission, the EU's supranational executive. But its uni-directional logic (integration could only go forward) was heavily criticized when European integration appeared to stagnate and even to reverse in the late 1960s and 1970s. Dissatisfaction with neofunctionalism, among some of its own proponents but especially among other international relations scholars, led to the development of alternative theoretical models, especially 'liberal intergovernmentalism'.

Most closely associated with Andrew Moravcsik (1993; 1998), *liberal intergovernmentalism* builds on earlier writings of international relations scholars who rejected the notion that national governments might not be supreme, or that nations would willingly relinquish sovereignty (see Hoffman 1995; Milward 1992). Marshalling impressive historical evidence, liberal intergovernmentalists argue that major choices—what Peterson (1995) calls 'history making decisions'—reflect the preferences of national governments rather than supranational organizations.

Each state's preferences reflect the balance of their domestic economic interests. The outcomes of EU negotiation are the result of *intergovernmental* bargaining; that is, bargaining between sovereign national governments (see Box 1.4). Any subsequent delegation to supranational institutions is calculated, rational, and circumscribed. In short, national governments are the dominant actors in shaping integration, and they are in control: 'governments first define a set of interests, then bargain among themselves to realize those interests' (Moravcsik 1993: 481).

A comparative politics approach

Analysts drawing on comparative politics approaches have challenged the primacy of the state in shaping European integration and the EU. Foremost among these approaches is **new institutionalism** which emphasizes the importance of institutions in shaping or even determining government preferences. In the EU context, new institutionalism demonstrates how the EU's common institutions (Commission, Council, Parliament, or Court) are more than impartial arbiters in the policy-making process: they are key players with their own agendas and priorities (Armstrong and Bulmer 1998; Bulmer 1998). For *new* institutionalists, 'institutions' refer not only to institutions traditionally defined—executives, parliaments, courts—but also to values, norms, and informal conventions that govern social exchanges between actors. These values and norms affect or 'frame' the way actors perceive the choices open to them. So, for example, the dominant rules (say majority voting among government ministers at the EU level) or informal practices (say the unwritten goal of seeking consensus whenever possible) can mould the behaviour of national government representatives in ways that governments neither plan nor control.

A second insight of new institutionalist analyses is the concept of 'path dependency': the notion that once a particular decision or path is chosen, 'it is very difficult to get back on the rejected path' (Krasner 1984: 225). Path dependency means that it is hard to change policy—such as an expensive common agricultural policy—even when it outlives its usefulness. The 'sunk costs' (time and resources already invested) of agreeing a policy in the first place are often considerable, and the idea of starting again on a long, time-consuming, and expensive process of agreeing a new policy is resisted for that reason (see Pierson 1996; Peterson and Bomberg 1999).

A public policy approach

A final theoretical approach of use to those studying the EU is the **policy networks** framework. Unlike neofunctionalism or liberal intergovernmentalism, this approach does not tell us much about the policy bargains struck between national governments, nor the history-making decisions (such as treaty reform) that set the broad direction of European integration. But network analysis is useful for uncovering the nitty gritty, behind-the-scenes negotiation and exchange that can shape policies at a day-to-day level. A policy network is 'a cluster of actors, each of which has an interest or stake in a given EU policy sector and the capacity to help determine policy success or failure' (Peterson and Bomberg 1999: 8). Policy networks at the EU level usually bring together institutional actors (from the Commission, Council, Parliament) and other stakeholders such as representatives from private firms, public interest groups, technical or scientific experts, and, perhaps above all, national officials. Networks lack hierarchy (there is no one actor in charge) and instead depend on resource exchange. That means participants need to bring with them some valued resource with which to bargain: information, ideas, finances, constitutional-legal power, or political legitimacy. According to network analysts, bargaining and resource exchange among these actors—rather than intergovernmental bargaining—determine the shape of actual EU policies.

Each of these theories has its own assumptions, strengths, and weaknesses (see Table 1.1; Nelsen and Stubb 1998). No one theory can explain everything treated in this book. But each school introduced here offers different insights about different key features of the EU: how integration evolves; the way policies are made and the role of different actors in this process. Students need not master all these theories to use this book. Rather, these theoretical insights—and their application in

Table 1.1 Explanatory theories of European integration and the EU

Theory	Proponents/ Major works	Assumptions	Criticisms
Neofunctionalism	Haas 1958	International institutions are capable of autonomous action; spillover is major impetus for integration	Cannot explain stagnation
Liberal inter-governmentalism	Moravcsik 1998	Member states control European integration	Too state-centric; neglects day-to-day policy-making
New institutionalism	Bulmer 1998; Pierson 1996	Institutions matter; path dependency	Overemphasizes power of the EU's institutions
Policy networks	Peterson 1995	Resource exchange within networks shapes policy	Cannot explain big decisions

subsequent chapters—are meant to encourage students to begin thinking about theory and its role in helping us understand and evaluate European integration and EU politics.

Structure and themes

Any book on European integration which aims to be at all comparative is bound to cover a lot of ground, both theoretical and practical. In explaining how the EU works it is necessary to look at the historical background of European integration and the major actors involved in EU politics and policy-making, as well as current issues and trends. The book's layout reflects this logic. In Part I, Chapter 2 tells us 'how we got here' by providing a concise historical overview of the EU's development. Part II (Chapters 3–5) focuses on the major actors: the EU's common institutions, the member states, and organized interests such as business groups and non-governmental organizations (NGOs). Part III focuses on process and governance. It provides an expert overview of key policies (Chapter 6), how they are made (Chapter 7), and the wider issues of governance and legitimacy arising from this process (Chapter 8). The last section features chapters covering major debates and developments, including enlargement (Chapter 9) and the EU's growing role as a global actor (Chapter 10). A conclusion draws together the main themes of the volume.

The book thus covers a lot, but it is held together by three common themes. All the chapters illustrate that the EU is:

1. An 'experiment in motion', an ongoing process without a clear end-state;
2. A system of shared power characterized by growing complexity and an increasing number of players;
3. An organization with an expanding scope, but limited capacity.

We introduce each of these themes below.

Experimentation and change

Since its conception in the early 1950s, European integration has been an ongoing process without a clear *finalité*, or end-state. In one sense its development has been a functional step-by-step process: integration in one area has led to pressure to integrate in another. As neofunctionalists would point out, the Union has developed from a free trade area to a customs union; from a customs union to a single market; and from a single market to an economic and monetary union. This development, however, has been neither smooth, automatic, nor predetermined. Rather, integration and the EU's development has progressed in fits and starts, the result of constant experimentation, problem-solving, and trial and error. European foreign policy, from failed attempts of the 1950s to the creation of a European Security and Defence Policy (ESDP) in 2000, is a good example of this evolution. With no agreed 'end goal' (such as a 'United States of Europe'), the EU's actors have reacted to immediate problems, but they have done so neither coherently nor predictably.

The nature and intensity of change are also varied. Constitutional change has taken place through Intergovernmental Conferences (IGCs)—special negotiations in which government representatives come together to hammer out agreements to alter the EU's guiding treaties. The first (resulting in the Treaty of Paris, 1951) created the European Coal and Steel Community. The Treaty of Nice, signed in 2001, reformed the institutions in preparation for enlargement (see Box 1.5). Yet another IGC is planned for 2004. Less spectacularly, legislative change has taken place through thousands of EU directives and regulations. Finally, the institutions, especially the Commission and European Court of Justice, have themselves acted as instigators of change, and have expanded the powers of the Union throughout its history. The point is that change is a constant in the EU. This book will explore its main sources and implications.

Power-sharing and consensus

Our second theme concerns power and how it is shared between different actors and across layers of government. The EU policy-making system lacks a clear nexus of power: there is no 'EU government' in the traditional meaning of the term. Instead, power is dispersed across a range of actors and levels of governance (regional, national, and supranational). Deciding which of these actors should do what, and at what level of governance, is a matter of on-going debate within the EU. The principle of *subsidiarity*—the idea that decisions should be taken at the level of governance 'closest to the citizens' compatible with policy success (see Box 1.4)—has been developed to address this problem, but without complete success (see Chapter 8).

The three most important sets of actors are the member states, institutions, and organized interests. Certainly, much about the evolution of the EU has been determined by the member states themselves, and in particular their different approaches to integration. Some member states want deeper integration, others do not, and this division continues to shape the speed and form of the integration process. Meanwhile, EU institutions have shaped the EU's development as they vie for power with the member states, as well as among themselves. Finally, organized interests—including representatives of lower levels of governance, private interests, citizens groups—now play an increasing role.

Part of what makes the EU unique is that these actors exist in a complex web where there are established patterns of interaction but no overall 'ruler' or

Box 1.5 The Treaties

When practitioners and academics use the term 'the Treaties' they are referring to the collection of founding treaties and their subsequent revisions. The founding treaties include the Treaty of Paris (signed in 1951, establishing the European Coal and Steel Community) and two Treaties of Rome, 1957: one establishing the European Atomic Energy Community (Euratom); the other the European Economic Community. The ECSC became void in July 2002. The Euratom treaty never amounted to much. But the **Treaty of Rome** (signed in 1957) establishing the EEC became absolutely central. It has been substantially revised in the:

- **Single European Act** (signed in 1986),
- **Maastricht Treaty** (or Treaty on European Union, signed in 1992),
- **Amsterdam Treaty** (signed in 1997), and the
- **Nice Treaty** (signed in 2001).

As Box 1.1 explained, the intergovernmental conference leading up to the Maastricht Treaty not only revised the Treaty of Rome (it is now formally called the Treaty establishing the European Community) but it also established the broader Treaty on European Union (TEU or Maastricht Treaty, 1992) which included two new pillars or areas of activity on foreign policy and justice and home affairs (see Box 1.2). The two core Treaties today are thus the **Treaty Establishing the European Community (TEC)** which covers the first pillar, and the **Treaty on European Union (TEU)** which covers the second and third pillars of EU activity.

These two key treaties, as revised in Amsterdam and Nice, are the basic toolkit of ministers, Commissioners, parliamentarians, and civil servants dealing with EU matters. Each piece of legislation is based on one of these treaty articles (of which there are nearly 700). The Treaties have grown increasingly long and complex. To improve the presentation and facilitate the reading of the Treaties, the articles were renumbered in the Amsterdam IGC of 1997. But the Treaties are hardly an easy read. Even many legal scholars would agree that the language borders on the incomprehensible. However presented, the EU treaties will never replace Harry Potter on the best-seller list. But they are important to the lives of European citizens. One of the objectives assigned to the 2004 intergovernmental conference was to simplify the existing texts and make them more readable.

government or even dominant actor. Instead, actors must bargain and share power in an effort to reach an agreement acceptable to all, or at least most. This dynamic has been captured in the term *'multilevel governance'* (see Box 1.4) which suggests a system of overlapping and shared powers between actors on the regional, national, and supranational level (Hooghe and Marks 2001). EU governance is thus an exercise in sharing power between states and institutions, and seeking consensus across different levels of governance. Coming to grips with this unique distribution of power is a key task of this book.

Scope and capacity

Our final theme concerns the expanding remit of the EU, and its ability to cope with this expansion. The EU has undergone continuous widening and deepening. It has grown from a comfortable club of six member states (Germany, France, Italy, the Netherlands, Belgium, and Luxembourg) to nine (UK, Denmark, and Ireland joined in 1973), to ten (Greece in 1981), to twelve (Portugal and Spain in 1986), and to the current fifteen (Austria, Finland, and Sweden joined in 1995), with over a dozen candidates including Turkey knocking on the door. It has 'deepened' in the sense that the member states have decided to pool sovereignty in an increasing number of policy areas.

This robust policy development has meant that the EU is managing tasks which traditionally have belonged to the nation-state. At the same time the EU is trying to dispose of its image as an economic giant, but a political dwarf. The Union is trying to stamp its authority on the international scene through the development of a Common Foreign and Security Policy (CFSP), which, according to the Treaties, 'might in time lead to a common defence'. These developments have challenged the EU's 'capacity'—its logistical and political ability to accommodate change. While the EU has taken on more members and more tasks, its institutional and political development has not kept pace. This mismatch—between the EU's ambitions on one hand and its institutional and political capacity on the other— raises questions about the EU's future and ability to adapt. It also represents the third theme of the volume.

Taken together these three themes address:

1. how the EU has developed and why (experimentation and change);
2. who are the main players and how do they interact (power-sharing and consensus);
3. what does the EU do, and how does it do it (scope and capabilities).

While these three themes correspond roughly to the first three sections of the book, each theme also appears throughout the entire volume, providing the glue necessary to hold together our investigation of the EU and how it works.

Discussion questions

1. If the EU is the most successful modern experiment in international cooperation, why is it increasingly unpopular amongst its citizens?

2. 'Neo-functionalism can explain the successes of European integration but not its failures'. Discuss.

3. Which theory offers the most compelling account of recent developments in European integration?

Further reading

Some of the key themes introduced in this chapter are inspired by broad studies of the EU including Hooghe and Marks (2001), Joerges, Mény, and Weiler (2000), Scharpf (1999), Siedentop (2000), Wallace and Wallace (2000), and Weiler (1999). Nelsen and Stubb (1998) offer a collection of seminal works on European integration theory and practice. Holmes (2001) provides a collection of 'Eurosceptical' readings while Leonard and Leonard (2001) counter with their 'Pro-European Reader'. For an incisive survey of different theoretical approaches applied to the EU, see Rosamond (1999). To explore in more depth some of the key theoretical approaches, see Haas (1958) on neofunctionalism; Milward (1992) and Moravcsik (1998) on liberal intergovernmentalism; Bulmer (1998) and Armstrong and Bulmer (1998) on the new institutionalism; and Peterson (1995) on policy networks.

Armstrong, K., and Bulmer, S. (1998), *The Governance of the Single European Market* (Manchester: Manchester University Press).

Bulmer, S. (1998), 'New Institutionalism and the Governance of the Single European Market', *Journal of European Public Policy* 5/3: 365–86.

Haas, E. (1958), *The Uniting of Europe: Political, Social, and Economic Forces, 1950–7* (Stanford, CA: Stanford University Press).

Holmes, M. (ed.) (2001), *The Eurosceptical Reader 2* (Basingstoke: Palgrave).

Hooghe, L., and Marks, G. (2001), *Multi-Level Governance and European Integration* (Lanham and Oxford: Rowman and Littlefield Publishers, Inc.).

Joerges, C., Mény, Y., and Weiler, J. H. H. (eds.) (2000), *What Kind of a Constitution for What Kind of Polity?* (Florence: European University Institute).

Leonard, D., and Leonard, M. (eds.) (2001), *The Pro-European Reader* (Basingstoke: Palgrave).

Milward, A. (1992), *The European Rescue of the Nation-State* (London: Routledge).

Moravcsik, A. (1998), *The Choice for Europe* (Ithaca, NY: Cornell University Press).

Nelsen, B., and Stubb, A. (eds.) (1998), *The European Union: Readings on the Theory and Practice of European Integration*, 2nd edn. (Boulder, CO: Lynne Rienner and Basingstoke: Palgrave).

Peterson, J. (1995), 'Decision-Making in the EU: Towards a Framework for Analysis', *Journal of European Public Policy* 2/1: 69–73.

Rosamond, B. (1999), *Theories of European Integration* (London and New York: Palgrave).

Scharpf, F. W. (1999), *Governing in Europe: Effective and Democratic?* (Oxford and New York: Oxford University Press).

Siedentop, L. (2000), *Democracy in Europe* (Middlesex: Allen Lane, the Penguin Press).

Wallace, H., and Wallace, W. (eds.) (2000), *Policy-Making in the European Union*, 4th edn. (Oxford and New York: Oxford University Press).

Web links

The EU's official website 'The European Union online' (**www.europa.eu.int**) is a very valuable starting point. It provides further links to wide variety of official sites on EU policies, institutions, legislation, treaties and current debates.

You can also use the web to access the *Official Journal (OJ)* which is updated daily in eleven languages. The *OJ* is the authoritative and formal source for information on EU legislation, case law, parliamentary questions, and documents of public interest. **www.europa.eu.int/ eur-lex/en/oj/**.

For lighter reading, the *Economist* (**www.economist.com**) provides useful general articles while *European Voice* (**www.european-voice.com**) offers insider coverage of EU policies and news. Note both of these charge non-subscribers a fee for certain articles.

Current debates and topics are also addressed in several think tank websites. Some of the better known include the Centre for European Policy Studies (**www.ceps.be**); the European Policy Centre (**www.theepc.be/**); the Centre for European Reform (**www.cer.org.uk**), and the Trans European Policy Studies Association (**www.tepsa.be**). Finally, 'Breakfast in Brussels' (**www.breakfastinbrussels.com/**) provides a news index and links to the international press as well as a light-hearted look at 'Brussels bureaucrats'.

Chapter 2
How Did We Get Here?

Desmond Dinan

Contents

Overview

European countries responded to a series of domestic, regional, and global challenges after the Second World War by integrating economically and politically. These challenges ranged from post-war reconstruction, to international financial turmoil, to the consequences of the end of the Cold War. Driven largely by national interests, Franco-German bargains, and American influence, Europeans responded by establishing the European Community and later the European Union. Deeper integration challenged cherished national concepts of identity, sovereignty, and legitimacy. Successive rounds of enlargement, which saw the EU grow in size from its original six member states, also generated institutional and policy challenges that have shaped the contours of European integration.

Introduction

The history of the European Union presents a fascinating puzzle: why did European states, traditionally jealous of their independence, pool sovereignty in an international organization that increasingly acquired federal attributes? This chapter argues that the answer is as simple as it is paradoxical: because it was in their national interest to do so. Political parties and interest groups did not always agree on what constituted the national interest, and governments themselves were sometimes divided. But at critical junctures in the post-war period, for various strategic and/or economic reasons, national leaders opted for greater integration.

This chapter aims to outline the history of European integration by focusing on national responses to major domestic and international challenges since the end of the Second World War. These responses gave rise to the European Community and later the European Union. France and Germany played key roles. The EC was a bargain struck between them for mutual economic gain. By strengthening post-war Franco-German ties, the EC also had an important political dimension. Indeed, Germany conceded a lot to France in the negotiations that led to the EC in order to deepen Franco-German solidarity, a key step towards binding the Federal Republic into the West. Subsequent milestones in the history of European integration also hinged on Franco-German bargaining.

Ideology—the quest for a united Europe—was not a major motive for European integration (see Box 2.1). The Preamble of the Rome Treaty, the EC's charter, called

---

Box 2.1 Interpreting European integration

Historians have offered different interpretations of how European integration has developed and why. Alan Milward (1984; 1992) is the foremost historian of European integration. He argues that economic interests impelled Western European countries to integrate, but that national governments shared sovereignty only to the extent necessary to resolve problems that would otherwise have undermined their legitimacy and credibility. Paradoxically, European states rescued themselves through limited supranationalism. More recently, Andrew Moravcsik (1998) has complemented Milward's thesis by claiming that national governments, not supranational institutions, controlled the pace and scope of integration. Moravcsik uses historical insights from a series of case studies, from the 1950s to the 1990s, to develop liberal intergovernmentalism as a theory of European integration. Intergovernmentalism generally is in the ascendant in the historiography of European integration, in contrast to the early years of the EC when the arguments of neofunctionalist scholars like Ernst Haas (1958) and Leon Lindberg (1963) dominated academic discourse on the EC (see Chapter 1).

for an 'ever closer union' among the peoples of Europe. This was a vague assertion of the popular aspiration for European unity, not a guiding principle for the EC. Some national and supranational leaders were strongly committed to federalism. But they succeeded in moving Europe in a federal direction only when ideological ambition coincided with national political and economic preferences. The language of European integration, redolent of peace and reconciliation, provided convenient camouflage for the pursuit of national interests based on rational calculations of costs and benefits.

This chapter also argues that the United States has been a major player in the integration process, both positively (as a promoter of integration) and negatively (as an entity against which Europe has integrated). *Globalization* (see Box 1.4) and its presumed association with Americanization, has driven European integration in recent years. Since the late 1980s, the EU has been in search of strategies to compete globally against the United States while retaining a social structure that is relatively egalitarian and distinctly not American.

Post-war settlement

The most pressing question at the end of the war was what to do about Germany. The question became acute with the onset of the Cold War. As the Soviet Union consolidated its control over the eastern part of the country, the Western Powers—the United Kingdom (UK), France, and the United States—facilitated the establishment of democratic and free market institutions in what became the Federal Republic of Germany (FRG). The German question then became how to maximize the economic and military potential of the FRG for the benefit of the West while allaying the understandable concerns of Germany's neighbours, especially France. France accepted a supranational solution to the problem of German economic recovery, but not to the problem of German remilitarization.

The US championed integration as a means of reconciling old enemies, promoting prosperity, and strengthening Western Europe's resistance to communism. The *Marshall Plan* (see Box 2.2) was the main instrument of American policy. European governments wanted American dollars for post-war reconstruction, but without any strings attached. For their part, the Americans insisted that European recipients coordinate their plans for using the aid. That was the extent of European integration in the late 1940s. The UK had no interest in sharing sovereignty. France wanted to keep the old enemy down and exploit Germany's coal-rich Ruhr region. Few countries were willing to liberalize trade. Winston Churchill's famous call in 1946 for a United States of Europe belied the reality of politicians' unwillingness to change the international status quo.

Box 2.2 Key concepts and terms (listed alphabetically)

The **'Empty Chair Crisis'** was prompted by French President Charles de Gaulle's decision to pull France out of all Council meetings in 1965 thereby leaving one chair empty. De Gaulle was protesting the Commission's plans to extend the EC's powers generally and subject more decisions to qualified majority voting.

The **Luxembourg Compromise** resolved the empty chair crisis. Reached during a foreign ministers' meeting in 1966, the Compromise was an informal agreement stating that when a decision was subject to qualified majority voting (QMV), the Council would postpone a decision if any member states felt 'very important interests' were under threat. In effect the compromise meant QMV was used far less often, and unanimity became the norm.

The **Marshall Plan** (1947) was an aid package from the US of $13 billion (a lot of money in 1947, 5 per cent of US GNP) to help rebuild West European economies after the war. The aid was given on the condition that European states cooperate and jointly administer these funds.

Qualified majority voting (QMV) can be used to reach most decisions on the Council of Ministers. Each member state is granted a number of votes roughly proportional to its population (Germany, UK, France, and Italy have the most; Luxembourg the least). The formula for deciding which country gets how many votes was revised after fierce debate at the Nice Summit in 2000 (see Chapter 3, especially Table 3.2).

The **Schengen Agreement** was signed by five member states in 1985 (Belgium, France, Germany, Luxembourg, and the Netherlands) and came into effect ten years later. It removes all border controls among its signatories which now include all fifteen member states (except Ireland and the UK) as well as Norway and Iceland. (Denmark has opted out of certain aspects of this agreement.)

It was Germany's rapid economic recovery, thanks in part to the Marshall Plan, that made the status quo untenable. The US wanted to accelerate German recovery in order to reduce occupation costs and promote recovery throughout Europe. A weak West Germany, the Americans argued, meant a weak Western Europe. France agreed, but urged caution. France wanted to modernize its own economy before allowing Germany's economy to rebound. Indeed, France agreed to establish the FRG only on condition that German coal production (a key material for war-making) remained under international control.

German expressions of resentment of French policy fell on receptive American ears. As the Cold War deepened, the US intensified pressure on France to relax its policy toward Germany so that Germany's economic potential could be put at the disposal of the West. Yet the US was not insensitive to French economic and security interests. Rather than impose a solution, Washington pressed Paris to devise a policy that would allay French concerns about the Ruhr region, without endangering Germany's full recovery. Given its preference for European integration, the US hoped that France would take a supranational tack.

Originally the US wanted the UK to lead on the German question. The UK had already taken the initiative on military security in Europe, having pressed the US to negotiate the North Atlantic Treaty (which founded NATO, the North Atlantic Treaty Organization). Yet the UK was reluctant for reasons of history, national sovereignty, and economic policy to go beyond anything but intergovernmental cooperation. The UK's prestige in Europe was then at its height. Continental countries looked to the UK for leadership. Such leadership, however, was absent, and under mounting American pressure, France came up with a novel idea to reconcile Franco-German interests by pooling coal and steel resources under a supranational High Authority.

Schuman Plan

This was the Schuman Plan, drafted by Jean Monnet, a senior French civil servant with extensive international experience. Being close to influential American officials and responsible for French economic planning, Monnet faced intense American pressure to devise a new policy towards Germany. Monnet believed in European unity and saw the Schuman Plan as a first step in that direction. More immediately, it would protect French interests by ensuring continued access to German resources, although on the basis of cooperation rather than coercion. The new plan bore the name of the French Foreign Minister, Robert Schuman, who risked his political life promoting it at a time when most French people deeply distrusted Germany.

Naturally, German Chancellor Konrad Adenauer endorsed the plan, which provided a means of resolving the Ruhr problem and rehabilitating Germany internationally. Schuman and Adenauer trusted each other. They were both Christian Democrats, came from the Franco-German borderlands, and spoke German together. Aware of the UK's attitude towards integration, Schuman did not bother to inform London of the plan. By contrast, the Americans were in on it from the beginning.

The Schuman Plan was a major reversal of French foreign policy. Having tried to keep Germany down since the war, France now sought to turn the inevitability of Germany's economic recovery to its own advantage through the establishment of a common market in coal and steel. The Schuman Declaration of 9 May 1950, announcing the plan, was couched in the language of reconciliation rather than *realpolitik*. In fact the initiative cleverly combined national and European interests. It represented a dramatic new departure in European as well as in French and German affairs (see Box 2.3).

Box 2.3 HOW IT REALLY WORKS

Rhetoric versus Reality in the Schuman Plan

Jean Monnet's drafting of the Schuman Plan in 1950 marked a diplomatic break-through on the contentious German question. More generally, the plan's proposal for a coal and steel community also advanced the goal of European unity. When outlining the proposal in the Schuman Declaration, a highly publicized initiative, Monnet emphasized the European and idealistic dimension of the proposal. Issued on 9 May, the Schuman Declaration proclaimed that:

> World peace can only be safeguarded if constructive efforts are made pro-portionate to the dangers that threaten it. . . . France, by advocating for more than twenty years the idea of a united Europe, has always regarded it as an essential objective to serve the purpose of peace. . . . With this aim in view, the French government proposes to take immediate action on one limited but decisive point. The French government proposes that Franco-German produc-tion of coal and steel be placed under a common 'high authority' within an organization open to the participation of the other European nations. . . . [This] will lay the first concrete foundation for a European federation, which is so indispensable for the preservation of peace.

But Monnet's primary concern was to defend French national interests. He wanted to ensure French access to German raw materials and European markets despite Germany's economic resurgence. In a private note to Schuman some days before the Declaration's unfurling, Monnet explained that France had little choice but to safeguard its interests by taking a new approach. On 1 May Monnet informed Schuman that:

> Germany has already asked to be allowed to increase its output [of steel] from 10 to 14 million tons [French output was 9 million tons at the time]. We will refuse but the Americans will insist. Finally, we will make reservations and give way . . . There is no need to describe the consequences [of not giving way] in any detail (quoted in Duchêne 1994: 198).

Instead of trying to block Germany's advance, Monnet advocated a European initiative—the Schuman Plan—in defence of French interests.

Participation in the plan was supposedly open to all the countries of Europe. In fact, the list of likely partners was far shorter. The Cold War excluded Central and Eastern Europe from the plan. In Western Europe, the UK and the Scandinavian countries had already rejected supranationalism. Ireland was isolationist; Spain and Portugal, under dictatorial regimes, were international outcasts; and Switzerland was resolutely neutral. That left the Benelux countries (Belgium, the

Netherlands, and Luxembourg), which were economically tied to France and Germany, and Italy, which saw integration primarily as a means of combating domestic communism and restoring international legitimacy. Consequently the European Coal and Steel Community (ECSC), launched in 1952, included only six countries. The ECSC soon established a common market in coal and steel products, with generous provisions for workers' rights.

European Defence Community

The same six countries ('the Six') signed a treaty to establish a defence community in 1952. The rationale for both communities was the same: supranational institutions provided the best means of managing German recovery. In this case, the outbreak of the Korean War in June 1950, which caused a war scare in Europe, made German remilitarization imperative. France at first resisted, and then acquiesced on condition that German military units were subsumed into a new European Defence Community (EDC). Like the Schuman Plan, the plan for the EDC sought to make a virtue (European integration) out of necessity (German remilitarization). Although the EDC was a French proposal, most French people fiercely opposed German remilitarization. The EDC became the most divisive issue in the country. In view of the treaty's unpopularity the government delayed ratification for two years. The French parliament ignominiously defeated the treaty in 1954.

Ironically, Germany formed an army anyway, under the auspices of the Western European Union (WEU), an intergovernmental organization comprising the UK and the Six and established in 1954. (The WEU also divided French opinion, but its intergovernmental nature and British sponsorship sufficed to ensure ratification in the French parliament.) Germany joined NATO via the WEU in May 1955 and effectively regained full formal sovereignty. Whereas the intergovernmental WEU endured (until it was folded into the EU; see Chapter 10), the European Defence Community was a bridge too far for European integration. At a time when the Six were setting up the ECSC, the launch of a similar supranational initiative in the much more sensitive defence sector was too ambitious. Even if it had come into existence, in all likelihood the EDC would have been unworkable. Resistance to its implementation, especially from the far left and far right, would have been intense. The EDC brought the idea of supranationalism into disrepute. The end of the affair allowed supporters of supranationalism to jettison the baggage of German remilitarization and concentrate on first principles: economic integration.

It is remarkable how quickly the idea of European integration bounced back to life. The ECSC was operating fully, but its political and economic impact was slight. Despite what some observers (and neofunctionalist theorists) predicted, there was little 'spillover' from supranational cooperation in coal and steel to other sectors. Monnet, who became President of the High Authority, was bored in Luxembourg, the ECSC's capital. He left office and returned to Paris in 1955, where he set up a transnational organization, the Action Committee for the United States of Europe, to advocate further integration. His pet scheme was for an Atomic Energy Community (Euratom), along the same lines as the ECSC. The French government was interested, but not for the same reasons as Monnet. Whereas Monnet saw Euratom as a further step towards European unity, the government saw it as a means of bolstering France's nuclear programme for civil and military purposes. Not surprisingly, this idea had little appeal for France's partners.

European Community

The relaunch of European integration after the EDC's collapse was due not to Monnet or support for Euratom, but to changes in international trade relations in the mid-1950s. Thanks largely to liberalization measures in the Organization for European Economic Cooperation (OEEC) and the General Agreement on Tariffs and Trade (GATT), intra-European trade was on the rise. With it, prosperity increased. European governments wanted more trade, but disagreed on the rate and range of liberalization. The British favoured further liberalization through the OEEC and the GATT, as did influential elements in the German government (notably Ludwig Erhard, the Economics Minister). The French were instinctively protectionist, although some influential politicians advocated openness. The Dutch, with a small and open economy, wanted full liberalization and were impatient with progress in the OEEC and the GATT, where intergovernmentalism constrained decision-making.

The Dutch had proposed a common market for all industrial sectors in the early 1950s. This would combine a customs union (the phased abolition of tariffs among member states and erection of a common external tariff, see Box 2.4) with the free movement of goods, people, services, and capital, as well as supranational decision-making in areas such as competition policy. They revived the proposal in 1955, arguing that the international economic climate was more propitious than ever for the launch of a common market.

Successful negotiations to establish the European Economic Community (EEC or EC) in 1956, so soon after the collapse of the EDC, owed much to the leadership of politicians like Paul-Henri Spaak in Belgium, Guy Mollet and Christian Pineau in France, and Konrad Adenauer in Germany. Because of France's political weight in Europe and traditional protectionism, Mollet and Pineau played crucial roles. But their advocacy of the EC came with a price for the other prospective member states. In order to win domestic support they insisted on a special regime for agriculture in the common market, assistance for French overseas territories (France was then in the painful process of decolonization), and the establishment of Euratom.

The negotiations that resulted in the two Rome treaties, one for the EC and the other for Euratom, were arduous. Because the UK opposed supranationalism and

Box 2.4 COMPARED TO WHAT?

Regional economic integration

Economic integration in Europe has proceeded through a number of steps or stages. A similar trajectory has occurred in other regions of the world, although nowhere has the level of economic cooperation matched that found in the EU.

In a **free trade area** (FTA) goods travel freely among member states, but these states retain the authority to establish their own external trade policy (tariffs, quotas, and non-tariff barriers) towards third countries. By allowing free access to each other's markets and discriminating favourably towards them, a free trade area stimulates internal trade and can lower consumer costs. But the lack of a common external tariff means complicated rules of origin are required to regulate the import of goods. One example of a FTA outside the EU is the European Free Trade Area (EFTA) which was established under British leadership in 1960 to promote expansion of free trade in non-EU western European countries. The UK left EFTA to join the EC in 1973, but Iceland, Liechtenstein, Norway, and Switzerland are still members. In North America, Canada, Mexico, and the US agreed to form a North American Free Trade Agreement (NAFTA) in 1992.

Regional organizations elsewhere have created closer economic ties which may develop into FTAs. For instance the Association of South-East Asian Nations (ASEAN) was established in 1967 to provide economic as well as social cooperation among non-communist countries in the area. A wider forum for regional economic cooperation is found among Pacific Rim countries within APEC (Asia Pacific Economic Cooperation) which includes Australia, China, Indonesia, Japan, Mexico, the Philippines, and the US.

A **customs union** requires more economic and political cooperation than an FTA. In addition to ensuring free trade among its members, a customs union has a common external tariff and quota system, and a common commercial policy. No member of a customs union may have a separate preferential trading relationship with a third country or group of third countries. A supranational institutional framework is required to ensure its functioning. Customs unions generally create more internal trade and divert more external trade than do free trade areas. The six founding members of the EC agreed to form a customs union in the Treaty of Rome and did so in 1968, well ahead of schedule. A customs union also exists in South America. Mercosur (Southern Cone Common Market) was established in 1991 by Argentina, Brazil, Paraguay, and Uruguay.

A **common market** represents a further step in economic integration by providing for the free movement of services, capital, and labour in addition to the free movement of goods. For various economic and political reasons the Six decided to go beyond the pure common market (the colloquial name for the EC)

Box 2.4 *Continued . . .*

by establishing additionally a common competition policy; monetary and fiscal policy coordination; a common agricultural policy (CAP); a common transport policy; and a preferential trade and aid agreement with member states' ex-colonies. Not all these elements were fully implemented. By the 1980s it was clear that the movement of labour and capital was not entirely free, and a host of non-tariff barriers still stymied intra-Community trade in goods and services. The '1992 project' or single market programme was designed to achieve a true internal market in goods, services, labour, and capital.

An **economic and monetary union** (EMU) is far more ambitious. It includes a single currency and the unification of monetary and fiscal policy. In the EU, plans to introduce EMU, outlined in the Maastricht Treaty, were successfully implemented in January 1999, with euro notes and coins circulating by January 2002 (see Chapter 6). No other region in modern times has come close to this level of economic cooperation.

the proposed agricultural regime, it did not participate. Germany succeeded in emasculating Euratom and grudgingly accepted the EC's overseas territories provisions. In the meantime, Adenauer resisted Erhard's efforts to jettison the common market in favour of looser free trade arrangements, arguing that the EC was necessary for geopolitical as well as economic reasons. French negotiators fought what they called the 'Battle of Paris', trying to assuage domestic criticism of the proposed common market while simultaneously driving a hard bargain in the negotiations in Brussels.

The ensuing Treaty of Rome establishing the EC was a typical political compromise. Its provisions ranged from the general to the specific, from the mundane to the arcane. Those on the customs union, calling for the phased abolition of tariffs among member states and erection of a common external tariff, were the most concrete. The treaty did not outline an agricultural policy, but contained a commitment to negotiate one in the near future. Institutionally, the treaty established a potentially powerful Commission, an Assembly (of appointed, not elected, members) with limited powers, a Council to represent national interests directly in the decision-making process, and a Court of Justice (see Chapter 3).

The Rome treaties were signed on 25 March 1957, and the EC came into being on 1 January 1958. Most Europeans were unaware of either event. Apart from the EDC, European integration had not impinged much on public opinion. Yet the ECSC and EC were highly significant developments. The Coal and Steel Community represented a revolution in Franco-German relations and international organization; the so-called Common Market had the potential to reorder economic and political relations among its member states.

Consolidating the European Community

The big news in Europe in 1958 was not the launch of the EC but the collapse of the French Fourth Republic and the return to power of General Charles de Gaulle. Events in France had a direct bearing on the EC. De Gaulle helped consolidate the new Community by stabilizing France politically (through the construction of the Fifth Republic) and financially (by devaluing the franc). On the basis of renewed domestic confidence, France participated fully in the phased introduction of the customs union, so much so that it came into existence in 1968, eighteen months ahead of schedule.

De Gaulle also pushed for completion of the Common Agricultural Policy (CAP). With a larger farming sector than any other member state, France had most to gain from establishing a single agricultural market, based on guaranteed prices and export subsidies funded by the Community. France pressed for a generous CAP and had the political weight to prevail. Nevertheless the construction of the CAP, in a series of legendary negotiations in the early 1960s, proved onerous. What emerged was a complicated policy based on protectionist principles, in contrast to the liberalizing ethos of Community policies in most other sectors (see Chapter 6). The contrast represented the competing visions of the EC held by its members, potential members, and the wider international community (see Box 2.5).

Implementation of the customs union and construction of the CAP signalled the Community's initial success, obscuring setbacks in other areas such as the failure to implement a common transport policy. The customs union and the CAP had a major international impact. For instance, as part of its emerging customs union the EC developed a common commercial policy, which authorized the Commission to represent the Community in international trade talks, notably the GATT. The CAP tended to distort international trade and irritate the EC's partners. It is no coincidence that the first transatlantic trade dispute was over the CAP (the so-called 'Chicken War' of 1962–3, sparked by higher tariffs on US chicken imports).

The EC's fledgling institutions also began to consolidate during this period. The Commission organized itself in Brussels under the presidency of Walter Hallstein, former top official in the German foreign ministry and a close colleague of Adenauer's. There were nine Commissioners, two each from the large member states and one each from the small member states (this formula would remain unchanged for nearly fifty years). The Commission's staff came from national civil services and from the ECSC's High Authority, which continued to exist until it merged into the Commission in 1967. In the Council of Ministers, foreign ministers met most often, indicating the EC's growing political as well as economic nature. The Council formed a permanent secretariat in Brussels to assist its work. Member states also established permanent representations of national civil

> **Box 2.5** HOW IT REALLY WORKS
>
> British accession and competing visions of Europe
>
> The integration of Europe is sometimes portrayed (not least in the popular press) as an inexorable process following some overarching agreed plan. But in practice integration has proceeded in fits and starts, the result of domestic and international pressures and competing visions of what the EU is or should be. The debates surrounding the UK's first application to join the EC illustrate the very different visions of Europe competing for dominance during the Community's early years.
>
> In a remarkable reversal of policy, the UK applied to join the EC in 1961. The UK wanted unfettered access to EC industrial markets, but also wanted to protect trade preferences for Commonwealth countries (former British colonies) and turn the CAP in a more liberal direction. De Gaulle was unsympathetic to the UK's application. Economically, he wanted a protectionist CAP. Politically, he espoused a 'European Europe,' allied to the United States but independent of it. By contrast, the UK acquiesced in America's Grand Design for a more equitable transatlantic relationship built on the twin pillars of the US and a united Europe centred on the EC, a design that disguised America's quest for continued hegemony in NATO. The US supported British membership in the EC as part of its Grand Design. By vetoing the UK's application in January 1963, de Gaulle defended the CAP and thwarted American ambitions in Europe. The episode suggests how international pressure, but also competing visions of Europe have shaped how European integration has evolved.

servants in Brussels, whose heads formed the Committee of Permanent Representatives (Coreper), which soon became one of the Community's most powerful bodies. The Assembly, later known as the European Parliament (EP), tried to assert itself from the beginning, demanding for instance that its members be directly elected rather than appointed from national parliaments. But the EP lacked political support from powerful member states. Working quietly in Luxembourg, the Court of Justice began in the 1960s to generate an impressive corpus of case law. In several landmark decisions, the Court developed the essential rules on which the EC legal order rests, including the supremacy of Community law (see Chapter 3).

Crisis and compromise

De Gaulle's arrival had a negative as well as a positive effect on the consolidation of the nascent EC. De Gaulle openly opposed supranationalism. He and his supporters (Gaullists) had resisted the ECSC and the EDC; they tolerated the EC, but primarily because of its economic potential for France. In de Gaulle's view, the nation state was supreme. States could and should form alliances and collaborate closely, but only on the basis of intergovernmentalism, not shared sovereignty. Yet de Gaulle thought that the Community could be useful politically as the basis of an intergovernmental organization of European states.

A clash over supranationalism was likely to arise in 1965 as, under the terms of the Rome Treaty, a number of decisions in key policy areas, including agriculture, were due to become subject to *qualified majority voting* (QMV) (see Box 2.2). Majority voting is a key instrument of supranationalism because member states on the losing side agree to abide by the majority's decision. De Gaulle rejected this on principle, seeing QMV as an unacceptable abrogation of national sovereignty. The looming confrontation erupted in June 1965, when de Gaulle triggered the so-called '*Empty Chair Crisis*' (see Box 2.2) by withdrawing French representation in the Council ostensibly in protest against Commission proposals to strengthen the EC's budgetary powers, but really in an effort to force other member states to agree not to extend the use of QMV. De Gaulle had a compelling practical reason to resist qualified majority voting: he wanted to protect the CAP against a voting coalition of liberal member states.

The crisis ended in January 1966 with the so-called *Luxembourg Compromise* (see Box 2.2). The Treaty's provisions on QMV would stand, but the Council would not take a vote if a member state insisted that very important interests were at stake. The Luxembourg Compromise tipped the balance toward intergovernmentalism in the Community's decision-making process, with unanimity becoming the norm. This had a detrimental effect on decision-making until the Single European Act took effect in 1987.

EC after de Gaulle

By 1969, when de Gaulle resigned, the EC was economically strong but politically weak. Supranationalism was in the doldrums. The Commission and Parliament were relatively powerless, and unanimity hobbled effective decision-making in the Council. De Gaulle had twice rebuffed the UK's application for EC membership, in 1963 and in 1967. Following de Gaulle's departure, British membership became inevitable, although accession negotiations were nonetheless difficult. Ireland, Denmark, and Norway negotiated alongside the UK, but a majority of Norwegian voters rejected membership in a referendum in 1972. The UK, Ireland, and Denmark joined the following year.

The EC's first enlargement was a milestone in the organization's history. Unfortunately it coincided with international financial turmoil and a severe economic downturn that slowed the momentum for further integration. Moreover, the UK's early membership was troublesome. A new Labour government insisted on renegotiating the country's accession terms. The renegotiations alienated

many of the UK's partners in the EC, especially France and Germany. At the end of
the 1970s a new Conservative government, under Margaret Thatcher, demanded a
huge budgetary rebate. The UK had a point, but Thatcher's strident manner when
pushing her case incensed other member states. The British budgetary question
dragged on until 1984, overshadowing a turnaround in the Community's fortunes
after a decade of poor economic performance.

Difficult decade

Because of the UK's early difficulties in the EC and prevailing stagflation in Europe,
the 1970s is generally seen as a dismal decade in the history of integration. Yet a
number of important institutional and policy developments occurred at that time.
On the policy side, the 1979 launch of the European Monetary System (EMS),
the precursor to the single currency, was especially significant. Concerned about
America's seeming abdication of international financial leadership, and eager to
curb inflation and exchange rate fluctuations in the EC, French and German leaders devised the EMS, with the Exchange Rate Mechanism (ERM) designed to regulate currency fluctuations at its core. The sovereignty-conscious UK declined to
participate. By the mid-1980s, the inflation and exchange rates of ERM members
began to converge. The Lomé agreement of 1975, providing preferential trade and
development assistance to scores of African, Caribbean, and Pacific countries,
was another important achievement for the beleaguered Community, as was
the launch of European Political Cooperation (EPC), a mechanism to coordinate
member states' foreign policies (see Chapter 10). In terms of greater European
integration, the development of EC environmental policy in the 1970s was even
more important.

Institutionally, the 1970s saw a gradual improvement in the Commission's political fortunes, especially later in the decade under the presidency of Roy Jenkins.
The first direct elections to the EP took place in 1979, raising the institution's
political profile and enhancing the EC's formal legitimacy. The inauguration of the
European Council (regular meetings of the heads of state and government) in 1975
strengthened intergovernmental cooperation. The European Council soon became
the EC's most important agenda-setting body (see Chapter 3), while direct elections laid the basis for the EP's institutional ascension in the 1980s and 1990s. The
Court of Justice continued in the 1970s to build an impressive body of case law that
maintained the momentum for deeper integration.

By the early 1980s, the EC had weathered the storm of recession and the challenge of British accession. The end of dictatorial regimes in Greece, Portugal, and
Spain in the mid-1970s presaged the EC's Mediterranean enlargement (Greece
joined in 1981, Portugal and Spain in 1986). By that time the EC was more than a
customs union but still less than a full-fledged common market. A plethora of non-
tariff barriers (such as divergent technical standards) hobbled intra-Community

trade in goods and services, and the movement of people and capital was not entirely free. Intensive foreign competition, especially from the US and Japan, began to focus the attention of political and business leaders on the EC's ability to boost member states' economic growth and international competitiveness. This was the genesis of the single market programme, which spearheaded the EC's response to globalization and ushered in the EU.

The emerging European Union

The single market programme for the free movement of goods, services, capital, and people emerged as a result of collaboration between big business, the Commission, and national leaders in the early 1980s. Several European Councils endorsed the idea. But the initiative only took off when the Commission, under the new presidency of Jacques Delors, unveiled a legislative roadmap (a White Paper on the 'completion' of the internal market) in 1985. To ensure the programme's success, the European Council decided to convene an Intergovernmental Conference (IGC) to make the necessary treaty changes. Chief among these was a commitment to use qualified majority voting for most of the White Paper's proposals, thereby ending the legislative gridlock that had hamstrung earlier efforts for full market liberalization.

As well as covering the single market programme, the Single European Act (SEA) of 1986 brought environmental policy into the treaty, strengthened Community policy in research and technological development, and included a section on foreign policy cooperation. It also committed the EC to higher expenditure on regional development (cohesion policy), partly as a side payment to the poorer member states, including new entrants Portugal, Spain, and Greece, which were unlikely to benefit as much from market integration as were their richer counterparts. Institutionally, the SEA's most important provisions enhanced the EP's legislative role through the introduction of the *cooperation procedure* (see Box 3.5). This was intended to improve democratic accountability at a time when the EC's remit and visibility were about to increase dramatically.

The single market programme, with a target date of 1992, was a success. Big business responded enthusiastically to the prospect of a fully integrated European marketplace. '1992' unleashed a wave of Europhoria. The EC was more popular than at any time before or since. Eager to remove barriers to the free movement of people even before implementation of the single market programme, France and Germany agreed in 1984 to press ahead with the abolition of border checks. This led to the *Schengen Agreement* (see Box 2.2) for the free movement of people, which gradually included most other member states and formally became part of the EU under the terms of the 1997 Amsterdam Treaty.

Economic and monetary union

The popularity of the single market programme emboldened Commission President Delors to advocate Economic and Monetary Union (EMU). He had the strong support of German Chancellor Helmut Kohl, an avowed 'Euro-federalist'. The Commission publicly justified EMU on economic grounds, as the corollary of the single market programme, but Delors and Kohl saw it primarily as a political undertaking. French President François Mitterrand also supported EMU, for both political and economic reasons. Thatcher opposed EMU vehemently, seeing it as economically unnecessary and politically unwise. Not only did Thatcher fail to turn the tide against EMU; her strident opposition to it contributed to her loss of the leadership of the Conservative Party and the country.

The European Council authorized Delors to set up a committee to explore the road to EMU. The 'Delors Report' of 1989 proposed a three-stage programme, including strict convergence criteria for potential participants and the establishment of a European Central Bank with responsibility primarily for price stability. The report reflected German preferences for EMU. That was understandable, given Germany's economic weight and German obsession with inflation. Even so, opinion in Germany remained sceptical about EMU, with the politically influential German central bank (Bundesbank) opposed to it.

Planning for EMU was well on track by the time the Berlin Wall came down in November 1989. By raising again the spectre of the German question, the end of the Cold War increased the momentum for EMU. Fearful of the prospect, however remote, of a rootless Germany in the post-Cold War world, other Community leaders determined to bind Germany fully into the new Europe, largely through EMU. Kohl was more than happy to oblige and cleverly exploited the concerns of Germany's neighbours to overcome domestic opposition to EMU, especially in the Bundesbank.

Maastricht and beyond

EC leaders convened two Intergovernmental Conferences in 1990, one on EMU and the other on political union, meaning institutional and non-EMU policy reforms. Both conferences converged in the Maastricht Treaty of 1992, which established the European Union with its three-pillar structure (see Box 1.2). The first pillar comprised the EC, including EMU; the second comprised the Common Foreign and Security Policy (CFSP), a direct response to the external challenges of the post-Cold War period; the third covered cooperation on justice and home affairs, notably immigration, asylum, and criminal matters. This awkward structure reflected most member states' unwillingness to subject internal security and foreign policy to supranational decision-making. Thus the Commission and the EP were merely associated with Pillar 2 and 3 activities. Within Pillar 1, by contrast, the Maastricht Treaty extended the EP's legislative power by introducing the far-reaching co-decision procedure, which made the Parliament a legally and politically equal legislator to the Council of Ministers (see Chapter 3).

The further extension of the EP's legislative authority, and the introduction of the principle of subsidiarity (whereby decisions should be taken as closely as possible to the people compatible with effective policy delivery), demonstrated EU leaders' concerns about the organization's legitimacy. Those concerns were fully vindicated in tough ratification battles in several member states, including the UK, France, and Germany, but especially in Denmark, where a narrow majority rejected the treaty in a referendum in June 1992. Voters approved the treaty, with special concession for Denmark, in a second referendum, in May 1993. This allowed the EU to come into being in November 1993.

At issue in Denmark and elsewhere was the so-called democratic deficit: the EU's perceived remoteness and lack of accountability (see Chapter 8). This issue remained a major challenge for the EU into the twenty-first century. The resignation of the Jacques Santer Commission in March 1999, amid allegations of fraud and mismanagement, increased popular scepticism, although it also demonstrated the Commission's accountability to the EP (the Commission resigned to avoid being sacked by the Parliament). Yet many Europeans saw the EP as part of the problem: few understood exactly the EP's role, and the turnout in direct elections declined yet again in June 1999. For its part, the Commission launched an ambitious reform effort under a new President, Romano Prodi, in 1999, while EU leaders attempted to improve transparency and efficiency in the decision-making process. Yet, as the negative result of the first Irish referendum on the Nice Treaty illustrated in 2001, public opinion remained highly sceptical of the EU.

Despite considerable public disquiet, the post-Maastricht period saw substantial policy development. The launch of the final stage of EMU in January 1999, in keeping with the Maastricht timetable, was one of the EU's most striking achievements. Euro notes and coins came into circulation in January 2002. The strengthening of the CFSP and the initiation of a European Security and Defence Policy, largely in response to the Balkan wars and uncertainty about US involvement in future European conflicts, was another important policy development. Reform of CFSP was the main outcome of the 1997 Amsterdam Treaty, which nevertheless ducked increasingly pressing questions of institutional reform necessitated by impending enlargement.

Post-Cold War enlargement

Enlargement was a major challenge for the new EU. As a result of the end of the Cold War, three non-aligned European states (Austria, Finland, and Sweden) joined in 1995. (Norway, a non-neutral, again chose not to join in another referendum in 1994.) The newly independent states of Central and Eastern Europe also applied for EU membership soon after the end of the Cold War (as did Cyprus and Malta). For the Central and Eastern European states the road to membership would be long and difficult, involving major political, economic, and administrative reforms. The slow pace of enlargement disappointed the applicant countries and their supporters in the United States, who criticized the EU for being too cautious. The EU countered that enlargement, an inherently complicated process, was even more complex in view of the applicants' history, political culture, and low level of economic development. The EU's approach reflected a widespread lack of enthusiasm for enlargement among politicians and the public in existing member states. Even so, negotiations with the Central and Eastern European applicants eventually began in 1998 (with the five front-runners) and in 2000 (with the five others). Cyprus also began accession negotiations in 1998, and Malta in 2000. The EU grudgingly acknowledged Turkey's candidacy in 1999. The EU agreed at the Nice Summit in December 2000 that enlargement could begin in 2004.

As Chapter 9 explores, enlargement will greatly alter the EU. The accession of so many poor, agricultural countries will have a profound effect on the CAP and cohesion policy. The EU reformed both policies as part of its Agenda 2000 initiative, in anticipation of enlargement, but the results were patently inadequate. Further policy reform is bound to coincide with or follow enlargement, inevitably giving rise to bitter budgetary disputes.

The EU's institutions also required reform because of enlargement. Member states avoided the contentious question of institutional reform in the Amsterdam Treaty, agreeing instead to undertake an institutional overhaul in another IGC in 2000. That conference resulted in the Nice Treaty of 2001, which changed the modalities of QMV in anticipation of enlargement, but in a way that complicated rather than simplified legislative decision-making. In other institutional areas the outcome of the 2000 IGC was equally disappointing. The messy compromises (see Box 4.3) demonstrated the growing difficulty of reaching agreement among member states on institutional issues, especially those which tended to drive a wedge between France and Germany as well as between the small and large member states. Behind the scenes, member states were more willing to reform institutional procedures that did not require treaty change, such as the complicated co-decision mechanism and the conduct of Council meetings. Such reform may hold the key to the EU's ability to function adequately after enlargement. In the meantime, member states, candidate countries, and EU institutions explored the EU's institutional arrangements in the 2002–3 Convention on the Future of Europe, which discussed the possibility of constitutionalizing the treaties and laid the basis for yet another IGC in 2004.

Conclusion

The history of European integration demonstrates the importance of opportunistic political leadership at a time of fluctuating economic and political fortunes. Early post-war Europe threw up a number of challenges to which European leaders responded with an initiative for limited integration, with strong US support. The ECSC was far from the grand design for European integration that the US had envisioned at the time of the Marshall Plan, but it fostered reconciliation in Franco-German relations and laid an economic foundation for further European integration.

The launch of the European Community in 1958 owed more to economic necessity (potential greater trade among the Six) than geopolitical concerns (the German question), and more to European initiative rather than American prompting. National interests and individual initiatives also played a definitive part. Despite his aversion to supranationalism, de Gaulle appreciated the EC's economic potential and ensured the organization's initial success. De Gaulle's support for the EC, however qualified, reassured Adenauer and strengthened Franco-German relations.

The Single European Act of 1986, which revitalized the EC, and the Maastricht Treaty of 1992, which gave rise to the EU, were also products of Franco-German bargaining. In both cases France and Germany sought to boost European competitiveness in a globalizing economic system while retaining Europe's distinctive social structure, in contrast to that of the United States. The Commission, under the energetic leadership of Jacques Delors, contributed to these developments, but only in association with France and Germany.

The dynamics of Franco-German relations and leadership in the EU are changing, not least because of enlargement. As the Nice Treaty illustrated, France and Germany remain far apart on institutional issues such as the modalities of QMV, the size and role of the Commission, and the composition of the EP. United Germany is showing signs of greater political assertiveness in the EU. Unsure of its place in the post-Cold War world and reeling from domestic political scandals, France seems to lack direction. Enlargement will shift the geopolitical balance of the EU eastward, in favour of Germany.

Yet the history of European integration shows how individual states can overcome institutional and policy differences for the sake of common economic and political interests. The end of the Cold War changed the context of European integration but not necessarily its substance. The challenge of globalization is greater than ever before. It is in the national interest of all member states to manage EMU and make a success of enlargement. They have little choice but to perpetuate European integration.

Discussion questions

1. Are France and Germany bound to lead in Europe?
2. How significant have federalist aspirations been in the history of European integration?
3. Is the United States the 'federator' of Europe?
4. What economic factors impelled integration during various stages of its history?

Further reading

Urwin (1995) and Dinan (1999) provide concise and readable overviews of EU history. For a neofunctionalist analysis of the EC's development, see Haas (1958) and Lindberg (1963). Milward (1984; 1992) is the most influential historian of European integration. Moravcsik (1998) blends political science and historical analysis to produce liberal intergovern-mentalism. Duchêne (1994) is excellent on Jean Monnet, and Gillingham (1991) provides an authoritative account of the origins of the ECSC.

Dinan, D. (1999), *Ever Closer Union: An Introduction to European Integration*, 2nd edn. (Boulder, CO: Lynne Rienner Publishers and Basingstoke: Palgrave).

Duchêne, F. (1994), *Jean Monnet: The First Statesman of Interdependence* (NY: Norton).

Gillingham, J. (1991), *Coal, Steel and the Rebirth of Europe, 1945-1955* (Cambridge: Cambridge University Press).

Haas, E. (1958), *The Uniting of Europe: Political, Social, and Economic Forces* (Stanford, CA: Stanford University Press).

Lindberg, L. (1963). *The Political Dynamics of European Economic Integration* (Stanford, CA: Stanford University Press).

Milward, A. (1984), *The Reconstruction of Western Europe, 1945-51* (Berkeley: University of California Press).

—— (1992), *The European Rescue of the Nation-State* (London: Routledge).

Moravcsik, A. (1998), *The Choice for Europe: Social Purpose and State Power from Messina to Maastricht* (Ithaca, NY: Cornell University Press).

Urwin, D. (1995), *Community of Europe: A History of European Integration Since 1945*, 2nd edn. (London: Longman).

Web links

The EU's official portal site has its own history page: **www.europa.eu.int/abc/history/**.
Leiden University's History Department offers a 'History of European Integration Site' with
links to primary sources and archives, papers and further sites (**www.let.leidenuniv.nl/
history/rtg/res1/index.htm**). The Florence-based European University Institute (EUI)'s
European Integration History Index provides internet resources (in all languages) on post-war
European history, with a particular emphasis on the EU (**www.iue.it/LIB/SISSCO/VL/
hist-eur-integration/Index.html**).

Part II

Major Actors

Chapter 3
The EU's Institutions

Elizabeth Bomberg, Laura Cram, and David Martin

Contents

Overview

All students of the EU need a basic idea of what its major institutions are and how they operate. This chapter describes the EU's institutions, but also emphasizes what makes them important and even interesting. The EU institutions are not just dry organizations (although they are complex); they are dynamic organisms exercising a unique mix of legislative, executive, and judicial power. We begin by introducing the EU's five most important institutions: the European Commission, the Council of Ministers, the European Council, the European Parliament, and the European Court of Justice. We outline their structures and formal powers (that is, what the Treaties say they can do), but we also focus on their informal power and procedures—including how they manage to 'squeeze' influence out of sometimes limited Treaty prerogatives. We then explain how these institutions interact and the changing dynamics between them. Finally we explore why these institutions matter in determining EU politics and policy more generally.

Introduction: institutions in Treaty and practice

A big part of what makes the EU unique is its institutions, several of which have no close counterparts at the national or international level (Peterson and Shackleton 2002: 2). Whereas the EU's Treaties designate several formal institutions (see Article 7 of the TEC) we step outside this legal definition to explore those five institutions exercising the most power and influence in EU policy and politics: the European Commission, the Council of Ministers, the European Council, the European Parliament (EP), and the European Court of Justice. Table 3.1 presents the formal powers conferred on each of these institutions by major Treaty reform. It does not, however, convey how informal powers have accrued over time, nor the incremental power shifts that may occur between Treaty reform. This section thus introduces the institutions' formal *and* informal powers, and how they have developed.

European Commission

The Commission plays a crucial role in the EU's institutional structure. A hybrid organization, somewhere between an executive and a bureaucracy, the Commission has no obvious counterpart at the national level. The Treaties designated to the Commission profoundly important tasks: to initiate policies and represent the general interest of the European Union; to act as guardian of the Treaties and ensure the correct application of EU legislation; and to manage and negotiate international trade and cooperation agreements. In practical terms, the Commission's power is exercised most spectacularly in competition policy (it has powers to vet and veto mergers), in its international lead in trade talks, and its right to propose policy. Together these powers have afforded the Commission a larger influence in the EU policy process than some member state governments might have preferred.

The Commission as a term is rather confusingly used to refer to two separate facets of this body: the College of Commissioners (or executive Commission) and the administrative Commission (the bureaucracy). The College is the powerhouse of the Commission. Headed by a President nominated by national governments and approved by the EP, the College is charged with specific policy tasks but is also expected to provide political direction for the Commission. The College is made up of twenty Commissioners (the number will change after enlargement) who generally have held high office in national politics before being appointed for a five-year term to serve in Brussels. The Commissioners meet once a week to develop and adopt proposals on new policies and legislation. Once a decision is taken, if necessary by majority vote but usually in the collegial spirit, it becomes the policy of all of the Commissioners who are then obliged to support it whatever their own private misgivings. This spirit of collegiality was severely tested in March 1999 when the Commission, under President Santer, was forced to resign *en masse* following some serious criticisms of individual Commissioners.

The Commissioners are each allocated a portfolio, such as agriculture or social policy, by the President of the Commission. The allocation of portfolios can be politically charged as member states seek to gain control over portfolios which are important to their state's particular national interests. For instance, the French for many years had great success in ensuring that a Frenchman controlled the agricultural portfolios, while a German traditionally had run competition policy. The President now has the power to allocate and reshuffle portfolios in an attempt to overcome this type of wrangling between member states.

Commissioners each have their own private staff or circle of advisers called a *cabinet*. These six officials may be drawn from inside or outside the Commission. They perform a very demanding and important role, keeping their Commissioner informed about important developments in their own policy areas as well as wider developments in the Commission bureaucracy. Like portfolio assignments, the role of *cabinets* can be highly controversial. According to the Treaties, Commissioners are sworn to act not in the interest of their national governments but in the general European interest. Yet Commissioners have been notorious for filling their *cabinets* with staff of their own nationality. Under Commission President Romano Prodi (installed in 1999) new codes of conduct were adopted in an attempt to bring an end to this practice. Prodi, a former Italian prime minister, set an example by initially appointing an Irishman to head his *cabinet*, though the Irishman was subsequently replaced by a Frenchman and then an Italian.

Controversy surrounding portfolio assignments and *cabinet* appointments suggest the assertion of national preferences in the Commission can never be entirely removed. Commissioners do not totally abandon their national affiliation once they arrive in Brussels. But too obvious a representation of national interests can backfire. In 2002, for instance, the Spanish Commissioner for transport was fiercely criticized for her alleged attempt to influence Commission fisheries policy along the lines favoured by Spain. At other times, Commissioners are chided by their home governments for ignoring entirely the government that put them there. In the 1980s, British Prime Minister Margaret Thatcher despaired at 'her' Commissioner's apparent failure to reflect the interests of the Thatcher government. Thus Commissioners face a tough balancing act: they must be aware of the national governments who have appointed them, but must also be sure not to undermine the ability of the Commission to act independently.

Each Commissioner is responsible for a number of *directorates-general* (DGs)—services or departments—which relate to his or her portfolio. These directorates, the Brussels equivalents of national minsters, cover the EU's main policy areas such as agriculture, competition, or environment, and are headed by a director-general who reports directly to the relevant Commissioner. There are over twenty

Table 3.1 The institutions from Rome to Nice: Treaty reform and powers conferred

	Rome (1957)	SEA (1986)	Maastricht (1992)	Amsterdam (1997)	Nice (2001)*
European Commission	Right to propose legislation; draft budget; act as guardian of Treaty; negotiate international trade agreements.	Right of initiative expands to new areas related to the completion of the single market.	Powers enhanced in economic and monetary union and in foreign policy; further extension of the right of initiative.	President's role strengthened and right of initiative extended.	Role of President enhanced; size of Commission stabilized to one Commissioner per member state (until EU reaches 27 member states; then size reduced and equal rotation established).
Council of Ministers	Power to pass legislation; appoint Commission; agree budget.	Increased use of qualified majority voting (QMV) in areas relating to the single market.	Further extension of QMV; right to propose legislation in justice and foreign affairs pillars together with the Commission.	Further extension of QMV and co-decision with the Parliament.	Continued expansion of QMV; re-weighting of votes between large and small member states (effective from 2005).
European Council	*not mentioned in Treaty*	Granted legal status.	Assigned responsibility of defining the general political guidelines of the Union.	Confirmed role in EMU and strengthened position in respect of CSFP.	*seat moved to Brussels*

European Parliament	Right to be consulted on legislation; right to dismiss the Commission.	Extension of legislative authority through the introduction of the cooperation procedure.	Right to amend and pass legislation in limited range of areas (co-decision procedure); greater role in appointing Commission.	Co-decision extended; right to approve appointment of Commission President and Commission as a whole.	Further extension of co-decision procedure; right to place matters before the Court on equal footing with Council and Commission; legal base established for party funding at European level.
European Court of Justice	Guardian of Treaties and EC Law.	Creation of Court of First Instance.	Power to impose fines against member states (but excluded from two intergovernmental pillars).	*increased jurisdiction in third-pillar matters*	Further sharing of tasks with Court of First Instance; creation of more specialized chambers to improve judicial capacity of larger Union; number of judges limited to one per member state.

* if ratified

such departments or services which together make up the *administrative Commission*—the EU's civil service or 'Euro-crats'. Although this Brussels bureaucracy is often portrayed in the popular press as an enormous body intent on taking over Europe, it is in fact relatively small. Approximately 15,000 administrators are employed in the administrative Commission. Only around 4,000 of these are in policy-making posts. Others are involved in the huge amount of translation and interpretation required by the Commission (the Union has eleven official languages) or in research and technological development. A comparison with national administrations is illuminating. Within member states, the average number of civil servants per 10,000 citizens is 322. For all the EU institutions the corresponding ratio is 0.8 civil servants per 10,000 citizens (Nugent 1999: 108). Put another way, the size of the Commission's entire staff is roughly equal to that of a large municipal authority (such as Barcelona) or a medium size national government department such as the French Ministry of Culture.

In practice it is difficult to draw a clear line between the administrative Commission and the more political College of Commissioners. While the College are ultimately responsible for any decisions which emanate from this institution, in practice many ideas are generated much further down within the administrative structures. In turn, some Commissioners will be more interventionist than others in seeking to influence the day-to-day functioning of 'their' directorate-general.

A key feature of the Commission bureaucracy is not only its complexity but its limited resources which must be stretched to cover fundamentally important—and expanding—tasks. The extent to which the member states desire the Commission to embrace these tasks fully has always been ambiguous. Even the Commission's power to initiate policy is not as exclusive as it may first appear (see Box 3.1). More generally, the history of the Commission has been fraught with, on the one hand, pressures to act in the 'European interest' and thus to fulfil its Treaty obligations and, on the other hand, constraints which are imposed by member states. When push comes to shove, many member states can be reluctant to relinquish their control over sensitive or politicized policies. For example, member states have been very cautious about surrendering control over policy areas such as immigration and defence (see Chapters 6 and 10).

The Commission faces further challenges to its position as new institutions with specialist capacities emerge (such as the European Central Bank, see Box 3.7), or as existing institutions, such as the Parliament, gain new powers. Traditionally, however, the Commission has proved adept at making the most of the powers given to it, and at squeezing additional areas of influence out of these. For example, using its place at the heart of EU policy-making, the Commission has conducted detailed cross-national research to support the need for new policies (and a new role for the Commission) in the area of environmental protection. Moreover, the Commission often has managed to create and engage policy networks of actors from the local and national levels and to create a constituency of support for the expansion of its

Box 3.1 HOW IT REALLY WORKS

Who initiates policy?

The formal right to initiate policies is considered one of the Commission's most precious and fundamental powers. Yet it is important not to overestimate the autonomy this right provides the Commission. Many initiatives emanating from the Commission are, in practice, a response to pressures from other sources. The Commission's 'own initiatives' thus account for only 10–20 per cent of proposals. Of all the Commission's proposals:

- **between 20 and 25 per cent** are a follow-up to Council or European Parliament resolutions, European Council initiatives, or requests on the part of the social partners (employers and employees).
- **around 30 per cent** arise from international obligations on the part of the Community.
- **between 10 and 15 per cent** have to do with existing obligations under the Treaty or secondary legislation.
- **around 20 per cent** involve updating existing Community legislation (e.g. adapting it to technical or scientific progress).

Source: Commission (2001e: 6)

policies. It has done so, for instance, in the area of social policy where member states often have been rather ambivalent about cooperation at the EU level. While, ultimately, member states can curb the powers of the Commission through their control over the Treaties, the Commission has shown again and again that it is far from simply being the servant of the member states.

Council of Ministers

The Council of Ministers (formally, the Council of the European Union) is one of the EU's most powerful institutions and its primary decision-making body. The Treaties state that the Council shall consist of 'a representative of each member state at ministerial level authorized to commit the government of the member state' (Article 203 of the TEC). In other words, it is there to represent the interests of national governments who comprise the EU. It is also responsible for *making* the major policy decisions of the Union. Alone or (increasingly) with the Parliament, it decides which EU legislation is adopted, and in what form.

The structure of the Council can be confusing because it has no permanent form or membership. The Treaties speak of only one Council, but it is made up of different ministers, depending on what policy area is being discussed (agriculture, finance, environment, and so on). Of the nine different compositions (as of 2002), the Council with the widest brief is the General Affairs and External Relations

Council (formerly the General Affairs Council) which brings together foreign ministers. It has dealt with general issues relating to policy initiatives and co-ordination, external political relations, or with matters which are politically sensitive (see Box 3.2). Other Councils—such as the Agriculture Council, the Transport Council, and so on—have dealt specifically with dedicated subjects or sectors, but ministers can (and do) refer to the General Affairs and External Relations Council issues which become especially contentious or difficult to resolve.

Box 3.2 Sample Council agenda

The following provides a glimpse of the full agenda facing foreign ministers in a General and Foreign Affairs Council. Note that 'A items' are items already agreed at Coreper level. They are not discussed unless a minister objects, but such objections are rare. The other issues are game for substantive discussion.

COUNCIL OF THE EUROPEAN UNION
Provisional Agenda / General Affairs and External Relations Council (Danish Presidency)

Date: 22 and 23 July 2002
Time: 10 H.00
Venue: Council Secretariat, Justus Lipsius Building,
Rue de la Loi 175, 1048, Brussels

1. Adoption of the provisional agenda
2. Approval of the list of 'A' items
3. Resolutions, decisions and opinions adopted by the European Parliament at its period of session in Strasbourg, 10/13 June 2002
4. Work programme for the Presidency
5. Enlargement
- Presentation of Presidency programme
6. Follow-up to the European Council in Seville
7. Progress of work in other Council configurations

External relations and European Security and Defence Policy
8. EU's priorities in the area of conflict prevention
9. Middle East
10. Western Balkans
11. Food crisis in Southern Africa
12. Zimbabwe (restricted session)
13. Afghanistan (restricted session)
14. Preparation of the World Summit on Sustainable Development
15. Any other business

The Council is aided by a small Secretariat headed by a Secretary-General who is also the High Representative of the CFSP (see Chapter 10). The Secretariat plays a powerful role brokering deals and crafting compromises amongst member states representatives. Even so, the burden on the General Affairs and External Relations Council has increased enormously, leading to a consensus that the 2004 IGC needed to find a way to allow EU foreign ministers to concentrate more directly on foreign policy (see Chapter 10).

The Council meets in some form every few days. The agricultural, economic, and finance (EcoFin) ministers meet at least once a month, the others from one to six times a year. The ministers' primary job is to agree legislation proposed by the Commission. The Treaties provide them with three basic ways of voting to reach a decision. Unanimity is required when a policy is considered particularly sensitive. It applies mainly to fiscal matters (for example tax harmonization) or constitutional questions (accession of new members) or new competences. In addition, it is required when the Council wishes to amend a Commission proposal against the Commission's wishes.

Today, majority voting is applied to most decisions. 'Simple majority', with each state wielding one vote, is used primarily for procedural questions. *Qualified majority voting* (QMV) (see Box 2.2) applies to the bulk of decisions, including most legislation related to the single market and proposals designed to implement or clarify existing policies or legislation. Each new treaty has expanded the areas in which QMV can be applied. Well over three quarters of all EU legislation was agreed by this procedure after 2000. Given the widespread use of majority voting, the question of how a majority is constituted is of critical importance. A qualified or weighted majority means that the more populous member states are given more votes than smaller ones. But how, precisely, weighting should be determined is a sensitive issue (see Chapter 4). The most recent change to this voting system, painfully agreed at the Nice European Council in 2000, made the QMV system far more complex. According to the Nice Treaty, decisions will require a so-called triple majority from 2005: decisions must garner support of a qualified majority of states, the backing of states representing at least 62 per cent of the EU's population, and the support of at least half the member states, whatever their size or population (see Table 3.2). The bottom line is that a qualified majority is now paradoxically more difficult to achieve.

In any case, although QMV *can* now be used in a wide variety of areas, it does not mean it *is* used. In fact, consensus is still widely sought in the Council and votes are seldom forced (see Box 3.3). Whichever decision method is used, these meetings and votes still take place behind closed doors, even if selected debates are now open to the public. A Commission representative attends, but no parliamentarian, no press, and no public is present during the meetings. Extensive leaks to the press ensure the meetings are not held entirely in secret, but these leaks reflect the 'spin' of the various national representatives doing the leaking rather than that of an outside observer. This seclusion makes consensus and agreement easier to achieve (and, some argue, nothing would be agreed without it), but it also makes the Council one of the few—if not only—legislative bodies in the democratic world that takes its main decisions behind closed doors.

Coreper

To help brief their ministers, each member state has its own national delegation (or *Permanent Representation*) in Brussels which acts as a sort of embassy to the EU. Taken together these fifteen permanent representatives form the 'Committee of Permanent Representatives', known by its French abbreviation Coreper. Led by national ambassadors to the EU, Coreper's job is to prepare the work of the Council and to carry out tasks assigned to it by the Council. Coreper itself is split (confusingly) into Coreper II, made up of the Permanent ambassadors who deal primarily with the big political, institutional, and budgetary issues; and Coreper I, led by Deputy ambassadors who deal with most other issues. Agriculture and economic policy have their own special preparatory committees.

  To the uninitiated (and many of the initiated), Coreper's operation is shadowy and complex. National ambassadors and senior civil servants preparing the

Table 3.2 Voting in the Council of Ministers

Voting in an EU of 15 Member States

Member state	Population (Millions)	Number of votes	Number of citizens per vote (Millions)
Germany	82.2	10	8.22
UK	59.6	10	5.96
France	58.7	10	5.87
Italy	57.7	10	5.77
Spain	39.4	8	4.93
Netherlands	15.9	5	3.18
Greece	10.5	5	2.10
Belgium	10.2	5	2.04
Portugal	10.0	5	2.00
Sweden	8.9	4	2.23
Austria	8.1	4	2.03
Denmark	5.3	3	1.77
Finland	5.2	3	1.73
Ireland	3.8	3	1.27
Luxembourg	0.4	2	0.20
Total	**375.9**	**87**	

Qualified majority: 62 votes (71 per cent)
Blocking minority: 26 votes (30 per cent)

Table 3.2 *Continued . . .*

Voting in an EU of 15 Member States

Member state	Population (Millions)	Number of votes	Number of citizens per vote (Millions)
Germany	82.2	29	2.83
UK	59.6	29	2.05
France	58.7	29	2.02
Italy	57.7	29	1.99
Spain	39.4	27	1.46
Netherlands	15.9	13	1.22
Greece	10.5	12	0.88
Belgium	10.2	12	0.85
Portugal	10.0	12	0.83
Sweden	8.9	10	0.89
Austria	8.1	10	0.81
Denmark	5.3	7	0.76
Finland	5.2	7	0.74
Ireland	3.8	7	0.54
Luxembourg	0.4	4	0.10
*** *** ***	***	***	***
Poland	38.7	27	1.43
Romania	22.5	14	1.60
Czech Rep.	10.3	12	0.86
Hungary	10.0	12	0.83
Bulgaria	8.2	10	0.82
Slovakia	5.4	7	0.77
Lithuania	3.7	7	0.53
Latvia	2.4	4	0.60
Slovenia	2.0	4	0.50
Estonia	1.4	4	0.35
Cyprus	0.8	4	0.20
Malta	0.4	3	0.13
Total	**481.7**	**345**	

Qualified majority: 255 votes (around 74 per cent), as well as a majority of member states, as well as 62 per cent of the EU's population
Blocking minority: 91 votes (around 26.5 per cent), or a majority of member states or 38.1 per cent of the EU's population

Sources: Commission (2001d); Galloway (2001); Wessels (2001).

ground for Council meetings are assisted by numerous working groups and committees of national delegates who scrutinize Commission proposals, get a feel for what amendments would or would not be acceptable, and hammer out deals in the run-up to the Council sessions. The vast majority of decisions (around 70 per cent) are taken here, before ministers ever get involved (Hayes-Renshaw and Wallace 1997: 15). This policy-making power prompted former President of the

Box 3.3 HOW IT REALLY WORKS:

Reaching decisions in the Council

Qualified majority voting now applies to most areas of decision-making in the Council, and any national representative on the Council can call for its use. Yet in practice, only around one-quarter of decisions which could be agreed under QMV are actually agreed that way (see Hayes-Renshaw and Wallace 1997: 53–4). Pushing for a formal vote too early or too often could create resentment that disrupts the mood and effectiveness of the Council. Thus, whatever the formal rules stipulate, decision-making in the Council usually proceeds on the understanding that consensus will be sought whenever possible.

How is this consensus achieved? Imagine a contentious item on the Council's agenda (say work and safety regulations). Perhaps a majority of states support the initiative but several are opposed or ambivalent. Well before proceeding to a vote, several attempts will be made to achieve some sort of consensus. This bargaining is most intense at the level of Coreper. Phone calls or informal chats between national representatives prepare the ground for subsequent meetings where agreements can be struck. Informal understandings or agreements might also be reached at the meals that are very much a part of both Coreper and Council meetings. Ostensibly a time for break and refreshment, these lunches provide opportunities for a delicate probing of national positions and willingness to deal. Similarly, a good chairman can make use of scheduled or requested breaks in the proceedings to explore possibilities for a settlement. These breaks feature off-the-record discussions or 'confessionals' between the chairman and national representatives or amongst representatives themselves. Lubricating these discussions are the familiarity and personal relationships that national representatives have built up over time. In the end, the objections of opposing states might be assuaged by a re-drafting of certain clauses, a promise of later support for a favoured initiative, or the possibility of a derogation (or postponement) of a policy's implementation for one or more reluctant state. The point is that the day-to-day practice in Coreper and the Council is characterized far more by the search for a consensus than by the straightforward mechanics of strategic voting.

Commission Jacques Delors to refer to Coreper as the 'powerhouse of Europe' (*Economist* 8 March 1997).

Council Presidency

Traditionally, the Presidency of the Council of Ministers has been held by a member state for six months on a rotating basis. The country holding the Presidency arranges and chairs all meetings of the Council, and has primary responsibility for coordinating the Unions' foreign policy (see Chapter 10). More generally their job is to build consensus and move decision-making forward. Holding the Presidency does not afford the host country extra formal power, but it can give that country added influence. By arranging the meetings and setting the Council's agenda the host attempts to determine which issues will be given priority and which will not. The Presidency also brings the member government a certain amount of prestige and visibility. Of course holding the presidency has disadvantages as well. The costs and time required of national officials are daunting if not overwhelming, especially for smaller states such as Ireland or Luxembourg. Moreover, a lot can go wrong in six months. EU crises (such as a failed referendum) can tarnish a Presidency whether or not the country holding it was responsible. On the other hand, six months is not usually enough to accomplish all or even most of that to which the host country aspires. It seemed possible that the days of the rotating Council presidency were numbered and the Convention on the Future of Europe prepared the ground for the 2004 IGC. The Convention's Chairman, Valéry Giscard d'Estaing, noted 'very extensive acceptance of the idea of ending the rotating presidency' in late 2002 (*Financial Times*, 7 October 2002).

Given their core function—representing member states' interests in the decision-making process—it would be easy to conclude that the Council of Ministers and Coreper are purely intergovernmental bodies, interested primarily in protecting national sovereignty and halting attempts for further integration. But regular ministerial meetings, informal contacts, and routinized bargaining at the level of Council and Coreper have provided the grounds for continual and close cooperation among executives from different member states. As a result, the Council has constructed a collective identity which is more than an amalgamation of national views, and which has helped push integration forward. In the final analysis, integration has proceeded only with the Council's sanction.

European Council (of Heads of State and Government)

The European Council began in the 1970s as an occasional series of informal fireside chats among the member states' heads of state (in the case of Finland and France whose Presidents are elected) and government. It is now much more: settling problems unresolved at lower levels of decision-making and providing political leadership for the entire EU. The European Council meetings (usually referred to in the media as Summits) are held three or four times a year. They are ordinarily hosted by the country holding the presidency and usually known by the name of their host city (although the Nice Treaty stipulates that all official European Council meetings will be held in Brussels after 2003). The location and even meal menus are carefully chosen to create an atmosphere conducive to open discussion, problem resolution and general *bonhomie*.

Over the years the European Council has climbed to the top of the EU's decision-making hierarchy and is now a major agenda-setter. Direct elections to the Parliament, monetary union, and the initiative for a EU rapid reaction force have all been launched at the European Council level. Major Treaty reform also is agreed at this level. The European Council's far reaching and dramatic decisions have helped propel their meetings into the public spotlight where they have become the focal point for media coverage of the EU. Hospitality, including for the press, is lavish. Photo opportunities are abundant and the final press conferences have become elaborately staged events.

The European Council's other broad function, however, is problem resolution, which is less amenable to public display. Issues which cannot be resolved at Coreper or Council levels often can be resolved at this elevated political level, perhaps through informal persuasion, perhaps through the forging of package deals which trade off agreement on one issue (say regional spending) in exchange for concessions on another (say CAP reform). Serious deadlocks on budget agreements often have been resolved only through such deals in late night meetings.

European Parliament

The European Parliament is the only directly elected EU institution. It is made up of 626 members (MEPs) elected every five years in elections across the fifteen member states. To its supporters, the Parliament is the voice of the people in European decision-making, but to critics it is little more than an expensive talking shop. Both of these portraits carry elements of truth. Compared to national parliaments the EP appears weak, and its role circumscribed. It does not initiate legislation, and its control of the EU's purse strings is limited. It began life as a consultative assembly, and was only directly elected for the first time in 1979. Its housekeeping arrangements are clumsy. Members must shuttle between Brussels (where committee and other meetings are held) and Strasbourg (where plenary sessions take place). But every Treaty change from the Single European Act in the mid-1980s up to the Nice Treaty of 2001 has strengthened the role of the Parliament in EU decision-making (see Table 3.1), and today it enjoys equal power with the Council in deciding most legislation. Moreover, the EP has proved adept at extracting maximum influence from limited formal powers (see Box 3.4).

The Members of the Parliament sit in political groups (not in national blocs), and most of the Parliament's activities are structured around these groups. The largest groups are comprised of identifiable political families such as the Christian Democrats or Socialists. Other groups are more ad hoc and bring together parties and individuals in loose coalitions in order to obtain the advantages (such as resources and speaking time) that membership of a group brings. The leaders of the party political groups, along with the Parliament's president and vice presidents, set the EP's agenda. But, like the US Congress, the detailed and most important work of the Parliament is carried out in seventeen standing Committees, organized by

Box 3.4 How the EP 'squeezes' power

The Parliament has always made the most of its limited powers. Even in the 1980s, when it had no power of veto or co-decision as it now has, the Parliament utilized several techniques to make its influence felt. One was the power of delay. Because the Council of Ministers could not vote on proposed legislation without waiting for the Parliament's Opinion, the EP might suggest to the Council that an Opinion could not possibly be delivered in a timely way . . . unless, of course the Council wished to rethink its opposition to certain amendments favoured by the EP (see Bomberg 1998: 152).

Similarly, in budget negotiations the EP's formal power is limited, but it does have the power to sign off—or not—on the agreed document. It uses this power selectively but effectively. For example, in the negotiations leading up to the 2000 budget, the EP bargained hard for increases in areas of particular importance (social and environmental policy, development aid). The Council abhorred such budget increases, but knew it needed the Parliament's approval. In the end, the EP got its increased spending not through a overall increase in the budget, but from a cut in agricultural spending.

New powers are often exploited to the fullest. The EP has on occasion threat-ened to use its Maastricht Treaty power to approve or veto the accession of new members. In the mid-1990s the Parliament threatened to scupper or at least delay accession of Austria, Finland, and Sweden if its call for an intergovernmental conference leading to the Amsterdam Treaty was ignored. Whether or not the EP would have blocked accession is less important than the effect its threats can have. Of course the threats must seem real, and for that to happen the EP must stay united. Such unity is not easy to come by in such a large and diverse institu-tion with 626 members from a vast array of parties and background. Thus despite its ability to 'squeeze' power, the Parliament does not always get its way.

policy areas (such as Transport, Agriculture, or the Environment). Although MEPs usually vote along party lines, national allegiances are never far from the fore. For an extreme illustration, consider the 2001 case in which virtually every German MEP supported their government's opposition to a directive designed to regulate cross-border company takeovers (see Box 5.5).

The Parliament's powers can be conveniently divided under three headings: supervisory (control), legislative, and budgetary. Its power has increased in all three areas, albeit to different degrees. The Parliament exercises *supervision* or control over the Commission and the Council through its right to question, exam-ine and debate the large number of reports produced by these two bodies. Its power directly to control the Council is weak but its assent is required before the Council can approve the accession of any new members (see Chapter 9).

The Parliament's increasing supervision over the Commission is more notice-able. When a new Commission is appointed by member governments, the EP must approve the Council's nominee for Commission President. It holds hearings with the nominee Commissioners and then appoints (or not) the whole Commission by a vote of confidence. More dramatically, the EP has the right to sack the entire Commission through a vote of censure. The Parliament has not yet wielded this 'atom bomb': to do so would require the support of an absolute majority of all MEPs and two-thirds of the votes cast. However, in 1999, following a report on the Commission's mismanagement by a committee of independent experts mandated by the EP, the Commission opted to resign rather than face formal (and certain) censure by the Parliament. In other words, the threat of censure—and not just its formal application—is itself a powerful weapon in the Parliament's arsenal of supervisory powers. But it cannot yet remove individual Commissioners, as many Parliamentarians wish it could.

The Parliament's *legislative* powers also have grown significantly since the Treaty of Rome. Originally Parliament only had the right to give an opinion on a Commis-sion proposal for legislation prior to adoption by the Council. Today, Parliament has the right of *co-decision* in a wide range of EU legislation (see Box 3.5). Under this procedure no text can be adopted without the formal agreement of both the Council and Parliament. The Council knows it must listen and accommodate the EP, which means many more Parliament amendments now find their way into EU legislation. Yet despite the wide use of co-decision, sensitive areas such as taxation and agricultural prices remain exempt. In these areas Parliament only gives an opinion which can be acted upon or ignored.

When it comes to *budgetary* powers the influence of the EP is uneven. On one hand, its powers over expenditure are significant. The annual budget only comes into force once the President of the Parliament has signed it. The Parliament has the last word in areas such as spending on the regions, social policy, culture, and education. Its importance is recognized by organized interests who lobby the EP intensely on these issues. On the other hand, the Parliament's budgetary role is strictly limited in important respects. It has virtually no say on the revenues side of the budget. Moreover, on issues of agricultural spending (which accounts for nearly half the budget) the Parliament can propose amendments but the Council has the last say.

The European Parliament has seen its powers grow significantly since direct elections were first held in 1979. However, many still question its ability to bring legitimacy to the EU decision-making process. Its claim to represent the peoples of Europe is seriously undermined by low and declining turnouts in European Parliament elections (49 per cent in the 1999 EP elections, and as low as 24 per cent in some member states). This lack of support, combined with the Parliament's image (accurate or not) as a profligate organization might well act as a break on any further increases in its powers. Ultimately Parliament's future role is tied up with larger questions of democracy and legitimacy in the EU (see Chapter 8).

Box 3.5 Key concepts and terms: legislative procedures

The EU has several different procedures for agreeing legislation, and the power of the institutions vary across them. The four most important are:

The **consultation** procedure was the original device used to decide most legislation, but today it is only used for a few policies relating primarily to agricultural policy as well as issues of asylum, visas, or immigration. Under the consultation procedure the Commission submits a proposal to the Council of Ministers. The Council is obliged to seek the opinion of the EP, but not to pay any attention to it (it often does not).

Under the **cooperation procedure** introduced in the SEA, the Parliament gained more influence. If the Parliament did not like what the Council had done with its proposed amendments it could ask for a 'second reading', a chance to review the legislation again and ask for further amendments. It could also reject the legislation under this procedure, but the Council could still overrule that objection. Today, cooperation applies only in limited areas of economic and monetary union.

The vast majority of EU legislation (over three quarters) now falls under the **co-decision procedure**. Under co-decision the European Parliament formally shares legal responsibility for legislation jointly with the Council of Ministers. The Parliament and Council must enter into direct negotiations if they cannot agree on a proposal. If these negotiations fail to reach agreement the legislative proposal fails. Essentially, co-decision gives the Parliament the power to veto any legislation that falls under this procedure. Yet its real significance is not the actual veto power it grants the Parliament (it wields this veto rarely). Rather co-decision has altered the way policy-making players view and interact with the Parliament. Knowing the Parliament 'matters' in ultimately deciding legislation, the Commission, the Council, and skilful lobbyists are keen to listen to, accommodate, and shape the Parliament's views when policies are being formulated.

Finally, the **assent procedure** is used to establish the EP's approval of major decisions concerning international treaties, most EU cohesion funding (see Chapter 6), and enlargement. The EP cannot propose amendments to these proposals. In most cases, the Parliament must agree to assent by an absolute majority. No decision requiring assent can be made without the EP's approval.

European Court of Justice

At first glance, the European Court of Justice (ECJ) seems neither a particularly powerful nor controversial institution. It is located in an unremarkable building in Luxembourg, and is comprised of fifteen judges (currently one per member state) plus six Advocate Generals who draft Opinions for the judges. It is supported in its work by the Court of First Instance, a lower tribunal created in 1989 to ease the growing workload of the Court (it had around 900 cases pending by mid-2002). The role of the ECJ is to ensure that in the interpretation and application of the Treaties the law is observed. In practice this function means that the Court is the final arbiter in disputes among EU institutions, and between EU institutions and member states. It is responsible for ensuring that the EU's institutions do not go beyond the powers given to them under the Treaties. It also ensures national compliance with EU Treaties and, since the Maastricht Treaty, can even fine firms or member states that breach EU (formally, Community) law.

More generally, the Court has been remarkably innovative in pushing the integration process forward. A series of decisions in the early 1960s widened the Court's jurisdiction and gave real substance to the EU legal system. Two landmark decisions during the 1960s developed the essential rules on which the EU legal order rests. In the 1963 *Van Gend en Loos* case, the Court established the doctrine of *direct effect*, which mandated that EU citizens had a legal right to expect their governments to adhere to its European obligations. In 1964 (*Costa v. ENEL*), the Court established the *supremacy* of Community law, which means that if a domestic law contradicts an EU obligation, European law prevails.

Community law is thus qualitatively different from international law in that individuals can seek remedy for breaches of it through their domestic courts. The process operates through the *preliminary ruling* system, which allows national courts to ask the Court for a view on the European aspects of a case before them. Such rulings have shaped national policies as diverse as the right to advertise abortion services and the age of retirement. These rulings also have contributed to the claim that the Court has, in effect, become a policy-making body in its own right (see Box 3.6).

However, the key contribution of the Court in establishing the direct effect and supremacy of Community law has been to create an important tool *other* institutions may use in the process of European integration. For instance in the 1979 landmark *Cassis de Dijon* case the Court established the principle of 'mutual recognition': a product made or sold legally in one member state (in this case a sweet French blackcurrant liqueur) cannot be barred in another member state (in this case, Germany). The principle is fundamental to the single market because it established that national variation in standards could exist as long as trade was not unduly impeded. But the full effect of the ruling was not apparent until the

Box 3.6 COMPARED TO WHAT?

The ECJ and the US Supreme Court

The European Court of Justice—like the EU more generally—is in many ways *sui generis*, an international body with no precise counterpart anywhere in Europe or beyond. But interesting parallels—as well as contrasts—can be drawn between the ECJ and the US Supreme Court, both in terms of their power and its limits.

There are some key differences between the two. The US Supreme Court's primary function is to uphold the US constitution, whereas the EU traditionally has had no such constitution. (Yet even here the difference may not be as stark as it first seems. For some legal scholars the cumulative impact of the ECJ's decisions over the years amounts to a 'quiet revolution' in converting the Treaty of Rome into a constitution for Europe (Weiler 1999).) Perhaps a more straightforward difference is jurisdiction, or the power to hear and decide cases. The jurisdiction of the Supreme Court is vast. It includes the consitutionally-conferred right to hear all cases involving legal disputes between the US states. More important is its appellate jurisdiction—the power to hear cases raising constitutional issues invoked by any national treaty, federal law, state law, or act. The ECJ's jurisdiction is far more confined. Its rulings on trade have had a fundamental impact on the single market and the EU more generally. But many matters of national law and most non-trade disputes between states fall outside its remit (see Cram 2001). Moreover, unlike the US Court the ECJ cannot 'cherrypick' a few select cases it would like to hear. Finally, recruitment, appointment, and tenure differ, with US Supreme Court justices seated for life following an involved and often highly politicized appointment and confirmation process. Judges on the ECJ, by contrast, are appointed with comparatively little publicity and they remain relatively unknown for their six-year renewable term.

Yet similarities are also telling. In both cases, the interpretations and rulings of these higher courts take precedence over those of lower or national courts. In both cases, these rulings must be enforced by lower courts. Moreover, like the US Supreme Court in its early decades, the ECJ's earlier decisions helped consolidate the authority of the Union's central institutions. But perhaps the most interesting similarities involve these Courts' power and political role. In the case of the US Supreme Court, concerns about politicization and activism of the Court are well known, especially in its rulings on abortion and racial equality (see McKeever 1995). In the EU, too, however, concerns about the Court's procedure, its ability to push integration forward, and the possible expansion of its authority have pro-pelled the Court into the heart of political debates about the future of the EU. Thus, whatever their differences, both these Courts have raised fundamental questions about the proper limits of judicial activism and the role of courts in democratic societies.

Commission used the principle as a cornerstone of its 1985 proposals to launch the single market (see Chapter 2).

The Court's own exercise of its powers remains contested. While most agree its policy-making role is inevitable, debate turns on when and to what extent such a role is appropriate (Bradley 2002). In part, perceptions of how activist or otherwise the Court should be depend on the prevailing political climate. In the 1960s and 1970s, a period normally characterized as one of stagnation and 'Euro-sclerosis', the Court played a vital role in pushing the integration process at the very time when political integration seemed paralysed by the use of the national veto. Scholars who take inspiration from neofunctionalist thinking often use this example to undermine the intergovernmentalists' claim that national interests alone dominate the rhythm of integration. But the Court's power is limited. Above all, it must rely on member states to carry out its rulings. The perception that it has tended to pursue integrationist goals has led member states to grant it only a very limited role in the justice and foreign policy pillars. In short, the precise policy-making powers of the Court—and how they should be wielded, remains a contested issue in EU politics.

Understanding institutional dynamics

What makes these five institutions particularly interesting and challenging is how they interact with the EU's other institutional bodies (see Box 3.7) and with each other. The relationship between the major institutions is both consensual and conflictual. Cooperation is unceasing because of the shared recognition that all institutions must compromise and work together to get a policy through or decision agreed. For instance, the Treaties say the Council has the 'power to take decisions' (Article 202 of the TEC). But in most cases the Council may only act on the basis of a proposal from the Commission and after consulting, cooperating, or co-deciding with the EP (see Chapter 7). Even decisions that appear to rest with one institution actually involve extensive institutional cooperation and compromise. Cooperation is encouraged by regular meetings and informal contacts between representatives of the Council, Commission, and Parliament (Stevens with Stevens 2001).

Inter-institutional rivalry also exists because each institution jealously guards its prerogatives (say to initiate policy or to share in decision-taking power). New institutionalists scholars such as Armstrong and Bulmer (1998) have underlined the importance of this institutional dynamic. Perceived attempts by one institution to encroach on another's 'turf' often elicit heated responses or fierce demonstrations of institutional loyalty. For example, in the run-ups to both the Amsterdam and Nice intergovernmental conferences the Council was extremely reluctant to allow the Parliament to take on a larger role in treaty reform because such reform was a traditional prerogative of the Council.

Box 3.7   Other institutional bodies

Several smaller institutions carry out a variety of representative, oversight, or managerial functions in the EU. By far the most significant of these specialized institutions is the **European Central Bank (ECB)**. Based in Frankfurt and modelled on the fiercely independent German Bundesbank, the ECB is charged with a fundamental task: formulating the EU's monetary policy, including ensuring monetary stability, setting interest rates, and issuing and managing the euro. The ECB is steered by an executive board (primarily made up of national central bank governors) and headed by a President who is chosen by member states, but who cannot formally be removed by them. The Bank's independence and power undoubtedly help ensure monetary stability but also have raised concerns about transparency and accountability. Its executive board is appointed by member states, and it must report to the EP several times a year. But its decisions are not made public and it enjoys considerable independence from other institutions or member states themselves (Article 108 of the TEU). Whilst still a young institution, the Bank is certain to become a more important, but also controversial player in EU politics (see McNamara 2002).

Exercising an oversight function is the **Court of Auditors** whose fifteen members are charged with scrutinizing the EU's budget and financial accounts. Acting as the 'financial conscience' of the EU, the Court has increased its stature and visibility in recent years as public concern over fraud and mismanagement has mounted. Its annual and specialized reports consist mainly of dry financial management assessments, but the Court has also uncovered more spectacular and often serious financial misconduct (see Laffan 2002).

Several smaller institutions carry out a primarily representative function (see Jeffrey 2002). For instance the **Economic and Social Committee (ESC)** represents various employer, trades union, and other social or public interests (such as farmers or consumers) in EU policy-making. Chosen by the national governments, these representatives serve in a part-time function advising the Commission and other institutions on various relevant proposals. Their opinions can be well researched but are not usually influential. The **Committee of the Regions and Local Authorities** suffers from a similar lack of influence despite being viewed initially by some as an embryonic European equivalent of the powerful German Bundesrat (see George 1996: 27). Created by the Maastricht Treaty, the Committee must be consulted on proposals affecting regional interests (cohesion funding, urban planning) and can issue its own opinions and reports. However it is internally divided and its membership debilitatingly diverse (powerful regional leaders from Germany and Belgium sit alongside representatives from English town parishes). It has yet to exert the influence its proponents originally envisioned, but does play a role as a channel of communication across several layers of governance.

The relationship between institutions is also constantly changing as power swings across and between institutions. This shift is not always reflected in formal treaty changes or reform. For instance, the Council of Minister's ability to impose its view has declined over the years as the bargaining power of the Parliament has increased (Hayes-Renshaw 1999: 36). The European Council's accumulation of agenda-setting power has usurped the Commission's traditional and legal right of initiative. Similarly, the emergence of European summits as problem solvers and package dealers has reduced the power and manoeuvrability of the Council of Ministers. Finally, the Court has significantly—even fundamentally—shaped integration and policy-making by issuing judgements with significant policy and institutional implications.

In general terms, both formal and informal institutional change has resulted in a blurring of powers among the core institutions. This blurring of power does not mean the formal rules do not matter. Rules and treaty provisions serve as the fundamental base of power from which institutions can and do act. But the formal powers are starting points only: knowing how the institutions exploit, compete for, and ultimately share power is also crucial for grasping how the institutions work.

Why institutions matter

Examining the EU institutions and how they work is essential for understanding wider themes in EU policy and politics. First, it gives us a starting point from which to examine the EU's policy process. Second, it helps us to identify the diversity of actors involved in EU politics, and to understand how they together determine the shape and speed of integration. Finally, it reminds us that there are many interesting questions still to be asked about the final destination for European integration. Are we heading towards a European state? How democratic or efficient will it be? Is it possible to reverse or are we locked into forward drive?

More particularly, the study of the institutions of the EU helps illustrate the three central themes of this book: (1) the extent to which the EU is an 'experiment in motion'; (2) the importance of power-sharing and seeking of consensus; and (3) the capacity of the EU structures to cope with the Union's expanding scope.

Experimentation and change

The EU's system of institutions reveals clearly the extent to which the Union has developed and changed since the establishment of the European Coal and Steel Community in 1951. As we have seen, the institutions have adapted over time to perform a variety of tasks. Some tasks are formally mandated by the founding

Treaties and others have developed in an informal manner. A variety of pressures have combined to encourage this informal 'task expansion' and the reinventing of the institutions over time. Sometimes institutions such as the Parliament or the Commission have actively sought to expand their influence. On other occasions, very real gaps in the capacity of the EU to respond to events and crises have resulted in an ad hoc expansion of the informal powers of the institutions. For example, the need for common action on the environment meant the informal environmental activities of the EU institutions predated the formal advances introduced by the Treaties. Sometimes member states themselves have felt a need to establish a greater degree of informal cooperation in certain areas, but were not quite ready to be legally bound by formal Treaties. A good example is the gradual expansion of the powers of the EU institutions in the area of the Common Foreign and Security Policy (see Chapter 10). Studying the institutional dynamics of the EU allows us not only to understand the extent to which the EU itself is subject to experimentation and constant change, but also to pose questions about where this process might be headed.

Power-sharing and consensus

Scholars of European integration have long (and fiercely) debated where power lies in the EU. Do supranational institutions drive the integration process forward, or do national governments remain in control of the process? The two sides of this debate have been taken up by neofunctionalists and intergovernmentalists respectively. Both sides can cite changes in formal EU rules to buttress their case. For example, as the Parliament has gained powers and the Council of Ministers has accepted more proposals on the basis of qualified majority voting rather than unanimous voting, it could be claimed that supranationalism is on the rise. On the other hand, as the European Council has come to dominate high level agenda setting, or as various countries have formally opted out of certain member states' policies (such as economic and monetary union) it could be said that intergovernmentalism is holding strong.

But depicting integration as a pitched battle between supranational institutions and the member states misses the point. Competition is fierce but so, too, is the search for consensus. Enormous efforts go into forging agreements acceptable to most. The overall trajectory of the integration process is thus a result of to-ing and fro-ing between a wide variety of actors and external pressures. This image is quite neatly captured in Wallace's (1996) description of EU governance as a pendulum, swinging sometimes towards intergovernmental solutions and sometimes towards supranational solutions but not always in equal measure (see Chapter 7).

In this type of system, institutional power is a product of how well institutions engage with other actors—lobbyists, experts, governments, and other international organizations—at different levels of governance. Peterson (1995) has tried to make sense of this complex mass by applying the concept of policy networks to the study of the EU. For example, in the area of agriculture these networks might include the Commission, the farmers' unions, environmental activists, and national farm ministers as well as international trade organizations. Focusing on the institutional structures of the EU and how they respond to these policy networks helps us to begin to make sense of the EU's very complex policy-making process.

Scope and capacity

The study of the EU institutions also helps us to understand the changing scope of the European Union's activity and the extent to which existing structures have the capacity to cope with these changes. With each successive enlargement, and as more and more competences have been formally adopted in the Treaties, the institutions have had to adapt accordingly. Increasingly, scholars have come to ask whether the existing institutional structures, originally conceived for a Community of only six member states, are adequate to cope with the demands of an EU of fifteen and soon more member states (see Chapter 9). The exhausting and ill-tempered negotiations at the Nice European Council reflected wider debates concerning how or if institutions should be reformed to meet these new challenges.

However, not all changes in the scope of the EU or its institutions are expansionary. The careful exclusion of the ECJ from Pillars 2 and 3 of the Maastricht Treaty is an important example. Similarly, the weak role played by the Commission and EP in most aspects of the Common Foreign and Security Policy reminds us of the potential of the member states to reassert control when required (see Jorgensen 2002). Finally, if there is one lesson to be learned from the study of the EU institutions it is in their remarkable ability to adapt and change as new requirements are placed upon them. This chapter has tried to show that while the capacity of EU institutions may be limited, their ability to adapt often seems limitless.

Conclusion

The EU's institutions and their interaction is complex, but so, too, is the diverse polity they help to govern. We have attempted to cut through this complexity by focusing on the institutions' powers, and what they do with them. We have stressed, too, the importance of cooperation and rivalry between the institutions. Each institution introduced here has its own agenda, but virtually no important policy area can be agreed without some (and usually, a quite large) measure of consensus spanning the EU's institutions. Institutions are as interdependent as the member states that make up the EU. In addition, we have highlighted why these institutions matter, and how they fit into the wider system of EU politics and policy-making. Above all, understanding institutions help us explore broader questions of how and why the EU works the way it does.

The role, number and importance of EU institutions is set to grow. As the EU takes on new tasks the burden on these institutions will increase. The EU's growing role in areas such as food safety, foreign and defence policy—to say nothing of monetary union—means other agencies, and bodies will join the institutional mix that helps govern EU politics. Further institutional reform is both necessary and inevitable, not least in preparation for enlargement. Such reform was the subject of the Convention on the Future of Europe in 2002–3 and will be a core feature of the IGC in 2004. But with future rounds of Treaty reform likely to require unanimous agreement by no fewer than twenty-five different member states, it seems likely that after the 2004 Intergovernmental Conference fundamental reform will prove extraordinarily difficult to achieve (see Peterson 2002a).

Finally, we have suggested that institutions do not operate alone. Today the EU's institutions must deal with an ever-broader range of actors including an increasing number of member states (see Chapters 4 and 9), but also an increasingly active group of organized interests (Chapter 5). The implications of this growing complexity for policy-making, issues of accountability, enlargement, and the EU's global role, are discussed in the remaining chapters of this volume.

Discussion questions

1. Which institution is most 'powerful' in your view and why?
2. Why has the balance of powers between the EU's institutions shifted over time?
3. Which institution could most accurately be described as the 'motor of integration'?
4. Is the relationship between the EU's institutions characterized more by cooperation or conflict?

Further reading

For a rich and insightful collection of chapters on all the EU's major institutions, see Peterson and Shackleton (2002). Nugent (1999) provides a thorough and detailed overview of the structure and operation of key institutions. Helpful examinations of individual institutions include: Hooghe's (2001) analysis of the Commission; Hayes-Renshaw and Wallace's (1997) classic study of the Council of Ministers which also includes analysis of the European Council; Corbett, Jacobs, and Shackleton's (2000) definitive account of the workings of the Parliament; and Joseph Weiler's (1999) provocative and thoughtful essays on the Court and EU's legal identity. Bulmer (1998) and Armstrong and Bulmer (1998) use the framework of new institutionalism to analyse the interaction of these institutions and how they affect EU policy and politics.

Armstrong, K., and Bulmer, S. (1998), *The Governance of the Single European Market* (Manchester: Manchester University Press).

Bulmer, S. (1998), 'New Institutionalism and the Governance of the Single European Market', *Journal of European Public Policy* 5/3: 365–86.

Corbett, R., Jacobs, F., and Shackleton, M. (2000), *The European Parliament*, 4th edn. (London: Cartermill).

Hayes-Renshaw, F., and Wallace, H. (1997), *The Council of Ministers* (Basingstoke: Palgrave).

Hooghe, L. (2001), *The European Commission and the Integration of Europe* (Cambridge: Cambridge University Press).

Nugent, N. (1999), *The Government and Politics of the European Union* (Basingstoke: Palgrave).

Peterson, J., and Shackleton, M. (eds.) (2002), *The Institutions of the European Union* (Oxford: Oxford University Press).

Weiler, J. H. H. (1999), *The Constitution of Europe* (Cambridge: Cambridge University Press).

Web links

Most of the EU's institutions have their own website which can be accessed through the EU's official portal site, 'The European Union online': (**www.europa.eu.int**). Below are the specific official websites of some of the institutions introduced in this chapter:

European Commission: **wwweuropa.eu.int/comm/**.
Council of Ministers: **www.ue.eu.int**.
European Parliament: **www.europarl.eu.int**.
European Court of Justice: **www.curia.eu.int**.
Court of Auditors: **www.eca.eu.int**.
Economic and Social Committee: **www.esc.eu.int/index800.htm**.
Committee of the Regions: **www.cor.eu.int/home.htm**.
European Central Bank: **www.ecb.int**.

Anyone brave enough to consider working as an intern or *stagiare* in one of the EU's institutions can find out more at **www.europa.eu.int/comm/sg/stages**. For recent updates on institutional developments, especially in relation to treaty reform, see **www.euractiv.com**. The London-based University Association for Contemporary European Studies (UACES) (**www.uaces.org**) announces regular workshops and lectures on the EU institutions held in the UK and (occasionally) on the European continent. For information on conferences and lectures held in the US, see the website of the US European Union Studies Association (EUSA) which can be found at **www.eustudies.org**.

Chapter 4
Member States

Brigid Laffan and Alexander Stubb

Contents

Overview

This chapter focuses on the EU's most essential component: its member states. It examines six factors that determine how any state engages with the EU: date of entry, size, wealth, state structure, economic ideology, and integration preference. We then explore how member states behave in the Union's institutions and seek to influence the outcome of negotiations in Brussels. We focus throughout on the informal as well as formal activities of the member states. The final section explores the insights offered by theory in analysing the EU–member state relationship.

Introduction

States are the essential building blocks of the EU. All EU treaties are negotiated and ratified by the 'high contracting parties'—the governments of the member states. By joining the European Union, the traditional nation-state is transformed into a member state. This transformation involves an enduring commitment to participate in political and legal processes that are beyond the state but that embrace the state. Membership of the Union has significant effects on national systems of policy-making, on national institutions, on national identity, sovereignty and democracy. Put simply, once a state joins the Union, politics may begin at home but no longer end there. National politics, polities, and policies become '*Europeanized*' (see Box 4.1).

But member states shape the EU as much as the EU shapes its member states. The decision to join the Union is a decision to become locked into an additional layer of governance and a distinctive form of 'Euro-politics' that is neither wholly domestic nor international but shares attributes of both. This chapter explores this interactive dynamic. We tackle questions such as: what is the role of the

---

Box 4.1 Key concepts and terms

Acquis communautaire is a French phrase that denotes the rights and obligations derived from the EU treaties, laws, and Court rulings. In principle, new member states joining the EU must accept the entire *acquis*.

Candidate countries will become member states pending accession negotiations and their acceptance of the *acquis communautaire* of the EU: Bulgaria, Cyprus, Czech Republic, Estonia, Hungary, Malta, Latvia, Lithuania, Poland, Romania, Slovakia, and Slovenia are all candidate countries. Turkey is a candidate country but had not started accession negotiations by late-2002.

Demandeur is the French term often used to refer to those demanding something (say regional funds) from the EU.

Europeanization is the process whereby national systems (institutions, policies, governments) adapt to EU policies and integration more generally, while also themselves shaping the European Union.

Flexible integration (also called 'reinforced' or 'enhanced cooperation') denotes the possibility for some member states to pursue deeper integration without the participation of others. Examples include EMU and the Schengen Agreement in which some member states have decided not to participate fully. The Amsterdam and Nice Treaties institutionalized the concept of flexible integration through their clauses on enhanced cooperation.

Tours de table allow each national delegation in a Council of Ministers meeting to make an intervention on a given subject. Today such rounds are still just manageable, but in an EU of 25 or more member states an intervention from each delegation will be time-consuming (even 5 minutes each would require over two hours).

member states in the EU system? What is it about the EU that has led the member states to invest so much in the collective project? How do member states engage with the EU? What factors determine how any member state behaves as an EU member?

Six determining features

The fifteen member states bring to the Union their distinctive national histories, state traditions, constitutions, legal principles, political systems, and economic capacity. A variety of languages and an extraordinary diversity of national tastes and cultures accentuate the mosaic-like character of Europe. The continental enlargement of the Union will deepen its pre-existing diversity. Managing difference is thus a key challenge to the Union. To understand how the EU really works, we must seek to understand the multinational and multicultural character of the European Union and its institutions.

Classifying the member states—including how and why they joined and how they operate within the EU—is key to understanding the member states' relationship with the EU. Six factors are extremely important. No one factor alone determines the relationship between the EU and a member state, but together they provide a guide to understanding member states' engagement with the EU.

Entry date

It is useful to deploy the metaphor of an onion to characterize the expansion of the Union from its original six states to nine, ten, twelve, fifteen, and to 27 or more states in the years ahead (see Figure 4.1). The core of the onion is formed by France, Germany, and the four other founding members. The European Union was the creation of six states that were occupied or defeated in the Second World War. It is the creation especially of France, a country that needed to achieve a settlement with its neighbour and historical enemy, Germany. From the outset the key relationship in the European Union was between France and Germany. As explained in Chapter 2, the Franco-German alliance and the Paris–Bonn axis—now Paris–Berlin—have left enduring traces on the fabric of integration. The Elysée Treaty (1963) institutionalized very strong bilateral ties between these two countries. The intensity of interaction should not be taken as evidence of continuous agreement between France and Germany on major European issues. Rather, much of the interaction has worked to iron out conflicts between them.

Close personal relationships between German Chancellor Helmut Schmidt and French President Valery Giscard d'Estaing in the 1970s and Chancellor Helmut Kohl and President François Mitterrand in the 1980s and early 1990s were key to

Figure 4.1 'Onion' chart of EU enlargements

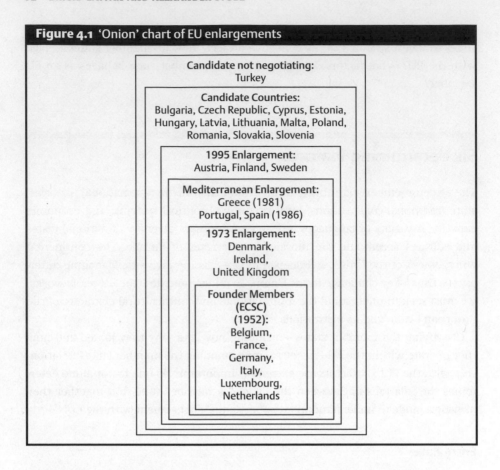

the creation of the European Monetary System (a precursor to EMU), the single market programme, and the euro. The Franco-German relationship was challenged by geopolitical change in Europe following the collapse of communism. German unification and the opening up of the eastern half of the continent altered the bilateral balance of power, with Germany no longer a junior political partner to France. The change was symbolically captured by the relocation of the German capital to Berlin. It is premature to talk of the demise of the Franco-German relationship; it remains important. But changing geopolitics and enlargement to the east profoundly alters the context within which it is played out. For instance, in 1997 the French launched a major defence initiative (called the St Malo initiative) with the UK, not Germany. Likewise, Germany and the UK joined forces through a joint Schröder–Blair letter on reform of the Council of Ministers on the eve of the Barcelona European Council in 2002.

The four other founder member states—Italy, Belgium, Luxembourg, and the Netherlands—see themselves as part of the hard core of the Union. The Benelux countries in particular (Belgium, Luxembourg, and the Netherlands) are usually at the centre of developments, often ready to push for deeper integration. They are deeply committed to the 'Community method' of law-making (institution-led rather than intergovernmental) and are supportive of a strong supranational element to the Union. The Benelux states form a particularly tight grouping. They typically engage in close policy integration and often issue numerous joint statements on the future of the Union. Again, close working relationships cannot guarantee a complete convergence of interests and preferences. For instance, during the 2000 Nice European Council, one of the most bitter disagreements concerned a proposal to give the Netherlands more votes than Belgium in weighted voting on the Council (to reflect a Dutch population that is nearly 50 per cent larger than Belgium's; see Table 4.1), thus breaking with the established tradition of parity between them. Yet this conflict did not prevent them from producing a joint Benelux memorandum on the *Future of Europe* soon afterwards (Benelux 2001).

Italy has oscillated between active involvement in EU diplomacy and a passive presence in the system. It has traditionally been enthusiastic about European institution-building, but hampered by endemic instability in its governing coalitions. Under the Berlusconi governments of the early twenty-first century, Italy tended to be more passive and in some instances opposed to closer European integration.

All states joining the EU after its initial formative period had to accept the pre-existing laws and obligations (or *acquis communautaire*, see Box 4.1), its institutional system, and way of doing business, all of which had been formed without their input. Thus for all latecomers, adjustment and adaptation to the EU was a process that began before the date of accession and continued well after membership. With the expansion of the Union's tasks, the burden of adjustment has grown for each successive wave of accession. As Chapters 6 and 7 indicate, over the years, the EU has taken on new policy areas ranging from environmental policy to police cooperation. (The *acquis communautaire* has grown to cover over 80,000 pages of legislation.) This expansion has made it even more difficult for outsiders to catch up and adapt to membership (see Chapter 9).

Size

As in all political systems, size matters in the EU. The distinction between large and small states is often evoked in political and media discussions about representation in the EU. At the cumbersome negotiations on the Treaty of Nice, which focused on the re-weighting of votes in the Council and the number of Commissioners each state could appoint, tensions between large and small states escalated. Afterwards, to paraphrase George Orwell's *Animal Farm*: all states remained equal, but some became more equal than others.

Whatever the debates between large and small, a more nuanced approach to size is warranted. The EU really consists of four clusters of states—large, medium,

Table 4.1 Clusters of member states and candidate countries by size

Current member states *(figure in brackets = approximate population in millions)*	Candidate countries
Large Germany (82) France (59) United Kingdom (59) Italy (57) Spain (39)	**Large** Turkey (66) Poland (38)
Medium Netherlands (16) Greece (10) Belgium (10) Portugal (10)	**Medium** Romania (22) Czech Republic (10) Hungary (10)
Small Sweden (9) Austria (8) Denmark (5) Finland (5) Ireland (3)	**Small** Bulgaria (8) Slovakia (5) Lithuania (3) Latvia (2) Slovenia (2) Estonia (1)
Micro Luxembourg (0.4)	**Micro** Cyprus (0.8) Malta (0.4)

small, and micro-states (see Table 4.1). The first cluster contains five large states: Germany, United Kingdom, France, Italy, and Spain together make up about 80 per cent of the population of EU-15. (Even here we find dissent: Germany, France, and the UK are certainly seen as the 'big three', with Italy seen as less powerful, and some would dispute Spain's categorization as a large state.) The next cluster consists of medium-sized states: the Netherlands, Greece, Belgium, and Portugal, whose populations range from 10 to 15 million inhabitants. The third cluster is one of small states: Sweden, Austria, Denmark, Finland, and Ireland, which all support populations between 3 and 9 million. The fourth category, micro-states, consists at present only of Luxembourg. All categories will have additional states as the Union enlarges, but the EU of the future will consist of proportionately more small and micro-states, thus raising concerns about its continued ability to reach consensus.

Size has implications for power and presence in the Union's political and economic system. The power of large states is not just expressed in voting power in the Council. It manifests itself in political, economic, and diplomatic influence. Large states can call on far more extensive and specialized administrative and technical resources in the policy process than small states, and their diplomatic presence is far stronger throughout the world. The German Chancellor, regardless of who holds the post, is usually the most powerful politician at European Council meetings. Small states, however, enjoy important advantages in EU negotiations. They tend to have fewer vital interests than larger states, their interests can be aggregated with much greater ease, and the potential for conflict and competing claims among different social groups is reduced. Luxembourg, for example, can concentrate all of its diplomatic energy on protecting its traditional industries, its liberal banking laws, and its presence in EU institutions.

Although size matters, it has little bearing on national approaches to substantive issues of EU policy that are formed by economic considerations, domestic interests, and the proposed nature of the change. Thus, small states are unlikely to band together against the large states in substantive policy discussions. Their interests, just like those of the larger states, diverge. Coalition patterns in the Council have always consisted of a mix of large and small states in any particular policy domain.

Small states do, however, have a common interest in maintaining the EU's institutional balance, the 'rules of the game', and their level of representation in the system. From the outset, the small EU states have been wary of proposals that privilege a *directoire* of larger states, which could dictate policy for the Union as a whole. Small states are thus keen supporters of procedural and legal orthodoxy in the Union. For example, during the preparations for the Maastricht Treaty negotiations the Dutch Government argued that:

The interests of small countries are best served by international co-operation based on legal structures with open decision-making processes. Large countries, on the other hand, also pursue structured negotiations but endeavour to protect their interests mainly by exploiting their position of power (The Netherlands, 1990: 3).

The key argument here is that the multilateral, institutionalized, and legal processes of the Union have created a relatively benign environment for small states.

How well has the EU accommodated large and small states? In the past the European Union successfully managed to expand its membership to include both large and small states without undermining the balance between them or causing undue tension. This began to change in the 1990s. The 1995 enlargement and the prospect of further enlargement to the east and south heightened the salience of the small-state/large-state divide in the Union. The need to strike a balance remained a central but tricky issue on the political agenda of the 1996 Intergovernmental Conference that led to the Treaty of Amsterdam. It was also one of the 'Amsterdam leftovers' (unresolved issues) that had to be tackled at Nice (see Box 4.2).

Box 4.2 HOW IT REALLY WORKS

The Nice European Council

A range of national sensitivities about state power and influence surfaced at the Nice summit in December 2000. Size was a major issue. The small states pushed to protect their rights to representation in the EU's institutions, while the large states expressed concerns that the Union might become unworkable with so many small states. Already worried about the loss of their right to appoint a second Commissioner, large states demanded a re-weighting of votes in the Council. Finding a formula on voting acceptable to states of all sizes led to one of the longest—and most arduous—European Councils in the EU's history.

   In addition to the small/large state divide, there were unseemly squabbles about the relative voting powers of states under qualified majority voting (QMV). France was determined to retain the same number of votes as Germany, and Belgium reacted very badly to the idea of breaking its voting parity with the Netherlands (France got its wish—in a manner of speaking—while Belgium did not). In the end, both small and large states could claim something from Nice. The larger states ensured that their relative voting power would not be eroded, and the smaller states made certain that all future qualified majorities would have to reflect a majority of states. The weight of the German population in the system was addressed, but only though the introduction of a complicated additional demographic criterion for votes in the Council. That is, a qualified majority also had to include states representing a majority of the EU's *population*. Nice showed how concerns about relative position and status can blind the member states to the increasing complexity of the decision-making process they have created. At this summit, at least, the EU's efficiency was sacrificed to national sensitivities.

Wealth

The original European Economic Community had only one serious regional poverty problem, the Italian Mezzogiorno, so 'cohesion' was not an important concern. The first enlargement in 1973 to include the UK, Denmark, and Ireland increased the salience of regional disparities in the politics of the Union. The UK had significant regional problems, with declining industrial areas and low levels of economic development in areas such as Northern Scotland, Wales, and Northern Ireland. Ireland as a whole had per capita incomes that were about 62 per cent the EU average at the time. The Mediterranean enlargements in the 1980s to include Greece, Spain, and Portugal (all relatively poor states) accentuated the problem of economic divergence.

   The Union as an economic space consisted of a 'golden triangle' which ran from southern England, through France and Germany to northern Italy and southern, western, and northern peripheries. Although committed to harmonious economic development from the outset, the Union did not have to expand its budgetary commitment to poorer Europe until the single market programme in the mid-1980s. Europe's poorer states successfully linked the economic liberalization of the 1992 programme with an enhanced commitment to greater cohesion in the Union. This manifest itself in a doubling of the financial resources devoted to declining regions, or those with a per capita income less than 75 per cent the EU average (see Table 4.2). In addition, four member states whose overall GDP was low—Spain, Portugal, Greece, and Ireland—were granted extra aid (in the form of a Cohesion Fund) as a prize for agreeing to monetary union. Of the four states, Ireland was the first to lose its cohesion status. Promoting economic and social cohesion will continue to resonate in the politics of integration well into the future as the candidate countries are all significantly poorer than the EU-15 average.

Economic divergence has a significant impact on how the EU works. First, it influences the pecking order in the Union. The cohesion countries are perceived as *demandeurs* in the Union, dependent on EU subsidies. Second, attitudes towards the size and distribution of the EU budget are influenced by contrasting views between net beneficiaries and net contributors. With the growth of the EU budget, a distinct 'net contributors club' has emerged in the Union, which is led by Germany but joined also by the United Kingdom, the Netherlands, Austria, Sweden, and Denmark. These states are committed to controlling increases in the EU budget and to limiting the budgetary costs of cohesion. On the other hand, the cohesion countries, as beneficiaries of financial transfers, tend to argue for larger budgetary resources and additional instruments.

Table 4.2 Gross Domestic Product in 2001 (1000 € per head of population)

European Union (15)	23.1	Candidate countries (13)	5.5
Luxembourg	47.4	Cyprus	12.4
Denmark	33.7	Slovenia	10.5
Ireland	30.2	Malta	10.2
UK	26.5	Czech Republic	6.1
Netherlands	26.5	Hungary	5.7
Sweden	26.3	Poland	5.1
Finland	26.0	Estonia	4.3
Austria	25.9	Slovakia	4.1
Germany	25.0	Lithuania	3.8
Belgium	25.0	Latvia	3.6
France	24.0	Turkey	2.4
Italy	21.0	Romania	2.0
Spain	16.1	Bulgaria	1.7
Portugal	12.1		
Greece	11.9		

Third, relative wealth influences attitudes towards EU regulation, notably in relation to environmental and social policy. The richer states have more stringent, developed systems of regulation that impose extra costs on their productive industries. They thus favour the spread of higher standards of regulation to peripheral Europe. By contrast, the poorer states, in their search for economic development, often want to avoid imposing costs of onerous regulation on their industries. Overall, environmental and social standards have risen in Europe, particularly in peripheral Europe but not to the extent desired by the wealthier states.

State structure

The internal constitutional structure of a member state has an impact on how it operates in the EU. The Union of 15 has three federal states—Germany, Austria, and Belgium; and two quasi-federal states—Spain and the United Kingdom. It has two regionalized states—France and Italy—and eight unitary small states that are more or less centralized. The subnational units in all three federal states have played a significant role in the recent constitutional development of Union. The German Länder, in particular, insisted in the 1990s that they be given an enhanced say in German European policy. They have been advocates of *subsidiarity* and the creation of the Committee of the Regions. In the 1992 Maastricht Treaty, they won the right to send Länder ministers and officials to represent Germany in the Council of Ministers. Representatives of the German and Austrian Länder, representatives of the Belgian regions and cultural communities, as well as ministers in the Scottish executive now sit at the Council table and can commit their national governments.

In addition to direct representation, there has been an explosion of regional and local offices in Brussels from the mid-1980s onwards. Increasingly, state and regional governments, local authorities, and cities feel the need for direct representation in Brussels. Their offices act as a conduit of information from the EU to the subnational level within the member states. They engage in tracking EC legislation, lobbying for grants and seeking partners for European projects. Not unexpectedly, there can be tension between national governments and the offices that engage in para-diplomacy in the Brussels arena (see Chapter 5).

Economic ideology

A lot of what the EU does is designed to create the conditions of enhanced economic integration through market-building. The manner in which this economic liberalization has developed has been greatly influenced by the dominant economic and social paradigms of the member states. Different visions of the proper balance between public and private power, between the state and market have left their traces on how the EU works.

Although all six founding member states might be regarded as adhering to a continental or Christian democratic model of capitalism, there are important differences amongst them. For instance, France traditionally has supported a far more interventionist EU than the German social market model would tolerate. Arguably, the French statist tradition has made little headway in the Union's system of economic governance.

Differences between France and Germany fade in comparison to differences between continental capitalism and the Anglo-Saxon tradition. The accession of the UK in 1973 and the radical deregulatory policies of successive Conservative governments brought the Anglo-Saxon economic paradigm into the Union. The UK has been a supporter of deregulation and economic liberalization in the Union but not of re-regulation at Union level, particularly in the social and environmental fields. The Anglo-Saxon tradition, however, has been somewhat balanced by the accession of the Nordic states with a social democratic tradition of economic governance and social provision, combined with a strong belief in market liberalization.

A battle of ideas continues in the Union, based on competing views about the right balance between state and market and the role of the EU in social regulation. Competing economic paradigms underpin national preferences. Hence, the Union is far more successful in constraining member state action through regulation than in building common policies in contested areas.

Integration preference

The terms pro- and anti-European, or 'good' European and awkward partner, are frequently bandied about to describe national attitudes towards the EU. The UK, Denmark, and Sweden are usually portrayed as reluctant Europeans (see Table 4.3). Whilst not entirely false, such categorization disguises at least three facts. First, attitudes towards European integration are moulded not just by nationality but (often more powerfully) by factors such as socio-economic class, age, or educational attainment. Second, in all states we find a significant split between the attitudes of those who might be called 'the top decision makers' and the mass public. A very high proportion of elite decision makers in the member states accept that their state has benefited from EU membership and that membership is in their state's national interest. These sentiments are not shared by the wider public in many states. Of course governments must take public opinion into account. When coherent, public opinion sets the broad parameters of what is acceptable policy. But public opinion toward the EU—however reluctant—is only one of several factors shaping a government's position.

Some states certainly are more enthusiastic about certain developments (say, enlargement or greater transparency) than are others. But there is often an important difference between rhetoric and reality in EU negotiations. Some

Table 4.3 Support for EU membership (by country)[a]

Country	Good thing	Bad thing	Neither good nor bad
Luxembourg	81	3	14
Ireland	78	4	12
Netherlands	71	6	17
Italy	69	3	22
Spain	66	5	23
Greece	64	5	27
Portugal	62	7	24
Denmark	60	16	21
Belgium	58	4	30
Germany	52	9	31
France	47	14	35
Finland	40	18	38
Sweden	38	27	32
Austria	37	16	41
United Kingdom	32	21	32
EU average	**53**	**11**	**28**

[a] *Question:* 'Do you think that membership in the European Union is a good thing, bad thing, neither good nor bad?' Figures show percentage of total polled who gave each response.

Source: Eurobarometer 57, 20 June 2002.

member states, including France and Germany, tend to use grandiose language in calling for deeper integration. However, around the negotiating table they are often the ones blocking an increase in qualified majority voting in, for example, trade or justice and home affairs. The opposite can be true for states such as the UK. Their ministers and officials are inclined to language that makes them seem reluctant about European integration. Yet, in negotiations on, for example, trade liberalization they are often in the forefront. In short, member states' attitudes towards integration are far more nuanced than is implied by the labels 'pro' or 'anti' Europe.

Different national preferences and attitudes are expressed most vividly during the Intergovernmental Conferences (IGCs) leading to treaty reform. These events are formally managed by the states holding the Council presidency and are finalized—amidst much media fanfare—at a European Council by the heads of state and government. An important feature of EU treaty change since the early 1990s has been the greater frequency with which states have been allowed to 'opt out' of certain policy developments. For example, Denmark has opted out of the euro, parts of the Schengen agreement on the free movement of people, and aspects of the Common Foreign and Security Policy.

In each IGC, member states need to decide what is negotiable and what is non-negotiable, or what they could trade in one area in return for concessions in another. The outcome is inevitably a series of complex package deals. Member states will trade off a concession on one issue (such as the size of the Commission) related to the Union's institutional order in exchange for the concessions of other member states on a separate issue (such as their voting weight under QMV, see Box 4.2).

Taken together, the six factors introduced in this section tell us a lot about how the EU works. Styles of economic governance and levels of wealth have a major influence on national approaches to European regulation, and on just how much regulation each state favours at EU level. A hostile or favourable public opinion will help determine the integration preferences of particular states. How states

---

Box 4.3 HOW IT REALLY WORKS

Intergovernmental Conferences

Article 48 of the Treaty on European Union states that 'the Government of any Member State or the Commission may submit to the Council proposals for the amendment of the Treaties on which the Union is founded' . If the Council decides that such a proposal has legs, it then calls for a 'conference of representatives of the governments', or what in EU-speak is called an intergovernmental conference (IGC), the means by which the EU changes its treaties (or enlarges). The outcomes of IGCs include the Single European Act, and the Maastricht, Amsterdam, and Nice Treaties.

An IGC is often a long and tedious process. The 2000 IGC on the Nice Treaty, for instance, witnessed a total of 370 official negotiating hours and required ten ministerial meetings and three European Councils. After months of discussions and seemingly endless *tours de table* (Box 4.1), which see the delegations state and restate their national positions, the Council's General Secretariat and Presidency draft a proposed set of Treaty amendments. Member states then suggest changes to the draft either in writing or orally in the meeting room. Finally a compromise is hammered out. Some issues can be solved by officials. Others demand the attention of the ministers. The most difficult questions are left to be resolved at the infamous all-night sessions of the European Council.

An IGC is always a cross-sectoral exercise, which has an impact on the whole administration of member governments. A sound relationship between the national capital and the Permanent Representation in Brussels is crucial for the proper functioning of the system. In many instances the actual IGC negotiators have positions that are closer to each other's than those between ministries at home. During negotiations it is usually not difficult to detect when a negotiator has been unable to coordinate the position at the national level. The code phrase is usually: 'we are still studying the question back home'.

represent themselves in EU business is partially determined by their state structure and domestic institutions. The point is that EU member states vary across
several cross-cutting dimensions, and this mix is part of what makes the EU unique.

Member states in action

Member states are not the only players in town (see Chapters 3 and 5), but national
governments retain a privileged position in the EU. What emerge as national
interests from domestic systems of preference formation remain central to how
the EU works. Member states are not unitary actors. Rather, each consists of a
myriad of players who project their preferences in the Brussels arena. National
administrations, the wider public service, key interests (notably, business, trades
unions, farming organizations, and other societal interests) all seek voice and
representation in EU politics. A striking feature of European integration is the
extent to which national actors have been drawn out of the domestic arena into
the Brussels system of policy-making.

As Chapter 3 highlighted, the national and the European meet in a formal sense
in the Council, the EU institution designed to give voice and representation to
national preferences. At any given time there are usually seventeen official meeting rooms in use in the Council building (named after the sixteenth-century
Belgian philosopher, Justus Lipsius) apart from the month of August when the
Brussels system goes on holiday. Formal meetings are supplemented by bilateral
meetings on the margins of Council meetings, informal chats over espressos, and
by media briefings. Thus the formal system of policy-making is augmented by considerable backroom dealing, arbitrage, and informal politics. In the evenings,
national officials (from some member states more than others) frequent the many
bars near the Rond Point Schuman, the junction in Brussels where several EU
institutions are housed. The evening trains to Zaventem (the Brussels airport) are
often full of national officials making their way back to their capitals after a long
day in Council working groups. Those within earshot can pick up good anecdotal
evidence of how the EU actually works when member states pick over the details
of EU proposals.

All member states have built up a cadre of EU specialists in their diplomatic
services and domestic administrations who are the 'boundary managers' between
the national and the European. Most are at home in the complex institutional and
legal processes of the Union, have well used copies of the EU treaties, read *Agence
Europe* (a daily bulletin on European affairs) every morning, know their field and
the preferences of their negotiating partners. The EU is a system that privileges
those with an intimate knowledge of how the Union's policy process works and
how business is conducted in the Council, the EP, and the Commission.

Members of the EU cadre seek to exploit their political, academic, sectoral, and personal networks to the full. With more member states, a widening agenda, and advanced communications technology, there has been a discernible increase in horizontal interaction among the member states at all levels—prime-ministerial, ministerial, senior official, and desk officer. Specialists forge and maintain links with their counterparts in other member states on a continuous basis. Deliberations are no longer left primarily to meetings at working group level in Brussels. Sophisticated networking is part and parcel of the Brussels game. Officials who have long experience of it build up extensive personal contacts and friendships in the system. Looking around a meeting room, one Brussels insider noted:

Around the table there were many familiar faces. There always are at European Union meetings. For individuals closely involved in European negotiations, the process gets into the bloodstream like malaria. Once its in the system, you never quite get rid of it (McDonagh 1998: 32).

In addition to a cadre of Brussels insiders, many government officials in national capitals find that their work has a European dimension. For most, however, interaction with the EU is sporadic and driven by developments within a particular sector. A company law specialist may have intense interaction with the EU while a new directive is being negotiated but may then have little involvement until the same directive is up for renegotiation.

The nature of EU membership demands that all member states must commit resources and personnel to the Union's policy process. Servicing Brussels—by committing time and resources to EU negotiations—has become more onerous with new areas of policy being added, such as justice and home affairs or defence. Once a policy field becomes institutionalized in the EU system, the member states have no choice but to service the relevant committees and Councils. An empty seat at the table undermines the credibility of the state and its commitment to the collective endeavour. Besides, the weakest negotiator is always the one who is absent from the negotiations.

Managing EU business

All member states engage in internal negotiations and coordination, above all between different national ministries and ministers, in determining what their national position will be in any EU negotiation. The coordination system in most member states is organized hierarchically. National ministers and/or the head of government will usually act as the arbiter of last resort.

In addition, all member states have either a Minister or a State Secretary of European Affairs. The Ministry of Foreign Affairs plays an important role in all member states, and most central EU coordination takes place here. However, there are a number of member states, such as Finland, where the Prime Minister's Office takes the leading role. With the increasing prominence of EU policy in national administrations, more EU business is generally shifting to the offices of Heads of government.

Each member state also has a Permanent Representation in Brussels, a kind of EU embassy. In most cases it is the most important and biggest foreign representation the country maintains anywhere in the world. It is, for example, usually much bigger than an embassy in Washington DC or Moscow or a representation to the United Nations. Although the official role or the Permanent Representation of each member state varies, they all participate actively in several stages of the co-ordination process. In certain member states they are the key player in the whole process.

Explaining member states' engagement

We have looked at the factors that determine the engagement of different states in the EU and at the member states in action. What additional purchase do we get from theory in analysing member states in the Union? The relationship between the EU and its member states has been one of the most enduring puzzles in the literature on European integration. From the outset, the impact of EU membership on statehood and on individual states has been hotly contested. At issue is whether the EU strengthens, transcends, or transforms its member states. Is the Union simply a creature of its member states? Are they still the masters of the Treaties? Or has the EU irrevocably transformed European nation-states? The relationship between the EU and its member states is a live political issue and not simply a point of contention amongst scholars. The theories and approaches introduced in Chapter 1 provide different lenses with which to analyse the member states in the Union.

Liberal intergovernmentalism provides a theoretical framework that enables us to trace the formation of domestic preferences in the member states and then to see how they are bargained in Brussels. It identifies the domestic sources of the underlying preferences and the subsequent process of interstate bargaining. The approach rightly concludes that the EU is an 'institution so firmly grounded in the core interests of national governments that it occupies a permanent position at the heart of the European political landscape' (Moravcsik 1998: 501). This approach is less helpful in tracing the impact of the EU on national preference formation or the cumulative impact of EU membership on its member states. Its focus on one-off bargains provides a snapshot of the Union at any one time rather than a film or 'moving picture' of how membership may generate deep processes of change (see Pierson 1996).

Contemporary theorists who view the EU through the lenses of *multilevel* (Hooghe and Marks 2001) or *supranational governance* (Sandholtz and Stone Sweet 1998) emphasize how the national and the European levels of governance have become intertwined. This meshing of national and European politics is fundamental in the EU. These approaches point to the influence of the supranational institutions—notably the Commission, Court, and Parliament—on the EU and its member states. The EU may be grounded in the core interests of the national governments, but the definition of core interest is influenced by membership of the EU and its continuous effects at the national level. Put another way, the EU has evolved into a political system in its own right that is more than the sum of its member states.

The *new institutionalism* offers at least two crucial insights concerning member states in the Union. First, its emphasis on change over time captures the give-and-take nature of EU negotiations and the manner in which norms and procedures are built up over time. Second, its concern with path dependency highlights the substantial resources that member states have invested in the Union. The costs of exit are very high, so high that no state would seriously contemplate it. At best member states have the choice of opting-out of various policy regimes. Even then there are costs associated with having no seat at the table.

Finally, a *policy network* approach captures the fragmented and sectorized nature of the EU. It highlights the fact that the degree and nature of national adaptation differs from one policy area to another, and according to the different mix of players involved. Some policy fields, and the networks that preside over them, have been intensely Europeanized (agriculture) while others have not (transport). This approach helps us to gauge this variation and the varying involvement of different layers of government and public and private actors in the EU system.

Conclusion

It is impossible to understand how the EU works without understanding the member states and their central role in the establishment and operation of the EU. In turn the EU has altered the political, constitutional, economic, and policy framework within which the member state governments govern. All of its member states, along with some states who aspire to join the EU, are part of a transnational political process that binds them together in a collective endeavour. Their individual engagement with the Union varies enormously depending on their history, location, size, relative wealth, domestic political systems, and attitudes towards the future of the Union. However, all of the member states are actively engaged on a day-to-day basis in Brussels. National ministers, civil servants, and interest groups participate in the Commission's advisory groups, the Council working groups, and meetings of the European Council. All member states engage in bilateral relations with each of their partners, with the Commission's services, and the Council Presidency in their efforts to influence the outcome of EU policy-making. In national capitals, officials and ministers must do their homework in preparation for the continuous cycle of EU meetings. Brussels is thus part and parcel of contemporary governance in Europe. The member states are essential to how the EU works, but in turn being a member of the EU makes a state something rather different from an 'ordinary' nation-state.

Discussion questions

1. What are the most important features determining an EU member state's attitudes towards integration?
2. Which is more powerful: the impact of the EU on its member states, or the impact of the member states on the EU?
3. How useful is theory in explaining the role of the member states in the EU?
4. How different are EU member states from 'ordinary' nation-states?

Further reading

The literature on the member states of the Union is very diffuse. There are a large number of country studies (see, for example, Lequesne 1993, George 1998, and O'Donnell 2000), a more limited number of comparative works (including Morgan and Bray 1986 and Bulmer and Lequesne forthcoming), and a very extensive body of policy-related work that throws some light on the EU and its member states (see for example Falkner 2000 and Laursen 2002). For discussions of the relationship between statehood and integration see Caporaso (1996), Hoffmann (1966), Milward (1992), and Moravcsik (1998). On national management of EU business and the impact of the EU on national institutions see Rometsch and Wessels (1996).

Bulmer, S., and Lequesne, C. (forthcoming), *The Member States of the European Union* (Oxford and New York: Oxford University Press).

Caporaso, J. (1996), 'The European Union and Forms of State: Westphalian, Regulatory or Post-Modern?', *Journal of Common Market Studies* 34/1: 29–52.

Falkner, G. (2000), 'How Pervasive are Euro-Politics? Effects of EU Membership on a New Member State', *Journal of Common Market Studies* 38/2: 223–50.

George, S. (1998), *An Awkward Partner: Britain in the European Community*, 3rd edn. (Oxford and New York: Oxford University Press).

Hoffmann, S. (1966), 'Obstinate or Obsolete: The Fate of the Nation-State and the Case of Western Europe', *Daedalus* 95/3: 862–915 (reprinted in S. Hoffmann (1995) *The European Sisyphus: Essays on Europe 1964–1994* (Boulder, CO, and Oxford: Westview Press)).

Laursen, F. (ed.) (2002), *The Amsterdam Treaty: National Preference Formation, Interstate Bargaining and Outcome* (Odense: Odense University Press).

Lequesne, C. (1993), *Paris-Bruxelles: Comment se fait la Politique Européenne de la France* (Paris: Presses de la Fondations Nationale des Sciences Politiques).

Milward, A. (1992), *The European Rescue of the Nation-state* (London and Berkeley: Routledge and University of California Press).

Moravcsik, A. (1998), *The Choice for Europe* (London and Ithaca, NY: UCL Press and Cornell University Press).

Morgan, R., and Bray, C. (1986), *Partners and Rivals in Western Europe: Britain, France and Germany* (Hampshire: Gower Press).

O'Donnell, R. (2000), *Europe: The Irish Experience* (Dublin: Institute of European Affairs).

Rometsch, D., and Wessels, W. (1996), *The European Union and Member States: Towards institutional fusion?* (Manchester: Manchester University Press).

Web links

For a comprehensive bibliographic guide to member state-EU relations see: **www.library.pitt.edu/subject_guides/westeuropean/wwwes/**.

The best place to search for websites of the member and candidate states' national administrations is **www.europa.eu.int/futurum/debate_en.htm**.

Useful links can also be found on the homepage of the European Commission **http://europa.eu.int/comm/index_en.htm**.

Chapter 5

Organized Interests and Lobbying in the EU

Rory Watson and Michael Shackleton

Contents

Overview

Member states and EU institutions are not the only influential actors in European Union policy-making. A host of other organized interests also make their presence felt—usually behind the scenes and at different times—in EU policy and politics. These interests range from pan-European trade associations and regional governments to lawyers, consultants, and multinational companies. The number of actors has grown as the responsibilities and membership of the Union have expanded with successive treaty changes and enlargements. This chapter will examine the nature of these organized interests, the reasons for their growth, their influence as lobbyists in the EU process, and the response of the various Community institutions to a phenomenon which was not foreseen when the first Treaties were drafted in the 1950s.

Introduction: identifying organized interests

The power and role of the different EU institutions are set out in the various Treaties. The status and influence of the many organized interests outside the formal institutions, but based in Brussels and involved in EU policy-making, are far less clear. The dramatic increase in their number and influence is one manifestation of the EU's expanding remit since the late 1980s (see Chapter 1).

It is useful—but not easy—to categorize this astonishing range of organized interests. In the early 1990s, the European Commission identified two categories: profit and non-profit making organizations (Commission 1993). We extend this characterization by identifying three broad and overlapping categories of organized interest, based on the main interests and membership of different groups (see Table 5.1):

- private interests, pursuing specific economic goals;
- public interest bodies, pursuing non-economic aims;
- governmental actors, representing different levels of government but not forming part of the national administrations of the member states.

No definitive figure exists for the number of people working in these different groups, but something close to 14,000–15,000 *lobbyists* (see Box 5.1) are employed by private and public groups in Brussels (Landmarks 2002). They are spread amongst organizations ranging in size from one to two people to large offices with scores of staff. As a comparison, it is worth noting that the combined personnel of all EU institutions and the Union's many specialized agencies is 33,600 (Court of Auditors 2001: 336).

Table 5.1 Overview of organized interests in the EU		
Type	**Approximate number of organizations**	**Examples**
Private	1300 (plus 270 law firms and consultancies)	Toy Industries of Europe, Philip Morris, UNICE
Public	300 (plus 40 think tanks)	ECAS, WWF, European Blind Union
Governmental	360	United States Embassy, Land of North Rhine Westphalia, Scotland Europa

Source: Landmarks 2002

> **Box 5.1** Key concepts and terms
>
> **Civil society** refers to the collection of associations and group activity between the individual and state. These groups are voluntary and outside the direct control of the state. Private firms, trade unions, and non-governmental organizations all make up civil society.
>
> **Lobbying** is an attempt to influence policy-makers to adopt a course of action advantageous, or not detrimental, to a particular group or interest. A *lobbyist* is a person employed by a group, firm, region, or country to carry out lobbying. Lobbyists in Brussels are also known as consultants or public affairs practitioners.

All lobbyists in Brussels try to make their voices heard in the formal, institutional EU decision-making structure as well as in less formal ways. In particular, organized interests provide a wealth of information to EU policy-makers and add depth to a legislative process that in formal treaty terms only involves the Commission, the Parliament, the Council, and two advisory bodies: the Economic and Social Committee and the Committee of the Regions. They also add to the complexity of policy-making, and increase rivalry between competing interests. There is no doubt that the impact of organized interests on EU policy-making has been profound. Their growing presence has prompted officials and others to ask how (or whether) to regulate their influence in EU decision-making. These issues are discussed below. But first, we explore in more detail the three types of organized interests.

Types of actor

Private economic interests

Of the three types of actor identified above, the largest category, including over 1,000 organizations, consists of private economic and business interests that come together to represent their points of view in pan-European trade federations or associations. They represent a staggering variety of business interests, ranging from the mighty (European Federation of Pharmaceutical Industry Associations) to the tiny (Hearing Aid Association); from the broad (European Youth Forum) to the specific (Association of European Starch Producers). Associations with powerful members such as automobile manufacturers, pharmaceutical companies, or food industries are extremely well-resourced and influential. Their main areas of interest are competition policy (particularly in connection with mergers), new regulatory measures, anti-dumping practices, product design, and any initiatives that they see as affecting their competitiveness. Major tobacco companies, for instance, have argued strongly against EU policies to restrict cigarette advertising.

The economic sector most heavily represented in Brussels is the chemicals industry which supports 150 organizations ranging from industry associations to public affairs consultancies. Second is the food and drink sector with 140 separate interest groups, followed by agriculture and fisheries (88) and the audiovisual, media, and publishing industries (70) (Landmarks 2002; Greenwood 1997).

While the variety of interests represented is striking, influence is not evenly spread. Those groups enjoying most access are those that can represent truly 'pan-European' economic interests—these tend to be pan-European umbrella economic associations such as the Union of Industrial and Employers' Confederations of Europe (UNICE) (representing business), the European Trades Union Confederation (ETUC) (trade unions), and the Committee of Agricultural Organizations in the EU (COPA) (agriculture). The heads of many of Europe's largest companies also meet in the framework of the European Round Table of Industrialists and regularly produce their own position papers on issues of concern to them.

It is not unusual for multinational companies or national business organizations to be members of a pan-European or international association, while also maintaining their own representation in Brussels. Major companies such as Six Continents (formerly Bass), Philips, IBM, GlaxoSmithKlein, Philip Morris, and others all have offices in Brussels specifically to monitor and influence EU developments that directly concern their activities. Some 320 major corporations have full-time EU public affairs directors or other executives dealing regularly in this area. But individual firms often find it useful to form alliances with other like-minded companies. Thus, the UK's Confederation of British Industry represents British industry as a whole through its office in Brussels, and is also a collective member of UNICE. National chambers of commerce come not just from member states such as the UK and France, but also from further afield: the US, Turkey, Norway, Morocco, or the Philippines. To this list should be added 270 or so law firms, political consultancies, and public affairs practitioners specializing in EU issues, all of whom represent clients in their relations with the formal institutions. Although all EU nationalities are to be found in these various groups, the majority tend to be British or American dominated, perhaps reflecting the greater ease and familiarity of Anglo-Saxon societies with lobbying when compared with their continental European neighbours.

Public interest bodies

Alongside national or sectoral economic groups has grown up a multitude of European non-profit organizations representing a wide range of public interests. These are now estimated to number over 300. Many of the smaller ones rely on EU funding for their existence. Among the most active are environmental, public health, human rights, and animal welfare non-governmental organizations (NGOs) such as Greenpeace, World Wide Fund for Nature (WWF), the European Consumers Organization (BEUC), the European Public Health Alliance, Human Rights Watch, or the International Fund for Animal Welfare. Environmental groups have built up particularly extensive contacts inside the different institutions and, with the help of certain 'greener' governments, have influenced the Commission's sustainable development policies.

Others, such as the Euro Citizen Action Service (ECAS) and the European Youth Forum are specifically concerned with citizens' rights inside the European Union. This type of public interest group often finds a welcome reception from MEPs, who recognize that many of their constituents share the same concerns and are aware of the potentially bad publicity if they fail to support 'worthy causes'. To illustrate the point, take an issue like the single currency. The European Monetary Institute, the forerunner of the European Central Bank, acknowledged that submissions from the European Blind Union led to design changes (such as special tactile marks and clearly visible numerals) being introduced to euro bank notes which make them easier to use by blind and partially sighted people (European Monetary Institute 1999).

Non-commercial interests are also represented by a handful of think tanks such as the European Policy Centre or the Centre for European Policy Studies and the leading Brussels-based conference organizer, Forum Europe. In addition to pushing their own ideas for, say, constitutional reform, these bodies provide useful fora for bringing together EU officials, academics, interest groups, and the media to analyse topical aspects of EU policy. However, the number and resources of think tanks in Brussels are modest compared to those in Washington DC as well as, for that matter, those in larger EU capitals (see Box 5.2).

Last but not least, mention should be made of the media in Brussels whose role has grown significantly in scale and importance over recent years as the scope of Union activity has expanded (see Box 5.3).

Governmental actors

Our final category includes governmental organizations and representatives. These comprise the 167 non-EU country embassies accredited to the Union, ranging from Albania to the United States. This category also includes local authorities or more powerful regional governments, such as the German Länder or the Scottish Executive. These embassies and regional offices maintain close links with all the main institutions. In the Commission, contacts are largely with the appropriate Commissioner or director-general and, at a lower level, with the desk officers handling their part of the world. In the Parliament, relationships are developed with individual MEPs with the relevant expertise, background, or

Box 5.2 COMPARED TO WHAT?

Lobbying in Brussels and Washington

At first glance, Brussels and Washington appear to have much in common as political capitals. Both are relatively small cities: Washington ranks only as the twenty-fifth largest city in the US, while Brussels' population is under one million, and is thus much smaller than London's (about 7 million) or Paris' (over 2 million). Both are federal-style capitals and centres of considerable power. Decisions taken in both affect the lives of citizens far removed from where policy is made. New-comers to both cities often express surprise at how much Brussels and Washington feel like 'villages': that is, the number of policy entrepreneurs seems rather small, everybody seems to know everybody, and nothing remains a secret for very long.

However, any lobbyist who approaches lobbying in Brussels in the same way as in Washington is doomed to fail. Lobbying in Brussels tends to be far more discreet, low-key, and informal than in Washington, where successful lobbying campaigns are often highly aggressive and public (Cowles 1996: 344-6). Success-ful lobbying in Brussels must be sensitive to fifteen different national cultures, and a big advantage comes from being able to speak multiple languages: English and French as a minimum, but also German, Spanish, and even Dutch. Since the EU has no elected government (or opposition), political campaign contributions are very rarely used to try to affect EU policy outcomes, in stark contrast to accepted practice—at least before recent campaign finance reforms—in Washington. Perhaps the biggest difference is in the value attached to reliable expertise and information. The EU's institutions are extremely resource-poor compared to their closest equivalents in Washington. For example, the European Parliament has nothing remotely similar to the respected and well-funded (US) Congressional Research Service. Brussels is home to only a handful of think tanks, which generate policy ideas and debates, while Washington boasts a large and diverse collection which are generally much better funded and more closely linked to major political parties (or factions within them). With fewer providers of expertise, and public institutions which are more desperate to acquire it, the power which comes from being able to gather, process, and disseminate reliable information may open more doors in Brussels than in any other political capital (Peterson and Cowles 1998).

Interestingly, one lobby group, commonly thought to be one of the most influen-tial on the Brussels 'circuit', appears able to thrive in a European lobbying environment despite having American roots. The EU Committee of the American Chamber of Commerce (of Belgium) brings together 'European firms of American parentage'—that is, US companies with large investments in Europe. Formed in

> **Box 5.2** *Continued . . .*
>
> 1985, the EU Committee of what is known as AmCham was one of the first major lobby organizations in Brussels to bring together firms in a wide array of different industries through direct membership (as opposed to being a 'peak organization' of national company associations or a single-industry lobby).
>
> Since the EU Committee of AmCham lacks a patron, national capital, or member government in Europe, it tends to ally itself more closely than most organized interests with the EU's institutions themselves. Meanwhile, no EU member government has any wish to alienate American investors, whose assets in Europe have grown from $72 billion in value in 1984 to $528 billion by 1999 (European–American Business Council 2001). US-headquartered firms directly employ over 3 million Europeans, mostly in jobs with unusually good pay, conditions, and benefits. But influence in Brussels policy-making is earned, not automatic. Successful lobbyists often must generate reliable and timely information and nearly always need to nurture access to key policy-makers. The EU Committee of AmCham's (2002) success in doing both may be reflected in its publication of a mid-term *Guide to the European Parliament 2002–4* in April 2002, well before anyone else produced anything comparable (AmCham's guide to the EP was still widely used months later *within* the Parliament itself).

responsibility, and with the parliamentary delegations engaged with specific countries or geographical areas (such as the Maghreb region of North Africa or South America). Third countries also nurture direct lines of communication with EU member state governments, often through the member states' permanent representations in Brussels. Most contacts between the EU and third countries focus heavily on commercial questions (how to boost trade and avoid disputes), but discussions increasingly encompass geo-strategic or human rights issues as the EU develops its common foreign and security policy and adopts joint positions on humanitarian and development aid.

Governmental actors from within the EU's existing member states are also well represented in Brussels. Most influential are regional governments which have established delegations (they are careful not to call them embassies for fear of angering national capitals) in Brussels. These delegations include the powerful German Länder—some of which, like North Rhine Westphalia, have a larger population and higher gross domestic product than many EU member states—but also many French, Spanish, and British regions. In all, it is estimated that there are now around 190 individual delegations in Brussels representing different regions, local authorities, and cities in the Union (Committee of the Regions 2001).

Box 5.3 Lobbying and the media in Brussels

While some newspapers and television channels may have particular editorial stances towards EU developments (think of the euro), influencing the EU decision-making process is not generally the aim of the media. Rather its role is to report, analyse, and comment. But this distinction is blurred and the media's role is crucial to understanding organized interests and policymaking.

First, lobbyists cultivate contacts with the media, looking to use these channels to present their case to a wider audience. It is not uncommon for a particular proposal or idea to be leaked to a favoured newspaper in an attempt to situate the debate in the most sympathetic light before details are officially in the public domain.

Second, with nearly 1,000 members, the Brussels-based media is the largest international press corps in the world, ahead of Washington. It contains full-time correspondents and freelance journalists from every EU member state, from the applicant states in central and eastern Europe and the Mediterranean, and from countries as far afield as Mexico and Japan. Among the most numerous are German and Spanish reporters, reflecting the strongly regionalized media in their countries.

The media shape policy by presenting news in a particular way. With few exceptions (such as, perhaps, the *Financial Times* or the Brussels-based *European Voice*) the media invariably view EU developments through a national prism. For example, a decision in January 2002 to move senior Commission officials who had been in the same post for more than seven years prompted the following headlines: 'Brussels braced for shake-up' (*Financial Times*); 'Britons set to lose out in big reshuffle by Prodi' (The *Times*); 'Britons on the advance in the EU institutions' (*Frankfurter Allgemeine Zeitung*); 'Brussels, French influence in decline' (*Libéra-tion*); and 'Kinnock kicks out fat cats' (*Daily Star*). What is reported (and how) in the media, and the tone adopted, can influence EU policy-making and politics as well as perceptions of the European Union held by ordinary people.

Emergence and rise of organized interests at the EU level

It is difficult to know precisely the number of economic, public, and governmental groups involved in EU affairs, but it is clear that their number has increased hugely over the past three decades. Recent scholarship by Gray (1998) and Wessels (1997) tracks the overall numbers of trade associations, interest groups, regions, national associations, think tanks, consultants, and lawyers from 400 in the 1970s to close to 2,000 by the late 1990s.

How can we explain this remarkable increase? Essentially, it has occurred as a result of, and in parallel with, the deepening and widening of the European Union itself. As more legislative responsibilities have been transferred to the supranational organization through successive treaty revisions, so national organizations have gradually realized that they need to argue their case in the corridors of Brussels, Luxembourg, and Strasbourg. Similarly, as the Union's budget has increased, particularly for overseas expenditure, so, too, has the interest of international NGOs and third countries.

Hence, different types of interests have congregated in Brussels in a series of waves. In the 1960s, the most dominant actors tended to be specific sets of commercial interests, namely agriculture and steel, corresponding to the responsibilities of the European Coal and Steel Community and the then European Economic Community. The importance and dominance of commercial interests continue. One of the largest single categories of trade associations remains the food and beverages industries. Its predominance is undoubtedly due to the existence of the Common Agricultural Policy—the first truly pan-European policy after coal and steel—and to the presence of a large number of agricultural and food committees which advise the Commission on various aspects of managing the market for different products.

While trade union, employer, and public sector organizations were well represented from the early days of the Union, broader public interest organizations, notably Europe's consumer (BEUC) and environment (European Environmental Bureau) organizations, did not mobilize in Brussels until the 1970s and the advent of increased legislation in these areas. For instance, the European Citizen Action Service (ECAS), formed in 1990, comprised a dozen or so different European NGOs. By 2001, it had three times that number.

Preparation for the single market programme in the late 1980s was a major catalyst for interest mobilization. Numerous trade associations and individual companies scrambled to Brussels to ensure that plans to encourage the free movement of goods did not damage their members' interests. They also were in a position to offer the technical advice EU legislators needed. Some large companies, preferring to represent their own interests directly, also opened, or strengthened, their offices. Many of these were American, reflecting their determination not to be excluded from the single market.

The late 1980s saw an increase in the presence of regional governments in Brussels (see Box 5.4). In particular, political decentralization across Europe, combined with a massive increase in the EU's budget for regional and social spending, sparked the creation of a plethora of regional offices during that period, as regional and local authorities throughout the EU realized the advantages of direct representation in Brussels and the funding it could bring (see Chapter 6; Laffan 1989). This presence led to, and was encouraged by, the 1993 establishment of the Committee of the Regions which was designed to raise the profile and input of regions in the Union (see Chapter 3).

Box 5.4 HOW IT REALLY WORKS

British Regions in Brussels

The strong presence of British regions in Brussels has been largely prompted by two factors: domestic constitutional changes inside the UK and the increasing impact of EU decisions on the policies and responsibilities of regional authorities. The arrival of the Scottish Parliament and the Welsh Assembly in 1999 and the rebirth of the Northern Ireland Assembly, were the catalysts for the creation in Brussels of separate offices representing the Scottish Executive, the Welsh National Assembly, and the Northern Ireland Executive. For English regions, the spur to develop their activities in Brussels was the UK government's decentralization initiatives in 1998 and 1999, which led to the creation of regional assemblies and development agencies.

Increased power on the domestic level also means greater interest in EU developments. The initial incentive for regional representations was undoubtedly the attraction of EU funding for regional and social projects. Today, economic development remains a high priority, but interests now are far wider, and regional offices kept far busier. For example, environmental policy is certainly a major concern of regional authorities. But they also want to know about EU programmes on social inclusion, life-long learning, support for business, and cultural and tourism activities. Regions with a strong university base are tapping into the Union's multi-billion euro research and development programme. Major political developments such as enlargement or moves to construct a comprehensive asylum policy are being closely monitored for their potential impact on regional economic and political development.

While developing their own direct contacts with the EU's various institutions, and establishing cross-border networks, British regions operate under the aegis—if not watchful eye—of the UK's Permanent Representation, since it is central government which formally represents the country inside the European Union. In this regard, few British regions enjoy the powers of their counterparts in (say) Belgium, where regional ministers occasionally represent the federal state in the Council of Ministers, or in Germany, where the regions have their own permanent observer in the Council.

Whatever their restrictions, the growing activities of British regions—like subnational authorities across the EU—also suggest that formal channels of representation such as the ESC or Committee of Regions (CoR) are deemed insufficient forms of representation for their interests. The CoR's limited power and lack of unified purpose (see Chapter 3) has encouraged a far more informal system of networking and lobbying through which representatives can put their case directly to the relevant policymakers, particularly those in the Commission and EP (see Jeffrey 2002). One cannot understand how the EU really works as a lobbying system merely by studying its formal institutions and their reputed purposes.

Increasingly robust regional representation is not without its problems. In particular, it has highlighted the possible tension between central and local/regional government in their dealings with the EU, particularly if regional priorities are not compatible with national ones. In the late 1990s, for instance, Scotland's Highlands and Islands region lobbied hard to keep its priority funding status in the carve-up of EU regional funds. The UK government, however, saw northern Scotland as a less deserving case and put most of its energies into ensuring that coveted status for Northern Ireland and parts of England and Wales. The episode, surely not the last of its kind, raises a broader point: as interest representation becomes more crowded, it also becomes more competitive and complex.

Organized interests at work

Whatever their type, non-institutional actors seek to shape EU decision-making through lobbying. Virtually all groups include in their strategies a focused effort to influence key EU institutions. Although the Council of Ministers is the most powerful institution, it is not usually the key target of most groups. It remains extremely difficult for EU lobbyists to obtain access to the Council, so attempts to influence member state governments tend to be concentrated at the national level or in individual member states' permanent representations in Brussels. But ease of access alone does not determine where lobbyists flock. For instance, most spend little time targeting their efforts at the Economic and Social Committee or the Committee of the Regions, even though both were specifically established to represent sectoral and regional interests. These institutions have neither the legislative clout nor institutional weight of the European Parliament or the Council of Ministers, nor the Commission's power to initiate legislation. And they receive legislation late in the game—usually after lobbyists want to make their views known. Thus the vast bulk of lobbying is directed towards the Commission and Parliament.

Lobbying the Commission

Most lobbyists worth their salt will seek to nurture relations with the Commission. It is, after all, the institution which most often initiates policy and drafts proposals. The Commission's basic approach is to maintain as open and wide a dialogue as possible with all interested parties, believing that this is beneficial both to itself and interested groups. The specialized knowledge of organized groups is a valued asset to an under-resourced Commission, providing it with an opportunity to explain to those most directly concerned what it is trying to achieve. The Commission insists that all groups should be treated equally and claims to make no

distinction in its handling of these relationships between private and public interests. However, it displays a distinct preference for dealing with pan-European
associations rather than with representatives of national or individual organizations, so it can glean and pursue the 'pan-European' interest. Moreover, the more
political and economic clout an organization has, the easier it is to gain access to
policy-makers and put across a case.

The contacts can either be formalized in the shape of advisory committees or
groups of experts, or conducted on an ad hoc basis. In the case of the former, the
Commission has developed a whole network of hundreds of specialized committees consisting of national officials or recognized experts in their field. These
committees assist the Commission both by helping to implement policy and by
considering amendments to existing legislation. (They might advise, say, on the
ethical implications of biotechnological advances or specific aspects of agricultural policy.) The Commission also hosts public hearings and issues consultative Green and White Papers. These actively solicit input from outside interests on
policy initiatives being considered by the institution (see, for instance, the White
Paper on Governance, Chapter 8).

Commission officials are in constant demand and relatively open to lobbyists'
courting. But most maintain that for budgetary and efficiency reasons (that is, to
balance conflicting demands on their time) a sensible compromise needs to be
struck when consulting outside interests. Noted one Commission official:

Sometimes people want to see the new text [of a proposal] every time a comma is changed in
a draft directive. That is unrealistic. The one big problem with consultation is that it length-
ens the process. You need to balance efficiency with respect for democratic values. . . . If we
can get the consultation structured and put draft documents on the Internet, then everyone
should benefit. It is also important that other organizations should be able to see who is in
contact with the Commission (Interview 26 June 2001, Brussels).

Yet the Commission, which already consults nearly 700 ad hoc bodies on a
wide range of policies, has committed itself to consulting outside organizations
and groups on an even more comprehensive basis. In the Commission's 2001
Governance White Paper and more recent communications, it has suggested
strengthening the partnership between itself and *civil society* (see Box 5.1)
(Commission 2001a; Commission 2001b).

The Commission recognizes that for consultation to be efficient, it is not sufficient simply to post a proposal on a web site. Guidelines are required on how the
information fed back should be properly processed and slotted into the legislative
machinery. Another delicate issue is the exact moment when civil society or cor-
porate interests should be consulted: before or after the European Parliament? If
before, then this could be seen as usurping the role of democratically elected
MEPs. If afterwards, then there might not be sufficient opportunity to take
account of contrasting outside views.

A particularly complex set of relationships exists between NGOs and the Commission. This is especially true for those small organizations that rely largely on EU funding for their existence. Several hundred NGOs in Europe and worldwide receive funding for projects from the Commission. The annual sums add up to over 1 billion euro. The major part is allocated to external projects (development cooperation, human rights, democracy programmes, and humanitarian aid), but internal EU social, educational, and environmental programmes and their NGO sponsors also benefit (Commission 2001a). Moreover, several NGOs sit on Commission consultative committees and a number act as agents for the Commission in the implementation of policy (in, for instance, the delivery of humanitarian aid). While such assistance undoubtedly helps these organizations and the Commission, critics argue that the close relationship lessens the independence of NGOs and makes them less willing to undertake forceful advocacy work, especially that critical of the Commission. Striking the right balance in the relationship can sometimes be difficult.

The Commission has no specific or formal rules—such as accreditation, registration, or codes of conduct—regulating relations with outside interest groups. However, it has consistently encouraged organized interests to draw up their own codes of conduct on the basis of minimum criteria proposed by the institution itself. The vast majority of public affairs consultants are members of two 'self-policing' organizations—the Society of European Affairs Practitioners (SEAP) and the Public Affairs Practitioners Group (PAPG)—which have adopted their own 12-point code. Signatories have agreed to resign voluntarily if they transgress its provisions.

The code, initially drawn up by the PAPG, is an official public document and can be accessed on the Commission's website (see Web links, p. 107). It stipulates that practitioners should declare the interest they represent, not sell copies of documents obtained from EU institutions to third parties for profit, nor disseminate false or misleading information. Internally, the Commission also has specific institutional rules to ensure clarity and probity in contacts between outside interests and its own officials. These cover the reception of gifts, engagement in outside activities, and employment after leaving the service of the institution. Yet the relationship between the Commission and lobbyists remains largely informal and ad hoc.

Lobbying the European Parliament

The Parliament's growing power over the last decade has prompted a dramatic change in its relationship with lobbyists. The change is neatly summed up by one long-serving MEP who said, only partly in jest: 'In 1979, we were begging people to come and see us. Now we are trying to keep them away' (Interview, 25 June 2001, Brussels).

The rules, too, have changed. Until 1994, a lobbyist needed the support of an MEP in order to obtain a pass giving access to the Parliament's premises. The Parliament has since adopted a more open and practical approach for regulating the relationship between the institution and outside interests. Now, anyone seeking a regular visitor's pass to the institution needs only to fill out a declaration and a letter of justification. In 99 per cent of cases, the request is approved. The information is contained in a register, which now holds around 3,400 names and may be consulted by the public, though only on the Parliament's premises. With the annual pass, lobbyists can enter the Parliament's buildings. But neither they, nor the media nor occasional visitors, have *carte blanche* to roam at will. Certain areas of the institution's premises in Brussels, Strasbourg, and Luxembourg are declared out of bounds to outsiders unless they have a specific invitation from an MEP.

Parliament has approved a code of conduct that the holders of passes must respect. The code contains provisions broadly similar to those adopted by lobbyists themselves (see above). However, it also states that any assistance which outside actors might give to MEPs, such as the provision of staff or office equipment, should be declared in a special register. To reinforce this principle, parallel rules have been introduced requiring MEPs to declare any outside financial support in their own register, which is now accessible via the Parliament website. While some MEPs feared that this rule would mean declaring every cup of coffee or meal they might accept as hospitality, the rough guidance now given is that anything costing over 100 euro is worth declaring. The idea is to dispel the image of the Parliament as a 'gravy train' while keeping the policy process accessible to a variety of interests.

In general, the activities of outside actors in relation to the Parliament are far more visible—and often more colourful—than those directed at the Commission. For example, during the lengthy debates in 1999–2000 over EU copyright legislation, the music industry successfully used the Irish pop group, The Corrs, to argue its corner. Not only did the band put forward arguments for ensuring that the interests of song writers were taken into account, they also embarked on a charm offensive with a special concert for MEPs and EU dignitaries. Similarly, in recent years, leading figures from the world of football, such as the manager of Manchester United, Sir Alex Ferguson, and the presidents of the sport's governing bodies have lobbied the Parliament when it became apparent that the EU's competition rules would affect the international soccer transfer system.

Intergroups in the EP—cross-party bodies of MEPs who share some kind of interest in a particular issue or theme—are another vehicle for injecting outside opinions into the formal EU process. In 2001, there were fourteen active intergroups with topics ranging from animal welfare, anti-racism, and the cinema, to hunting and minority languages. The group's secretariat is usually provided by an outside body, either an NGO or a consultancy. Helping to administer these groups allows outside interests to focus the attention of MEPs from different parliamentary committees and political groups on a specific subject. The enthusiastic sponsorship of intergroups by organized interests suggests that as the EP's power grows, the attention of individual MEPs becomes increasingly valued by interests keen to shape policy.

Successful lobbying

Information and alliances

The art of lobbying has come a long way in the EU. In the view of one heavily lobbied MEP: 'Now, we have far higher skills and standards in the lobbying industry. You very rarely get the utter fool you would have encountered some years ago' (Interview, 25 June 2001, Brussels). The information provided by lobbyists is crucial to making the policy-making system work, but it must be tailored appropriately. The European Commission attaches special attention to accurate, unbiased information that will provide officials with the necessary technical expertise in drafting legislation. For individual governments, assessments of how proposed EU initiatives will impact on specific national concerns will be listened to. MEPs need information from their constituents as well as specific interests. Successful lobbyists will target their expertise accordingly.

Another skill common to successful lobbyists is an ability to build alliances or networks across nationalities, institutions, and groups in a common cause. As explained in Chapter 1, policy networks which link together stakeholders in specific policy sectors can play a crucial role in shaping EU policies. Coalitions of like-minded actors, which sometimes bring together some unlikely partners, can 'load' the policy process in favour of certain outcomes. In 1995, for instance, the EU's proposed biotechnology patenting directive was soundly rejected in the European Parliament (240 votes to 188 with 23 abstentions) as MEPs expressed their concerns about the 'patenting of life'. By May 1998, when a second draft directive was put to the Parliament for its final approval, it won the support of 432 members with only 78 MEPs totally opposed. The turnaround was achieved through lobbying by a carefully constructed network made up of the pharmaceutical industry in alliance with patient groups, many of whose members hoped that the new technology would deliver new cures for disease. More recently, as Box 5.5 illustrates, a coalition of national and business interests played a determining role in blocking planned EU legislation on company takeovers.

New technology and old techniques

More than in most political capitals, new technology has made its presence felt in Brussels. In particular, electronic means of communication help organized interests to put their message across swiftly and efficiently. Emails are a convenient way to maintain a dialogue with Commission and national officials and

Box 5.5 HOW IT REALLY WORKS

Lobbying and the Takeovers Directive

On 4 July 2001 the plenary of the European Parliament rejected—on a tied vote—the 'Takeovers Directive'—a proposal designed to facilitate cross-border take-overs of firms in the EU. The plenary voted on the outcome of arduous negotiations between a delegation of its members and the Council of Ministers. The vote was the culmination of just over two months of frantic activity by a wide array of organized interests across the EU.

At the end of April, the German Chancellor, Gerhard Schröder, was approached by the head of Volkswagen, Ferdinand Piech, who argued that the proposed directive would put his and other German companies in danger of hostile take-over. Following the meeting, the German government changed tack. It withdrew its suppport for the 'common position' which it had supported along with the other fourteen member states in 2000, and lobbied strongly against the directive in the European Parliament. The Parliament had already begun a 'conciliation process' with the Council (part of the co-decision procedure, these talks between delegates of the Council and Parliament are designed to agree a draft legislative text). Despite German opposition, delegations representing the Council and Parliament reached an agreed position in June 2001. However, the whole Parliament still had to ratify the agreement. In the month preceding the vote, MEPs were subject to fierce lobbying from all sides and from unlikely alliances of interests.

Opposing the directive, the Brussels-based European Trade Union Confederation issued a statement, arguing that the provisions for consulting the workforce were insufficient, therereby encouraging many Socialist MEPs to vote against. In Italy and Spain, there was anxiety amongst electricity producers about hostile takeover bids from Electricité de France, itself protected from hostile takeovers by its status as a French public (that is, state-owned) company.

Supporters of the directive, including national employees' groups, such as the Swedish trade unions in Stockholm, argued forcefully in favour, as did representatives of financial interests, like the Association of British Insurers. The Commission too was strongly committed to improving the operation of financial markets, by reducing the obstacles to takeovers.

The final result was dramatic: a tied vote meant the directive failed and German interests prevailed. The case suggests that issues as contentious as the takeover directive cannot be resolved without taking account of the strong concerns of national, but also specific organized (industrial, labour and consumer) interests in the EU. It also raises concerns about the continued ability of one member state—especially one of the larger ones—to veto some agreements in EU decision-making which are supported by all other member states.

parliamentarians and their assistants, although an increasing number of MEPs complain that they are being deluged with unsolicited messages. However, e-mails remain an enormously handy and time-saving device for widely disseminating draft amendments and a useful instrument for quickly gathering together a coalition of interests.

These advantages are particularly valuable to pan-European trade associations which have huge logistical problems trying to secure the agreement of each of their national member organizations to a coordinated position. Equally, technology increases the effectiveness of national organizations eager to influence EU policies. For instance, the human rights pressure group Statewatch, which monitors the EU's policies on civil liberties and transparency, has embraced these techniques in its campaign for more public access to internal Commission and Council documents. With the click of a mouse, it can engage sympathetic MEPs, other like-minded groups, and journalist federations to quickly construct a broad coalition behind its cause. Websites are proving to be another useful lobbying tool; both EU institutions and other organizations use sites to publicize background information and allow easy access to it.

But these technological developments are no substitute for old-fashioned face-to-face contact, particularly at the outset of a lobbying relationship. Personal contacts over a drink or meal or in a private meeting are still seen as essential ingredients needed to insert outside views into the formal EU decision-making process. Consultants, lobbyists, and pressure groups inevitably try to break into the busy agendas of European and national officials and parliamentarians in Brussels and Strasbourg. Despite the time required to travel to the Alsatian capital from Brussels (a 4-hour journey by train), Strasbourg is an especially popular venue for lobbying because virtually everyone who travels there for EP plenaries is away from home and has evenings free. The particular rhythm of business there—to say nothing of the fine wine and food—means that it is generally easier for MEPs and officials to find time for external visitors. Thus, whatever the cost and other disadvantages of the MEPs' 'travelling circus' from Brussels to Strasbourg and back again, it does allow the possibility for an impromptu word on the train, in hotel lobbies, and in airport lounges.

Timing

A successful lobbyist is also sensitive to the timing and stages of EU decision-making. At the outset, when legislation is being mooted, their focus of attention tends to be the European Commission where the proposed text is being drafted. Lobbyists are aware that it is far harder to change something once it is put down in writing than when an official is faced with a blank sheet of paper. Once the proposal has been formally adopted by the Commission, the focus of attention usually moves to national governments and the European Parliament, particularly if the measures under consideration are subject to co-decision, as is the case with around

75 per cent of EU legislation. Organizations interested in the contents of the draft legislation, especially those keen to amend it, will try to put their views across to individual MEPs. They will pay particular attention to the parliamentary *rapporteur* (the MEP responsible for the text), and the members of the relevant parliamentary committee which will examine the proposal. At this committee stage, it is a fairly common practice for interested outside parties even to draft amendments for sympathetic MEPs in the hope that these will be tabled and win wider support. Most of this lobbying occurs well before the proposal is submitted to a plenary session for the institution's formal opinion.

Conclusion

What impact do organized interests have on the EU and how it works? The question is central to debates about the EU's democratic deficit (see Chapter 8) and opinions certainly differ. On the one hand, it is widely recognized that well-resourced organizations with a clear mission can lobby very effectively, whereas smaller or less well-funded bodies generally find it harder to put their particular message across. Very broad coalitions of pan-European interests—such as UNICE or the ETUC—often find it more difficult to agree internally to a clear, common position than do individual private firms or mission-oriented NGOs. The EU may be less technocratic and more open to lobbying than it once was—and arguably more open than are many member states—but resources are by no means distributed evenly. This imbalance concerns writers such as Mark Aspinwall (1998) who argues that EU policy is determined by a few well-resourced interest groups at the expense of other public interests which cannot employ the same sort of well-resourced lobbyists. Put another way, the EU favours private interests that are most powerful at the domestic level.

Others have found that the EU provides an alternative arena where groups that are not gaining access at the national level have a second chance to be heard. Research by Wallace and Young (1997) and Peterson (1997) suggests more diffuse interests have managed to shape decision-making over time, usually by forming alliances with the Commission (environmental groups) and the EP (consumer groups), or learning to use the European Court of Justice (in the case of women's rights groups).

A related question concerns the overall effect of the growth in the number and range of such interests. Has it generally been a positive phenomenon? Or does it represent a danger for democracy and efficiency in the EU? On the positive side, the range of subjects now covered by the EU is so wide that virtually any actor can find its specific interests reflected somewhere on the agenda. NGOs and public interest groups have helped ensure that many issues of public concern—sustainable development, employment, social inclusion, and public health—are now discussed at the very highest levels of EU decision-making, including at the level of the European Council. The growing involvement of these groups, as well as regional and local authorities in EU affairs, can also encourage governments and the Union's institutions to involve individual citizens more closely in Europe's development and thus divert the criticism that decisions are taken by an inner elite, detached from the concerns of ordinary citizens.

The upsurge in the number and range of interests also has a downside. The most obvious is that of overcrowding and the imbalances it may cause. Outside groups are now so numerous that hard-pressed officials within the institutions have less and less time to listen to individual concerns, thereby potentially reducing consultation to a formality without real substance. Enlargement is likely to exacerbate this problem. The number of staff in the institutions is unlikely to grow substantially, but there will be an ever wider set of interests outside chasing after the 'eartime' of relatively few and ever more harassed officials.

In short, by no means does everyone believe that the arrival of civil society in Brussels has been a positive development. For some, it represents a move towards a political process where outcomes depend on the relative strength of determined lobbyists and backroom deal-making. What is needed is a more open policy debate in which more voices are heard by EU policy-makers.

Yet it seems highly improbable that we will return to the situation which prevailed before the arrival of these groups. Demands for transparency and pressures for outside groups to see, and seek to influence, what is happening inside the institutions are powerful and gaining in strength. Perhaps the key issue is to make explicit the terms under which such activity takes place so that all can be aware of the role played by those outside and the links they enjoy with those inside. If these terms are perceived to be fair and transparent, it is reasonable to argue that the developments described in this chapter could be part of the solution to the democratic deficit in the European Union, rather than part of its cause.

Discussion questions

1. Does the greater and increasing involvement of outside interests in the EU's decision-making process make for better policy?

2. Is democracy strengthened or undermined by the presence of non-elected interest groups in the EU decision-making process?

3. Should sub-national layers of government be given a stronger formal role in the EU's decision-making process? If so, how could this be achieved?

4. What are the arguments against giving 'civil society' a more powerful role in EU decision-making?

Further reading

For detailed information on the European Parliament, including its intergroups, see Corbett, Jacobs, and Shackleton (2000), Chapter 10. The edited collection by Claeys et al. (1998) provides a useful mix of academic and practitioner analyses of lobbying. For an insider's account of lobbying on the biotechnology patenting directive, see Earnshaw and Wood (1999). A detailed examination of different interests groups is found in Greenwood (1997). For a general overview of the many different organized interests involved in the EU process, see *The European Public Affairs Directory*, published by Landmarks (2002).

Claeys, P.-H., Gobin, C., Smets, I., and Winand, P. (eds.) (1998), *Lobbying, Pluralism and European Integration* (Brussels: European Interuniversity Press).

Corbett, R., Jacobs, F., and Shackleton, M. (2000), *The European Parliament*, 4th edn. (London: Cartermill).

Earnshaw, D., and Wood, J. (1999), 'The European Parliament and Biotechnology Patenting: Harbinger of the Future?', *Journal of Commercial Biotechnology* 5/4: 294–307.

Greenwood, J. (1997), *Representing Interests in the European Union* (Basingstoke and New York: Palgrave).

Landmarks (2002), *The European Public Affairs Directory* (Brussels: Landmarks sa/nv).

Web links

The Commission has established a directory of non-profit pan-European organizations. This electronic database, known as 'Consultation, the European Commission and Civil Society' (Coneccs), now holds details of nearly 1,000 European bodies grouped by category—for instance trade unions, professional federations, and religious interests. The site provides basic data on each organization and lists representatives with which the Commission has formal and structured consultations. It can be found at: **www.europa.eu.int/comm/civil_society/ coneccs/**. The websites of the major umbrella organizations mentioned in this chapter (UNICE, ETUC, COPA) can all be accessed via the Coneccs site.

The voluntary code of conduct for lobbyists can be found at: **www.europa.eu.int/comm/ secretariat_general/sgc/lobbies/code_consultant/codecon_en.htm**.

Some of the organized interests discussed in this chapter are also represented through formal institutions. See the websites of the Committee of the Regions (**www.cor.eu.int/ home.htm**) and the Economic and Social Committee (**www.esc.eu.int/**). Finally, the websites of several think tanks mentioned include the Centre for European Policy Studies (**www.ceps.be**); the European Policy Centre (**www.theepc.be/**); the Centre for European Reform (**www.cer.org.uk**); and the Trans European Policy Studies Association (**www.tepsa.be**).

Part III

Policies and Policy-Making

Chapter 6
Key Policies

Alberta Sbragia

Contents

Overview

Public policies in the European Union vary, and so does the EU's role in formulating them. Some policies fall under the jurisdiction of the European Union but others are carried out in partnership with the national governments. Still others are primarily under national control. Policies which seek to build markets are largely formulated in Brussels and encourage economic liberalization. They are designed to increase economic efficiency within the EU so as to increase economic growth and prosperity. Other policies attempt to mitigate the consequences of market forces. In these areas, the European Union tends to 'co-govern' with the national governments and the Commission plays a key role. Finally, policies which are not related to the market—such as justice and home affairs (JHA) and common foreign and security policy—are helping to build a political community or 'polity' while reserving a central role for the EU's Council of Ministers. This chapter introduces the EU's most important policies and examines how they have developed, and with what effect.

Introduction: policies in the EU

The European Union sets policies in so many areas that it is difficult to think about national policy-making in Europe in isolation from Brussels. While the euro—the common currency used by twelve of the EU's fifteen member states—is perhaps the most visible manifestation of European integration, a diverse set of *public policies* (see Box 6.1) affecting the everyday lives of Europeans are shaped by

---

Box 6.1 Key concepts and terms

Agenda 2000 refers to the major budgetary reforms agreed in 1999 in preparation for enlargement. In the area of cohesion policy, 213 billion euros were budgeted for the period 2000–06. 195 billion of these were allocated to the 'structural' funds which are spent on declining or disadvantaged regions in both rich and poor countries.

Benchmarking is the use of comparison with other states or organizations (on issues such as pension reform or employment practices) with the aim of improving one's own performance by learning from the experience of others.

A **directive** is the most common form of EU legislation. It stipulates the ends to be achieved (say, limiting the emissions of a harmful pollutant) but allows each member state to choose the form and method for achieving that end. It can be contrasted with a regulation which is binding in its entirety on all member states.

Federalism is a constitutional arrangement in which the power to make decisions and execute policy is divided between national and subnational levels of government. In a federal system both national and subnational units wield a measure of final authority in their own spheres and neither level can alter or abolish the other. Each derives its authority from a 'higher' source the other does not control, usually a constitution.

A **market** is a system of exchange bringing together buyers and sellers of goods and services. In most markets, money is used as means of exchange. Markets are regulated by price fluctuations that reflect the balance of supply and demand. To function properly markets require the existence of law, regulation, and property rights. Virtually all markets are subject to some sort of regulation.

Polity here refers to an organized community or political system for allocating valued resources such as security.

Public policy is a course of action (decisions, actions, rules, laws, etc.) taken by government in regard to some public problem or issue.

the decisions taken at the EU level. Agriculture, environmental protection, international trade, the movement of goods, services, labour, and capital across borders, justice and home affairs, and foreign and security policy are all affected by the decisions taken in Brussels. In fact, roughly half of all the legislation adopted at the national level is linked somehow to European Union policies. Moreover, as the Union enlarges and admits new members, its influence will be felt throughout Europe, including in countries which thus far have only indirectly been affected by the EU and what it does (see Chapter 9).

Yet the role of the EU should not be overestimated; it is not a 'superstate' exercising control over all areas of policy. It should be thought of as a 'selective' policymaker whose power varies significantly across policy areas. Most of the policies for which it is responsible are related to markets—some build markets, some protect producers or consumers from market forces, some try to cushion the impact of market forces. Some are non-market related, and this category, while still a distinct minority, is increasing in importance. In still other policy areas (such as most kinds of taxation), the EU is absent and it is likely to remain so.

The differentiated role of the EU across policy areas is not unusual if we compare it to existing *federal* systems where power is shared between the national and subnational level (see Box 6.1). In such systems the national level may choose not to legislate in many areas, leaving policy discretion to the constituent units. Canadians, Australians, and Americans, for example, take for granted that many decisions affecting their lives will be taken at the state or provincial level rather than at the national level. In the European Union, citizens are becoming accustomed to such a system of differentiated policy responsibilities. Just as Washington lets each state decide whether to allow the death penalty within its borders, the European Union does not directly legislate on Ireland's abortion policy or Sweden's alcohol control policy or Spain's policy on bullfighting (see below). Citizens of a federal polity accept that at least some unequal treatment comes with living in a federation. In a similar vein, it matters a great deal—and will continue to matter—where one lives within the European Union.

However, the impact of the EU is such that its member states are, in many ways, much more alike now than they were fifty years ago. In certain policy areas, especially those related to economic activity, member state governments as well as private firms either have had to engage in new activities (such as environmental protection) or alternatively change their traditional practices. This is part of the process of 'Europeanization' referred to in Chapter 4. And of course the introduction of the euro in twelve member states has not only changed the landscape of monetary affairs but also made the average citizen constantly aware of that changed landscape.

The world of money and business has been changed by EU policies in very fundamental ways, but so have many related areas. Environmental protection, gender equality in the workplace, and occupational health and safety have all moved the EU toward a system in which many of the negative consequences of market activity are addressed in Brussels rather than in national capitals. This expansion in the EU's remit is the result not of some well-orchestrated plan but rather the product of constant problem solving, bargaining, and experimentation.

This chapter introduces some of the key policies adopted by the European Union. It does not provide a comprehensive inventory of all policies, but rather focuses on those policy areas which account for most of the EU's expenditure, staff time, and legislative output. The chapter begins by outlining the key features of EU policies, and how they differ from national policies. It then introduces market-building policies such as competition policy, trade policy, and EMU. It next addresses those policies which attempt to change or cushion the impact of the market. The Common Agricultural Policy (CAP), cohesion policy, and environmental and social policies fall into this category. The final set of policies are those which are involved in constructing a political community or *polity*—(see Box 6.1) outside the economic realm. Here justice and home affairs policies play a particularly important role (as does foreign and security policy which is discussed in Chapter 10). The final part of the chapter compares the different policy fields.

Key features of EU policies

Differences between national and EU policies

Policies in the European Union differ in some important ways from policies decided at the national level by its member state governments. At their most basic level, EU policies are different because the European Union and its member states are structured and financed very differently. Varying financial structures lead to three wider differences between national and EU policies:

- with a few exceptions, EU policies typically involve the spending of very little money, whereas national policy typically involves spending a good deal of it;
- the distance between those who formulate policy and those who actually execute it in practice is far greater in the EU than it is in most of the national systems which make up the EU;
- the EU is active in a much narrower range of policies than are national governments.

Thus, knowing about national policies is not a particularly good template for understanding EU policies. Let us examine each of these differences in more detail.

Money

One way to understand the European Union's relative poverty in the area of public finance is to compare its budget with the budgets of central governments in its member states. There is no direct 'euro tax' equivalent to the national income tax paid directly by citizens, and the EU's budget is significantly smaller than national budgets. As Table 6.1 illustrates, even though the central governments of France, Germany, and Italy are each responsible for only a fraction of the EU's total population, each of those central governments spends a great deal more than does Brussels. Another useful comparison is with the federal government's budget in the United States. The European Union has a larger population than does the United States, but the budget of the US federal government is roughly thirty times as large as the EU's budget (see Table 6.1).

The Union therefore relies on the power of law (as embodied in legislation and court decisions) rather than money to carry out most of its decisions. The lack of money shapes what the content of policies can be. The Union can have only a small number of policy areas which cost a great deal, whereas national systems typically have a large number of expensive policy areas, including those which fall under the rubric of the welfare state. The Union, given its current fiscal structure, could not, for example, finance health care for EU citizens or provide old age pensions or finance systems of public education. Overwhelmingly, the EU regulates economic activity; that is, subjects it to rules and standards.

Legislation vs. execution

In most national systems, the national government makes policy decisions and then has numerous ways of ensuring that those policies are actually executed 'on the ground'. Even in federal systems, national decision-making and execution are linked. Although that link is far from perfect in actual practice, it is far tighter in most national systems than it is when EU policy is involved. A policy decided in Brussels faces several hurdles before it can be successfully executed on the ground.

Table 6.1 EU and national budgets compared[a]				
EU budget (2002)	German federal budget (2001)	French central budget (2001)	Italian central budget (2001)	US federal budget (2002)
€98.6 billion	€250 billion	€266 billion	€389 billion	€2,280 billion

[a] Budgets are extremely difficult to compare as each government defines a 'budget' differently and includes different types of expenditures. The figures in the table should be understood as illustrative of differences in magnitude rather than precise calculations. The figures include general central government expenditures plus social security expenditures for which the central government is responsible. The figure for Italy includes interest payments but not monies used to redeem debt.

Sources: European Economy; International Monetary Fund; Delegation of the European Commission to the United States; Embassy of the Federal Republic of Germany to the United States.

The first step is known as 'transposition'. That is, most laws (known as *directives* or regulations, see Box 6.1) adopted by the Council of Ministers in Brussels need to be 'transposed' into national legal codes before they can be executed by the member state's public administration or formally shape the behavior of private actors in significant ways. Such transposition is not usually timely. In fact, the EU finds it difficult to ensure that legislation adopted in Brussels is transposed at the national level when it is supposed to be. For example, the Commission reports that of the eighty-three directives which should have been transposed in 2000, only five of them had been transposed in all member states (Commission 2001*b*).

Even when transposition does occur, the Commission may feel (and argue to the European Court of Justice) that the transposition does not adequately reflect the intent of the EU's legislation. If the ECJ upholds the Commission's position, the national government will need to transpose the EU's legislation in a different way. Thus, Union policies do not become 'policy' at the national level uniformly across the EU's member states. For example, a directive transposed in Finland shortly after its adoption in Brussels may not be transposed in France or Greece until several years after the Finnish action.

These differences suggest that Brussels formulates and adopts policy but its actual impact will be shaped by national systems of governance (see Chapter 4). National governments play a central role in the EU's policy process because they hold a monopoly of power in the actual execution of most policies adopted in Brussels. In some federal and nearly all non-federal state systems, central agencies have field offices throughout the national territory to monitor the work of sub-national administrators involved in executing national policy. But the EU has no administrative presence within the member states. The Commission, for example, has no field offices in national capitals from which it can monitor the execution of EU law. It must instead rely on complaints from citizens, firms, and non-governmental organizations. Even then, it can only try to persuade national governments to improve execution.

The difficulties surrounding execution and monitoring mean that policies which affect a dispersed set of actors are less likely to be executed uniformly than are those policies which affect a few. For example, environmental policy, which attempts to shape the behaviour of huge numbers of both public and private actors, is executed with a tremendous degree of variability within the Union. By contrast, the Commission's decisions about mergers and acquisitions are implemented uniformly. The number of firms affected by any single Commission decision is very small and a non-complying firm would be very visible.

Jurisdiction

A third difference between EU and national policies concerns policy competencies (see Box 6.2). While certainly broader than that of international organizations, the EU's policy remit is narrower than that of national governments. Health care,

Box 6.2 The policy competencies of the EU

Policy competence refers to the primary legal authority to act in particular policy areas. The different types of competencies, which are based on the Treaties, are traditionally divided into three categories: *exclusive* competencies of the EU, *shared* competencies between the EU and its member states, and competencies belonging mostly to the *member states*.

1. The EU has **exclusive** competence in few, but important, policy areas: external trade in goods and some services, monetary policy, customs and fisheries.
2. The majority of policy competencies are **shared** between the EU and its member states. Shared competencies include, for example, environmental policy, consumer protection, mergers and acquisitions, development aid, transport policy, visas, asylum and immigration.
3. Finally there are policy areas where the **member states** are the main players, even if the EU is involved in some general coordination or is engaged in a few specific projects. Education, culture, employment, public health, research, social and urban policy, and most foreign and security policy fall into this domain.

In some policy areas it is difficult to place policies in one of these categories because the line between shared competencies and member state competencies is blurred. In foreign and security policy, for instance, it is often unclear how much weight the EU has because the member states in the final analysis must allocate the resources necessary to execute the EU's foreign and security policy (see Chapter 10).

old age pensions, poverty alleviation, urban regeneration, abortion, prison administration, and education, for example, are not subject to EU legislation because the EU has not been given competence in those areas by the member states. Other areas remain under national control because of the decision-making rules which apply to them. In the areas of taxation and energy, for example, the decision-making rule is unanimity. Since the member states have been unable to agree on any single policy, those policy areas remain under national control.

Nor does the EU deliver social services. A battered wife or an abused child would be cared for by local or national service providers, not by EU social workers. Recently, various 'soft' measures such as *benchmarking* (see Box 6.1) have been used to encourage national governments to emulate successful policies formulated elsewhere (see also Chapter 7). But in general the 'welfare state' and the direct provision of social services is primarily under national control with the notable exception of agriculture (see below).

Policies which have a moral or cultural dimension also remain under national control. The Irish do not permit abortion, for example, and the EU does not have the power to tell Ireland either to change its abortion law or to keep it. The Swedish and Finnish alcohol control system has been under strain due to the ability of individual revellers to bring liquor in from other EU countries, but alcohol control policy in both Sweden and Finland remains under national control. Paulette Kurzer (2001: 6), after analysing the distinctive Irish policy on abortion, Dutch policy on drugs, and the Finnish and Swedish alcohol control policies, concludes that changes brought about by EU membership have been modest and due primarily to 'the abolition of borders and the desire of consumers to enjoy goods and services not easily available at home'.

Although the EU does not have a direct effect on these policies, it is important to note that the EU can and often does have important indirect effects. For instance, energy *policy* (energy taxation especially) is still under national control because EU policy-making requires unanimity in that area. But the energy *market* is being liberalized as the EU requires national governments to allow (selected) consumers a choice of electricity suppliers. Similarly, the commitment of the EU to meet the Kyoto Protocol requirements to combat global climate change will, once implemented, constrain energy policy in all the member states. To take another example, education at both pre-university and university level are under national control, but the EU has been a prime mover in encouraging university students to study in another EU member state. The Commission's programmes on student mobility have led to major changes in universities' administrative structures and have encouraged university rectors to work toward much greater cross-national standardization in degree programmes (such as the length of time required to receive a degree). In short, the lack of formal competence at the EU level does not mean that Brussels lacks influence in shaping the terms of debate within a policy area. The programmes that Brussels adopts, while not legally binding in the way that legislation is, provide national and subnational governments with important incentives to carry out certain activities (see Table 6.2).

The primacy of economic integration

Policies related to economic integration form the core of what the EU does. The EU's unique history and development has privileged some areas as important for the EU while leaving others aside. As Chapter 2 explained, European states in the 1950s chose to defend each other within a transatlantic rather than a 'European' organization (NATO includes Canada and the United States). Policy areas concerning defence as well as foreign policy and security, therefore, were not central to the integration process and have become salient only recently. Even now the role of NATO shapes significantly the way the EU member states address the Common Foreign and Security Policy.

Table 6.2 Indirect effects of European Union policies	
Policy area under national control	**Role of European Union**
Alcohol control policy	Free movement of people and goods makes control more difficult
Higher education	Encourages student exchanges; gradual convergence in universities' administrative structures
Poverty	EU's concept of 'social exclusion'—emphasizing the marginality of the poor from the larger society rather than focusing exclusively on their lack of money—helps shape new ideas about social assistance at the national level
Pensions	Encourages 'best practice', 'benchmarking', and stipulates gender equality provisions

By contrast, economic cooperation was viewed as a politically acceptable way of increasing integration while laying the groundwork for political cooperation at a future date. Consequently, policy areas related to economics have been privileged from the very beginning. The 1957 Treaty of Rome, by calling for a customs union and a common market (now referred to as a single or internal market), steered the process of European integration toward the liberalization of cross-border trade, a unitary trade policy vis-à-vis non-members, and the free movement of capital, goods, services, and labour. The process of creating an operational single market is still in process, but the centrality of that effort to European integration symbolizes the importance that economic integration has within the European Union. The next sections explore a range of policies linked directly or indirectly to the goal of closer economic integration.

Market-building policies

The focus on liberalization and creation of a single market highlights the EU's concern with 'market-building' and what is sometimes termed 'negative integration'. Building markets involves both *removing* barriers to trade and carrying out regulatory reform. So negative integration means eliminating various tariff and non-tariff barriers to trade, regulatory reform in the area of economic regulation, and ensuring that competition among firms is encouraged. The goal is to facilitate cross-border economic transactions with the expectation that the resulting greater efficiency will lead to higher levels of prosperity for the citizens of Europe. This same approach has characterized the main institution shaping the global economy, the General Agreement on Tariffs and Trade (GATT, founded in 1949), and underpins its successor, the World Trade Organization (WTO). It also has been the goal of other regional economic organizations which have emerged in the 1990s such as the North American Free Trade Agreement and Mercosur (see Box 2.4; Fawcett and Hurrell 1996). Cross-border trade is thought to lead to greater prosperity, and the single market programme emphasized the removal of 'invisible' barriers to such trade.

The political economy of the member states has been profoundly affected by the privileging of economic policies at the EU level (Sbragia 2001). In this arena, policies adopted in Brussels frequently 'pre-empt' national policies and the EU is said to have 'exclusive competence'. Monetary policy falls under this category (though it only applies to the twelve members of the eurozone), as do some other areas of the single market (see Box 6.2).

In general, the kind of 'negative integration' which characterizes the EU is far more penetrating than that found at the global (World Trade Organization) level or in other regional arrangements. The EU's ambitions in market-building are very serious and their scope very wide. The foundation of the single market involves the 'four freedoms'—freedom in the movement of capital, goods, services, and labour. However, a single market such as that envisaged by the founders of the Community does not occur simply by removing obstacles to trade. Other interventions (such as the break-up of monopolies, or standardizing of rules) must be put into place to ensure that the hoped-for market will operate smoothly and efficiently. For that reason, the construction of the European market has led to widespread regulation from Brussels. The central role of regulation in the EU has led Giandomenico Majone (1999) to label the EU a 'regulatory state'. Whereas a welfare state engages in redistribution and spends a great deal of money in providing social welfare (such as pensions), a regulatory state exercises its influence primarily by passing legislation which regulates the behaviour of actors in the economy. A welfare state provides unemployment benefits, for example, while a regulatory state would regulate pollution.

The development of a far-reaching regulatory regime in Brussels also has led to frequent complaints from those affected by such regulation—who typically blame 'Eurocrats' even when the blame should be placed elsewhere (see Booker 1996). Complaints about 'goldplating'—that is, enforcing EU regulations more stringently than common sense would seem to justify—are heard most often in the United Kingdom. The British civil service is known for its competence and thoroughness, virtues which seem to become vices when applied to EU regulations (see Box 6.3).

Box 6.3 HOW IT REALLY WORKS

'Goldplating' and EU policy

The extent to which seemingly anodyne EU directives can be transformed into nightmare regulations is illustrated below with some examples from the UK.

Whisky and Water
Directive 78/659, the EU's 'Fresh-water Fisheries Directive' stipulated that water taken from a stream and replaced must not be so hot as to harm fish. Temperatures should not exceed 1.5 degrees centigrade above normal temperature, but member states shall set these values, and they are allowed to grant regional exceptions if they can show fish would not be harmed.

Goldplated Application
The Scottish River Purification Board defined compliance as heating the water in a stream no more than precisely 1.5 degrees centigrade above its original temperature, and they warned that criminal prosecution would occur in case of non-compliance. This zealous interpretation caused difficulties, not least for Scottish whisky distillers who use huge amounts of water from rivers which are also home to salmon and trout. In their operations distillers sometimes heat the water slightly more than 1.5 degrees above its original temperature, although they argue that they are careful to protect the nearby fish. To constantly keep the water from being heated more than precisely 1.5 degrees would in fact be impossible because the technology had not yet been developed which could regulate the warming of water to the extent required by the Purification Board (Booker 1996: 191). The Purification Board's inflexible interpretation led many whisky distillers to view EU regulations as going beyond anything that common sense would dictate. In this case as in others, however, the directive might have been sensible but its interpretation was not.

Social Assistance and Lifting
Directive 90/269, known as the 'back-ache' directive, ruled that workers should not be asked to lift loads which could injure them. No specific weight limits were established.

Goldplated Application
The implementation of this directive is found in the UK's 'Health and Safety Executive's Manual Handling Operations Regulations 1992' which suggests that the limit for a load to be carried by a woman might be 16.6 kilograms. But the UK's National Health Service Executive adopted the guidelines as firm limits and prohibited nurses from lifting loads above 16.6 kilograms (Booker and North 1996: 23). The result was that elderly patients who had been bathed at home by female nurses could not now be bathed because female nurses were prohibited from lifting them to help them in the tub. Thus a directive that starts out reasonably enough can become increasingly less so with each subsequent 'goldplated' interpretation.

Competition policy

One of the most important market-building powers given to the EU—the Commission specifically—is over competition policy. The Commission operates as an independent institution in this policy area. The Council of Ministers is not involved in decisions regarding competition policy. In essence, competition policy is about encouraging competition among firms and battling monopolistic or oligopolistic practices, or those which privilege national producers over those in other EU member states. The requirements can be tough for any member state, but competition policy poses particular challenges for accession states from Central and Eastern Europe. Moving from an economy which was largely under public control to one in which the market is dominant is difficult, and the rigour of the EU's competition policy makes that transition even more onerous.

The Commission has the authority to rule on many mergers and acquisitions, fight cartels, and rule on the appropriateness of many forms of state aid given by national or regional authorities to firms. In this policy area, the Commission is an international actor as well as an EU actor. For example given the level of foreign direct investment in Europe by American firms, the Commission has the power to veto mergers between American firms with extensive operations in Europe, even if the American anti-trust authorities have approved the merger. It has exercised that veto in several high profile cases, notably vis-à-vis a proposed merger between General Electric and Honeywell.

Trade associations and firms as well as member state authorities and ministers (and at times prime ministers as well as the French President) lobby, especially informally, when the Commission considers specific competition cases. However, the Commission needs to engage in far less negotiation than is required in other policy domains and has turned a deaf ear to lobbying, even by very important national politicians. In this area, the directorate-general for competition and the Commissioner for competition are central and powerful actors.

Commercial (trade) policy

The key goal of the Treaty of Rome was to create a common market across national borders. This objective required liberalizing many national markets (that is, allowing imports to compete with domestically produced goods) which had been heavily protected for many decades. Over time, the national economies of the member states have become far more interdependent with intra-EU trade accounting for over 60 per cent of the overall trade of the individual member states in 1999. However, trade with countries outside the EU is still very important for many member states.

The application of a single external tariff (which is applied to non-EU producers) in the late 1960s led to the decision that the European Economic Community (as the EU was then known) would need to speak 'with one voice' in negotiations involving international trade policy. The Treaty of Rome gave the EEC competence in international trade negotiations involving trade in goods. The Commission was granted the power to act as sole negotiator for the Community in, for example, world trade talks, and that power was strengthened in the Treaty of Nice, which gave the Commission the right to negotiate (with certain exceptions) trade in services. However, the competence to decide the EU's position in international trade negotiations was given to 'the member states operating through the European institutions', not to the Commission acting on its own. Therefore, although the Commission is the negotiator, the member states play a key role in shaping the negotiating mandate which the Commission pursues. In practice, the relationship between the member states (or at least selected ones) and the Commission is often conflictual as both argue for maximum institutional power in setting the terms of the negotiations.

Economic and monetary union (EMU)

The decision at Maastricht to adopt a common currency was momentous. For the first time since the Roman Empire, Western Europe would have a common currency. It was thought that a common currency would help keep a unified Germany tied to the project of European integration, would help increase economic efficiency in the EU and thereby raise the standard of living, and would help develop a sense of 'European' identity. A common currency requires a single central bank, and the European Central Bank (ECB) was set up to develop monetary policy with the goal of price stability (anti-inflation) as its top priority.

Part of the 'bargain' which underpinned the decision to move to a single currency by 1999, however, was an agreement that states wishing to adopt the euro must meet certain public finance requirements. Furthermore, public debt had to be constrained. The decisions were taken by the heads of state and government, but the preparation which underpinned those key political decisions was carried out by finance ministers and a relatively small group of national civil servants and central bank staff. Private businesses such as banks were not intimately involved, and the policy process was relatively closed.

The domestic political economy of states adopting EMU (the so-called eurozone countries) has been profoundly affected by EMU membership. The budget deficit requirements forced the restructuring of public finances in several eurozone member states. In the Italian case, the restructuring was so profound that the country's ministerial organization and budgetary process had to be radically transformed. Following the adoption of the euro in 1999 (notes and coins became available on 1 January 2002), several other member states found their macro-economic policies under scrutiny as they struggled to meet the budget deficit requirements of EMU membership. More generally, membership of the euro means these countries no longer have an independent monetary policy. The European Central Bank, headquartered in Frankfurt, makes decisions about monetary policy which apply to all member states using the euro. National governments therefore can no longer control the level of interest rates, a control which previously gave them some leverage over the direction of the economy. For example, in the pre-EMU era, governments could try to give priority to job creation or alternatively to price stability. Now, the European Central Bank is mandated to privilege price stability and thereby avoid inflation. The Bank has been criticized by some who would prefer it to adopt lower interest rates so as to stimulate the eurozone economy and hopefully create more employment. The Bank, however, has argued that job creation requires more flexible labour markets and more liberalization of markets in general. It has not tailored its interest rate policy to the wishes of the member states, nor to societal actors. The ECB has become an important, and very independent, actor in economic policy-making.

Market-correcting and -cushioning policies

Although policies related to building markets have been a central feature of the Union's policy activity, the Union also has been very active in policies which might be viewed as 'market correcting'. These policies attempt to either compensate for the cost to particular groups imposed by the building of markets, to channel or constrain the market itself, or to limit inequality.

Common Agricultural Policy

Perhaps the best-known policy designed to offset market forces is the Common Agricultural Policy (CAP)—of which the European Union has almost exclusive competence. In fact, some analysts argue that only in agriculture does 'the scale of political governance reach proportions resembling those of a federal government' (Rieger 2000: 181). The CAP is unique in the amount of money it receives from the EU budget (see Figure 6.1), the degree of power the EU exercises, and the amount of contestation it causes. Although the CAP created a market for agricultural goods within the EU, its market-correcting properties have been the most controversial outside the EU because the CAP distorts global prices for many agricultural products, thus affecting (negatively) non-EU agricultural producers.

Although welfare state policies have been peripheral to the EU's policy agenda, the CAP is an exception to that rule as well. As Elmer Rieger (2000: 182) has

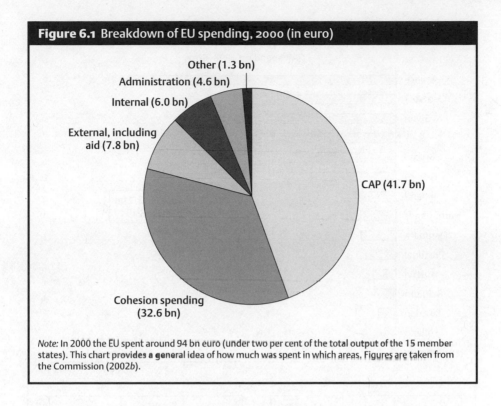

Figure 6.1 Breakdown of EU spending, 2000 (in euro)

Other (1.3 bn)

Administration (4.6 bn)

Internal (6.0 bn)

External, including aid (7.8 bn)

CAP (41.7 bn)

Cohesion spending (32.6 bn)

Note: In 2000 the EU spent around 94 bn euro (under two per cent of the total output of the 15 member states). This chart provides a general idea of how much was spent in which areas. Figures are taken from the Commission (2002b).

written, 'The key to understanding this policy domain is to see the CAP as an integral part of the west European welfare state.' The CAP keeps food prices in Europe higher than they would be if imported food would be allowed to enter at the world price, and in that way the CAP supports the incomes of European farmers. While the CAP has been cut back to some extent due to pressure at the global level, especially during the 1980s Uruguay trade round, it is still a major point of contention with other countries which would like to export farm products to the EU without facing very high barriers.

The CAP stirs up plenty of internal debate as well. The benefits of the CAP are distributed very unequally across member states. On a per capita basis, Ireland, Greece, Denmark, France, and Spain are the winners in this policy area while Luxembourg, the United Kingdom, and Germany are the losers. As Figure 6.2 shows, Italy, the Netherlands, and Belgium do not do too well either. In fact, of the original six founding member states, only France does very well. Moreover, whereas the CAP was introduced to ensure that farmers' income would not fall behind that of other societal groups, the distribution of funds does not necessarily help poor countries. For example, Portugal on a per capita basis receives far less from the CAP than does France.

Although attempts have been made to reform the CAP, such efforts have been stymied for many years. Typically, France was able to defend the status quo while

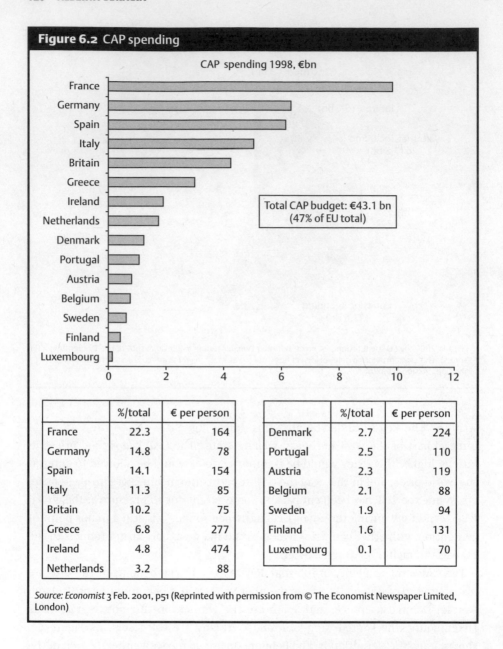

Figure 6.2 CAP spending

CAP spending 1998, €bn

Total CAP budget: €43.1 bn
(47% of EU total)

	%/total	€ per person
France	22.3	164
Germany	14.8	78
Spain	14.1	154
Italy	11.3	85
Britain	10.2	75
Greece	6.8	277
Ireland	4.8	474
Netherlands	3.2	88

	%/total	€ per person
Denmark	2.7	224
Portugal	2.5	110
Austria	2.3	119
Belgium	2.1	88
Sweden	1.9	94
Finland	1.6	131
Luxembourg	0.1	70

Source: Economist 3 Feb. 2001, p51 (Reprinted with permission from © The Economist Newspaper Limited, London)

Germany gave higher priority to issues other than CAP reform. Under the pressure of enlargement, the German government pushed for a restructuring of this policy area and the Commission introduced a radical reform proposal in 2002. But reform is extraordinarily difficult in this sector. The CAP has come to symbolize the very process of European integration and the path dependency which constrains it (see Chapter 1).

Cohesion policy

Cohesion policy was introduced to reduce inequality among regions and compensate governments of poor countries for the costs of economic integration. To help offset some of the costs faced by member states in adjusting their economies to EU standards, cohesion policy was introduced after the first enlargement (which admitted the UK, Denmark, and Ireland). Cohesion policy has increased in importance over time, and after significant budget increases in 1988 became a key policy area. It now represents one of the most important areas for public expenditure, although its overall claim on the EU's budget is declining somewhat.

The policy area has undergone several major revisions, including a major reform package, the so-called *Agenda 2000* negotiations, agreed in 1999 (see Box 6.1). The Agenda 2000 agreement budgeted over 200 billion euros to cover the period 2000–6. Most of the money went to the 'structural' funds which are spent on declining regions in rich countries as well as poor areas in poor countries. Another 18 billion went towards the 'cohesion fund' which is designed only for the poorer countries of the EU (Spain, Portugal, Greece, and Ireland).

As Figure 6.1 illustrates, the budget for cohesion policy represents roughly one-third of all the funds spent by the EU (the CAP accounts for nearly half). Every member state receives some cohesion policy monies, although the importance of these funds for a poor country such as Portugal is clearly far greater than it is for a rich country like France. But most go to the neediest regions; nearly three-quarters of the funding is spent in regions whose per capita GDP is below 75 per cent of the EU average (see Box 6.4). Regions with specific problems (such as a declining

---

Box 6.4 Poor regions

(Regions with per capita GDP below 75 per cent of the EU average, 2000–2005)

All of Greece

Spain (except Catalonia, Cantabria, the Basque Country, and Madrid)

Portugal (except greater Lisbon)

West and north-west Ireland

Southern Italy (including Sardinia and Sicily but not Molise)

Eastern Germany (except Berlin)

Western fringe of the United Kingdom (Cornwall, West Wales, and the Valleys, Merseyside, and South Yorkshire)

Remote northern regions of Sweden and Finland

Eastern border region of Austria (Burgenland)

Overseas French territories (but not Corsica)

Source: Hooghe and Marks (2001: 85)

industrial base) also receive funding even if they are part of a wealthy member state.

The distribution of structural funding across many member states has rendered it one of the most visible of the EU's policies, with road signs often signifying that a road or other public work is being financed with EU funds. It also features actors across levels of governance: regional, national, and EU policy-makers are all centrally involved in decisions surrounding the allocation of structural funds and their implementation. The interaction of actors from several levels of governance, and the sharing of power between them gives rise to the notion of the EU as a system of multilevel governance (see Chapter 1). Because regions in all member states have so far benefited from some form of regional spending, cohesion policy has escaped some of the intense controversy surrounding CAP. But the prospects of enlargement and the accession of far more (and much needier) member states means cohesion policy is now both the target of reform and the object of fierce political battles (see Chapter 9).

Environmental and social regulation

Although the CAP and cohesion policy are probably the best-known of the EU's policy areas outside of the single market, other policy areas have become far more important over time. Such policy areas are grouped under the rubric of 'social regulation' and they are designed to regulate the social effects of the market. Occupational health and safety legislation is one such area in which the EU acted rather early. Another important type of social regulation is that concerned with the protection of the environment. In environmental policy (especially in the area of pollution control) the EU became active after a customs union had been created, but before many of its member states had become environmentally conscious. Environmental policy was initially put on the agenda because of its international salience and because it affected trade in goods such as automobiles. Over time, the focus was enlarged into areas which are not market-related, such as the protection of environmentally sensitive habitats.

In many areas of environmental policy (primarily those outside of pollution control), national governments are free to supplement EU legislation with more robust standards or additional environmental requirements. Some do. In general, the Nordic member states, Austria, the Netherlands, and Germany are the most active in supplementing EU legislation with their own. But most member states choose not to go beyond EU requirements. Their decision means the EU is *de facto* the primary 'standard setter' in the area of European environmental policy.

Another area of 'social regulation' is consumer protection. A series of food scares and concern over genetically modified organisms (GMOs) has propelled this issue up on the EU's agenda and has resulted in the establishment of a Food Safety Agency. Social regulatory policies which are related directly to the single market (such as regulations on product safety) pre-empt national policies, whereas in other areas (such as hygiene standards) the EU stipulates minimum standards which national governments can exceed if they so wish.

The EU has also been active in the area of gender equality. National pension systems have had to be restructured to treat men and women equally. More generally, the EU has been a significant actor in the move toward equal pay (both in terms of income and benefits) in the workplace (Caporaso 2001). Most recently, the EU has passed laws against sexual harassment. While some member states already had tough laws, Spain, Portugal, Greece, and Italy had no laws which held employers responsible for harassment in the workplace, and Germany defined sexual harassment more narrowly than did the EU legislation. Member states can adopt stricter definitions of harassment, but now the EU legislation provides a 'floor' for any national legislative activity in that area.

Polity-building (non-market) policies

The Maastricht Treaty began the process of what might be viewed as polity-building. That is, the Union became active in areas which were not related to the market but which had the effect of making the EU a more powerful political system. As explained in Chapter 1, the Maastricht Treaty's creation of three pillars identified those policy areas related to the Union's traditional core economic activities (Pillar 1) but also highlighted two additional pillars of EU activity, foreign and security policy (Pillar 2) and justice and home affairs (Pillar 3) (see Box 1.2). Pillars 2 and 3 therefore brought under the EU's remit policy areas which had no direct connection with the market and were absolutely central traditional concerns about sovereignty. Precisely because of these concerns, leaders at Maastricht originally put these areas under the primary jurisdiction of the Council of Ministers and the supranational institutions were not allowed to exercise their usual powers in these fields.

But EU-wide cooperation in the area of immigration, asylum, and internal security evolved considerably in response to external events and new challenges. The 1997 Treaty of Amsterdam marked a turning point for the area of Justice and Home Affairs. The Treaty called for the development of an 'area of freedom, security, and justice'. Several policy areas (asylum, immigration, judicial cooperation in civil matters) were transferred to Pillar 1 and the Commission was to be given its traditional powers of initiative after a five-year waiting period. Police cooperation and judicial cooperation in criminal matters, however, remained in Pillar 3, where the Commission's normal monopoly over the right of initiative did not apply. Following the Tampere European Council in 1999, the general area of Justice and Home Affairs developed so quickly that, after the 11 September 2001 terrorist attack on the United States, a single arrest warrant and a common legal definition of terrorism were approved, both of which would greatly facilitate cross-border law enforcement. Furthermore, Europol, the European Police Office designed to improve the effectiveness with which police forces across the EU could cooperate across national borders, was strengthened. And in December 2001 the EU concluded a bilateral agreement with the United States to combat terrorism.

Because of its wide remit and development, the area of justice and home affairs is among the most complicated to understand. It blurs elements of intergovernmentalism and supranationalism and functions under several different kinds of legislative procedure (see Box 3.5). However, it has also been the most important in demonstrating that the EU is no longer an institution concerned only with markets and economics.

The development of Pillar 2 and a Common Foreign and Security Policy has developed more slowly due to the sensitive nature of defence, the central role of NATO in these areas, and the different foreign policy histories and colonial legacies of the EU's various member states. These dynamics and their consequences are explored in Chapter 10.

Comparing EU policy types

Each category of EU policy presented above has certain characteristics which distinguish it from the others. While the categories are clearly not watertight in the real world, they do differ in significant ways along a number of dimensions highlighted in Table 6.3. First, those policies which fall under 'market-building' stimulate market forces and encourage regulatory reform. Because of their emphasis on competition, such policies tend in practice to favour (although not require) privatization and the withdrawal of the state from those areas in which it has protected national producers. Many of the policies in this category are regulatory. In general, they tend to be made by the Community method (see Chapter 7) in which the Commission, the Council of Ministers, the European Parliament, and the ECJ are most active (although when it comes to external trade policy the European Parliament is largely excluded). In the market-building category the Union's competence tends to be most comprehensive and national policy activity is largely pre-empted.

The creation of markets is also marked by a variety of political dynamics and a range of political actors. The different theoretical approaches introduced in Chapter 1 shed light on these different dynamics. A few policy areas, such as energy and pharmaceuticals, feature what Peterson and Bomberg (1999: 81) conclude is 'a relatively stable and cohesive policy network'. That is, policies are shaped by a tight and insular group of actors. Similarly, the area of monetary policy is quite

Table 6.3 Policy types in the EU

Type	Level of EU competence	Key characteristics	Primary actors	Examples
Market-building	Nearly exclusive; covering extensive range of policies	Emphasis on liberalization and increasing economic efficiency; strong role of supranational institutions	Business groups; EU institutions; national finance officials; central bankers	Internal market policies (such as telecommunications or air transport); EMU
Market-correcting	Often exclusive but only in limited areas	Controversial; has redistributive implications; effective exclusion of Parliament	Farm lobbies; national officials; Commission	Common Agricultural Policy; Cohesion Policy; Fisheries
Market-cushioning	Shared with member states	Significant implementation problems	Supranational institutions; sectoral ministers; public interest groups	Environmental protection; Occupational health and safety; Gender equality in the workplace
Non-market policies (polity-building)	Subordinate to member states	Exceptionally strong role of national governments; supranational institutions marginal; sensitive sovereignty concerns	Council of Ministers; specialized lobbies	Selected aspects of immigration; police cooperation; asylum procedures; foreign policy

insulated from actors outside the central banking community. But most other areas related to trade do not exhibit such single-mindedness among the key actors who interact in what are often fragmented and internally divided networks.

Market-correcting policies differ from market-building in that they tend to protect producers from market forces. Most are redistributive—from consumers to farmers, and from rich regions to poor regions. Because they are overtly redistributive rather than regulatory, they tend to be very difficult to change as the impact of any change is quite transparent. For this reason, market-correcting policies tend to be dominated by intergovernmental bargaining rather than by the EU institutions. Liberal intergovernmentalism shows how major decisions in these areas are dominated by national governments responding to strong societal actors (say, agricultural lobbies) but national ministers ultimately decide when other considerations will trump the demands of those lobbies.

Market-cushioning policies try to minimize the harm economic activities impose on nature and humans. These policies tend to be regulatory in nature, impose demands on private actors, and fall under the 'shared competence' of the EU because both Brussels and national capitals typically 'co-govern' in these areas. The role of institutions in propelling these areas forward provides fertile ground for the new institutionalists' claim that 'institutions matter'. Brussels here is represented by the full panoply of EU institutions, and societal actors also attempt to influence the outcome. Such societal actors, however, are often weaker than one might expect, in part because they vary so much across the EU itself. Environmental groups, for example, are far stronger in Germany and Sweden than they are in France or Italy. It is difficult, therefore, to mobilize a European interest group which wields the same degree of power in Brussels as do producer groups (see Chapter 5).

In the *'polity-building'* areas of Justice and Home Affairs, and Common Foreign and Security Policy, different actors dominate. Thus far, civil servants have played a central role and societal actors are much less important than they are in areas related to market activity. For example, ministers of the Interior and Justice and their officials deciding JHA policies are much more insulated from interest groups than are ministers for Telecommunications or Transport. Moreover, the Telecommunications and Transport councils have been very much affected by decisions taken by the European Court of Justice, whereas the JHA Council is more insulated from ECJ rulings. Foreign policy and internal security have traditionally been the province of national public administrations, not civil society, and that same pattern is being reproduced at the EU level (see Chapter 10).

Conclusion

It is helpful to categorize policies into types, and this chapter has outlined the key features of each. But what makes studying EU policies enormously challenging—as well as fascinating—is that each of the policies introduced has its own unique features and trajectory. To illustrate, let us review some of the policies introduced in this chapter. Liberalization of markets has proceeded in a variety of ways. Often the European Court of Justice has played a key role—as it did in the case of tele-communications and aviation. The energy market, however, has been particularly difficult to liberalize because France has resisted so strongly. French firms, operating within a protected market, have bought (or attempted to buy) energy companies in countries which have liberalized, sparking outrage and calls for further powers to be given to the Union in this sector.

The euro for its part was introduced exactly according to a timetable drawn up at the time of the Maastricht Treaty negotiations in 1991. The 'virtual euro' was created on schedule in January 1999, and coins and notes followed in 2002. The introduction of this single new currency was in fact so smooth that it is easy to overlook what an enormous political, economic, and logistical achievement it represents.

The area of Justice and Home Affairs, introduced in 1993, initially received little attention and was not viewed as central to the process of integration. Ten years later, it had become a major policy area and took up a great deal of the Council of Ministers' time. External events were critical to the evolution of this policy area as was the relative insulation of this arena from societal actors. Environmental policy experienced a somewhat similar trajectory, but here the explanation lies with the leadership of a key state (Germany), international obligations, and the mobilization of environmental groups and public support (see Sbragia 2000). By contrast, the CAP has been very resistant to change. An entrenched 'policy community' has developed over many decades, and only external pressure from the global trading system seems able to serve as a catalyst for change in this policy area.

In sum, at any single point in time, the European Union's policies will range from those in which the European Union is the key actor, to those in which the Union and national governments 'co-govern', to those in which the Union exercises little formal or direct power. There is little uniformity across types of policy areas within the Union. Coupled with the Union's unusual institutional architecture, such diversity makes the Union's policy role terrifically complex. Furthermore, policy change in the European Union does not follow a single and predictable path. A policy area such as environmental protection or justice and home affairs can become important rather quickly while others can remain at a low level of salience for decades. As Chapter 1 noted, the contingency and fluidity of the Union's policy role is one of the features which makes it especially interesting to students of politics and public policy.

That same fluidity also makes the policy role of the Union of real concern both to politicians and ordinary citizens. The debate on the future of the EU, culminating in the 2004 Intergovernmental Conference, revolves around a simple question. What should the EU do? Where should it do more and where should it do less? Public opinion suggests the EU's citizens want the EU to be more active in the fields of international crime, food safety, environmental protection, and security, both internal and external. It is not clear, however, how popular the EU's emphasis on increasing economic competition and the liberalization of markets is with the citizenry. National and subnational policy-makers, for their part, seem to want the EU to adopt less detailed legislation, leaving more discretion to policy-makers in national systems. However, such discretion may harm the effectiveness of the single market which lies at the core of economic integration. Finally, the decisions taken at the Intergovernmental Conference will have to address the EU's limited capacity to take on an increasing range of policies in an increasingly enlarged Union. In particular, decisions to strengthen the EU's role in security, food safety, or environmental protection will have limited impact unless the EU's budget is increased over time. Policies, to be effective, require the expenditure of public monies. If the financial position of the European Union is not strengthened, its capacity to deliver policies will remain limited.

Discussion questions

1. Why has the EU privileged economic policies over social welfare policies?
2. Why is the EU budget so much smaller than that of its major member states?
3. What implications does a single monetary policy have for the development of other types of policies within the EU?
4. Which policies seem to have been affected primarily by pressures *internal* to the EU, and which by pressures or events *external* to the EU?

Further reading

For an excellent in-depth analysis of the EU's major policy areas, including those discussed in this chapter, see Wallace and Wallace (2000). For a good discussion of a more limited set of sectoral policies (telecommunications and energy policy for example) see Andersen and Eliassen (2001). Egan (2001) analyses the construction of the European internal market in a particularly comprehensive and insightful fashion, and Hooghe (1996) considers how the politics of cohesion policy contribute to the process of European integration. Zito (2000) presents a sophisticated explanation for the evolution of EU environmental policy, while McCormick (2001) delivers a comprehensive overview of environmental policy. Majone (1996) provides an excellent analysis of regulation and the 'regulatory state' in Europe while Majone (2000) offers a sophisticated analysis of various problems associated with the EU's regulatory system. Finally, Azzi (2000) explains the unique difficulties associated with executing EU policies on the ground.

Azzi, G. (2000), 'The Slow March of European Legislation: The Implementation of Directives', in K. Neunreither and A. Wiener (eds.), *European Integration after Amsterdam: Institutional Dynamics and Prospects for Democracy* (Oxford: Oxford University Press): 52–67.

Andersen, S., and Eliassen, K. (eds.) (2001), *Making Policy in Europe*, 2nd edn. (London: Sage).

Egan, M. (2001), *Constructing a European Market: Standards, Regulation, and Governance* (Oxford: Oxford University Press).

Hooghe, L. (ed.) (1996), *Cohesion Policy and European Integration: Building Multi-Level Governance* (Oxford: Oxford University Press).

Majone, G. (1996), *Regulating Europe* (London and New York: Routledge).

—— (2000), 'The Credibility Crisis of Community Regulation', *Journal of Common Market Studies* 38/2: 273–302.

McCormick, J. (2001), *Environmental Policy in the European Union* (Basingstoke and New York: Palgrave).

Wallace, H., and Wallace, W. (eds.) (2000), *Policy-Making in the European Union*, 4th edn. (Oxford: Oxford University Press).

Zito, A. (2000), *Creating Environmental Policy in the European Union* (Basingstoke and New York: Palgrave).

Web links

To locate EU publications covering policy, try the EU portal EUR-Lex at **www.europa.eu.int/eur-lex/**. It is bibliographic in nature, but contains links to many fulltext documents. For a record of EU legislation, search this site from the European Parliament: **www.europarl.eu.int/guide/search/docsearch_en.htm**. More information on the policy implications of Agenda 2000 can be found at: **www.europa.eu.int/comm/agenda2000/index_en.htm**.

For fulltext, non-EU documents; and analyses on the web, see the websites 'European Integration Online Papers' at **www.eiop.or.at/eiop/** and 'European Research Papers Archive' at **www.eiop.or.at/erpa/erpaframe.html**.

Chapter 7
The Policy-Making Process

Alexander Stubb, Helen Wallace, and John Peterson

Contents

Overview

This chapter explores how policies are made in the European Union. The aim is to show that there is no one EU policy process, but rather three different ones—the Community method, the coordination method, and the intergovernmental method. Sometimes the EU institutions run the show. At other times national policy officials work together with each other and their counterparts in the EU institutions. In some areas member governments organize and control cooperation themselves. The main players and the rules of the game vary depending on the policy area in question. One of the only common denominators linking the three variants of the policy process is the common aim of achieving agreement, preferably by consensus.

Introduction

The European Union's (EU) policy process matters, not least because EU rules have a profound impact at the national and subnational levels in Europe, and sometimes beyond. Chapters 3, 4, and 5 outlined the main actors in the EU game—that is, *who* makes the Union tick. Chapter 6 six dealt with the key policies of the EU—it illustrated *what* the EU does. This chapter examines *how* the EU makes decisions and policies.

The EU is active in a wide array of policies and its scope has been significantly extended, particularly in the past fifteen years. However, its policy remit has not been extended in any standard way. Being a fundamentally experimental system, the EU has experimented with a wide array of decision rules and procedures. The same EU institutions and national policy-makers operate in different ways depending on the policy—sometimes the specific issue—in question. And the policy process has varied over time. The same policies, for environmental protection or promoting cooperation in research, have been subjected to different procedures at different times. There is no single catch-all way of capturing the essence of EU policy-making, except to say that the central aim is almost always consensus, or something like it.

This chapter starts by reviewing the main players and the rules of the EU game. It then describes how the different categories of policy outlined in Chapter 6—'market-building', 'market-correcting and cushioning', and 'polity-building'—tend to be made. The bulk of the chapter examines three basic ways in which a proposal can travel the long road from proposal to decision. First we look at the policy process when the EU's institutions drive the process: what is known as the *Community* method. We then examine policy-making in areas where the powers are shared between the EU and its member states and/or attempts are made to coordinate national policies at the EU level: what we call the *coordination* method. Here policy-makers from both EU and national institutions are engaged. Finally we look at the process when the member governments effectively run the show: the *intergovernmental* method.

Different rules govern each method, and each produces a different form of governance that empowers different kinds of actor. As such, there is no shortage of power struggles between different member states, and between them and the EU's institutions, for policy 'turf' and competencies. One result is frequent change in how particular policies are made. To help explain why the EU's policy process is subjected to almost constant reconstruction, we introduce the idea of a 'policy pendulum', which swings between more and less collective policy-making, while also spelling out the many different motives for European cooperation.

The main players and the rules of the game

Before looking at *how* EU policy is made, it is important to recall the main players in the EU game. As Chapter 3 indicated, the main institutional players are the European Commission, the Council, the Parliament, the Court of Justice, the European Council, now complemented by the European Central Bank. These institutions do not, however, exist in a European vacuum: they do not 'stand alone' in Brussels (or Luxembourg or Strasbourg) without links to national capitals as well as other international organizations. A hallmark of multilevel governance in Europe is the embedding of the EU's policy process in its subnational, national, and international counterparts, and vice versa.

More specifically, most EU policy-makers are also, even mainly, *national* policy-makers (see Chapter 4). National officials and ministers, even many MEPs, spend the majority of their time in their home countries dealing with national policy concerns. For them, as well as many subnational actors, the European dimension is an extension of their 'home' policy arenas, not a separate activity. Many spend very little time in Brussels. The same is true of many representatives of private firms, non-governmental organizations, and other social and economic groups which seek to influence the development and content of EU policy (see Chapter 5). Meanwhile, a growing number of EU officials—some formally part of the Commission or Council—represent the Union, and seek to advance its interests, in international organizations including the United Nations and the World Trade Organization (WTO). Most of these actors try to affect what happens in their policy 'backyard', wherever that may be, by trying to influence the EU's policy process in Brussels.

It is thus important not to lose sight of the domestic and international games in which the players are engaged even as they manoeuvre for advantage in the Brussels policy process. Take, for example, bargaining between different ministries and agencies in the member states themselves when the 'national interest' in defined in any EU policy debate. Often, clashes over what should be the national position are greater *between* ministries in a single member state than between the *same* ministries of different countries. Perhaps naturally, environment ministries often find agreement easier among themselves in Brussels than agreement with their 'own' industry ministries back home.

Meanwhile, the emergence of the EU as a global actor (see Chapter 10) means that European foreign policy-makers increasingly seek to use 'Brussels' to further their own objectives, be they national or international, economic or political. The UK managed to engineer a collective EU condemnation of Argentina's invasion of the Falkland Islands in 1980, despite the hesitations of several member states. One of the most notorious episodes in the history of European foreign policy saw

Germany basically bludgeon the Union as a whole into supporting the right to independence of the former Yugoslav republics in 1991 (Peterson and Bomberg 1999: 242–3).

Thus, the EU is a crossroads where subnational, national, supranational, and international policy-making all intersect. It thus comes as no surprise that the EU policy process has differentiated outcomes, with significant variations between countries, since most of what is decided in Brussels is implemented or enforced by actors who are only marginally connected to the EU policy process. Some never participate at all. Still, Brussels is an important political capital primarily because of its links to other political capitals, in Europe and beyond, and *not* because it simply dictates policies which actors elsewhere must obey.

Three variants of the policy-making process

At first glance, the EU's policy process seems hopelessly complicated. There are over thirty specific and different legal instruments and procedures at the disposal of the Union. One of us, concerned to give a complete picture, has identified no fewer than five different EU policy 'modes' (H. Wallace 2000*b*: 28–35). Here, we simplify somewhat and identify three main variants of the EU's policy process.

The basic rules of the most commonly used process are quite simple. Where powers are clearly assigned to the EU (see Box 6.2), the Commission generally has a monopoly over the right of initiative: nothing may become EU policy unless it tables a formal proposal. The Council of Ministers takes the final decision after consulting other EU institutions. The Parliament's powers vary between policy sectors, but the so-called co-decision procedure, which makes the EP a political and legal equal to the Council, has gradually become something like the template rule. The European Court of Justice (ECJ) is called upon to resolve legal disputes, and generally acts to reinforce the power and prerogatives of the EU institutions, as well as the force of European law. Thus, we have the main features of the classical *Community* method of policy-making. Typically it is contrasted with the *intergovernmental* method: where the member governments are clearly in charge, the Commission is an invited guest to intergovernmental discussions but has no formal power, and the EP has only a consultative voice and the Court has little or no jurisdiction. Usually, the EU policy process is portrayed in the form of a simple dichotomy between these two basic methods, with the Community method dominant in the first pillar, and the intergovernmental method employed in the other two.

Yet, this dichotomy oversimplifies and ignores considerable nuances in the policy process. A number of new innovations have emerged recently, which together may be labelled the *coordination* method. Increasingly we find cases where member governments engage in study and discussion of shared problems at the EU table, or attempt to coordinate national policies more effectively with Brussels policies. But they avoid strict, legally binding EU directives or regulations. Instead, the co-ordination method involves governments and national agencies seeking to learn from each other and to mimic 'best practices', or policy solutions that have been shown to work. The central aim is to coordinate national policies, as opposed to trying to find a 'one size fits all' EU solution to problems that manifest themselves in very different ways in different national settings.

In examining these three variants (below) we find that each tends to encourage a different kind of policy outcome. Different outcomes even emerge from the application of a single method to different policy sectors. What they all share, however, is the goal of achieving agreement, be it a minimal, lowest-common-denominator policy that all can accept, or something more ambitious.

The Community method

The Community method emerged in the early years of the European Community as the main way of developing common policies, shaped by the new supranational institutions, to replace national policies. A case in point is the Common Agricultural Policy (CAP) after member governments agreed to common product prices and a common financing system. Another is competition policy, where the Commission became in effect an independent agency with formidable powers to prevent cartels and other anti-competitive behaviour (see Chapter 6).

The traditional Community method produces a form of supranational governance, in which powers are transferred from the national to the EU level. The EU's institutions are the main players and even the Council is as much a 'supranational' institution as a forum for intergovernmental bargaining. It is important to note that the Community method is not uniform in the way that it operates. The European Parliament, for instance, is not much involved in trade and agricultural policy, which are both subject to the Community method, whereas the EP has full powers of co-decision on the internal market. Nonetheless, the main characteristics of the Community method can be summarized as:

- A strong role for the European Commission, in particular through its monopoly on the right of initiative but also because it brokers policy compromises and supervises policy execution.

- A powerful role for the Council of Ministers, which engages in strategic bargaining and often engineers package deals.

- A potent role for the European Parliament in most legislative matters and (with the exception of agricultural spending) on budgetary questions.

- An important role for the European Court of Justice in reinforcing the legal authority of the Community regime.

■ The monitoring of policy implementation by committees of national officials which are chaired by the Commission, via the so-called 'comitology' procedure (see Box 7.1).

■ Openness to lobbies and interest groups that seek to influence EU policy and which provide expertise crucial to the design of effective policy solutions.

Market-building

At the heart of the EU policy process lies the goal of making the European economy function as an internal market. The Community method mostly focuses on market regulation or what Chapter 6 calls market-building policies. Policy-makers strive to develop rules, standards, and practices that will enable goods, services, and capital to move freely within the single market. This market embraces the economies of the member states, and also, increasingly, the economies of other, neighbouring countries.

In practice, the EU process is usually highly accessible to organized interests who seek to influence the building of markets. As Chapter 5 indicated, a range of interest groups, including pan-European trade associations, regional govern-ments, and multinational companies, are active lobbyists. Organized interests exercise influence through elaborate consultations with the Commission, the EP, and the member states. Consumers and others concerned about market regulation have a voice. National ministries and agencies, too, are recurrently involved in discussions and deliberations with the Commission, and with each other.

Market regulation is, however, an arena easily dominated by technicians and private actors. Most opinion polls suggest that ordinary EU citizens often feel themselves to be at a considerable distance from the process of regulating EU markets, and baffled by or uninterested in efforts to harmonize market standards such as solvency ratios for banks or safety regulations for combustion plants, even though both may be highly relevant to their daily lives.

In the Community method, the European Parliament provides an important institutional safeguard. Most EU market-making legislation is co-decided by the Council and the European Parliament. In practice MEPs scrutinize such legislation closely and frequently propose successful amendments, often responding to pres-sures from the lobbies that are active around the EU institutions. In principle there are opportunities for national parliaments to intervene as well in transposing EU directives into national law. In practice the attention paid by national parliaments to EU market legislation is erratic and sporadic.

Market-correcting and cushioning

Over time, the EU policy process has become increasingly caught up in distri-butional policy-making, involving the allocation of resources to different groups, sectors, regions, and countries. Some EU policies are redistributional, and take

---

Box 7.1 Key concepts and terms

Comitology. Most EU decisions are purely administrative and concern the implementation of policies on competition, agriculture, and so on. The Commission has primary responsibility for such decisions, but a complicated committee procedure exists under the decidedly unsexy name of comitology, which allows national officials to monitor the execution of EU policies. The number of committees has mushroomed to over 500 (plus subcommittees). There is debate about how much comitology limits the power of the Commission. What is clear is that the only person who truly understands it is the doorman at 35 Avenue Brochart in Brussels (the venue for most meetings) who can survey the hundreds of national and EU bureaucrats and experts walking in and out of comitology meetings on a daily basis.

Epistemic communities are a specific category of network consisting of experts with specialized and recognized expertise in a given policy domain. They are widely viewed as powerful in international policy-making generally and in the EU particularly, since so much European policy is highly technical in nature. Interestingly, the concept of epistemic communities has been developed primarily by Peter Haas (1999), the son of one of the academic fathers of neofunctionalism, Ernst Haas.

Open method of coordination (OMC) refers to a relatively new policy method involving comparison of national policies and the dissemination of 'best practices' in areas such as social and employment policy. The central aims are to exchange experiences, encourage policy-learning, and sometimes to agree and apply non-binding European guidelines to national and regional policies, whilst still respecting national and regional differences and steering clear of EU legislation.

Soft convergence is the idea that national policies should gradually become more alike through voluntary exchanges of information between officials (such as via the open method) on what has worked at the national level to achieve shared policy goals. The process usually involves creating scoreboards which rank the performance of national policies, thus shaming under-performers, as well as identifying 'benchmarks', or high standards to which all national policies should aspire.

---

from the rich to give to the poor: examples include cohesion policy (Hooghe 1996) and, by some accounts, research policy (Peterson and Sharp 1998: 165–7). In Chapter 6 we called these policies either market-correcting (the CAP, cohesion, and fisheries) or market-cushioning (environment, consumer protection, and gender equality).

The CAP and common fisheries policy have always had strong redistributional elements. Negotiations centre on sharing out allocations from the EU budget. The EU is unusual among transnational organizations in having an independent (if small) budget and its own spending programmes. Thus there is scope for the EU institutions to distribute resources to favoured clients and constituencies, as well as to transfer resources between the richer and poorer parts of the EU.

Despite its modest size—just over 1 per cent of EU GDP—the allocation of money from the EU budget generates a good deal of lively argument and competition. Debates about who should get how much engage national governments, regional and local authorities, and the representatives of different economic sectors of society. Practically all EU spending involves the EP, Council, and Commission. Spending programmes not only open up competition for resources but also create opportunities for stakeholders to try to influence decisions about what policy goals should be. For instance, the growing engagement of subnational govern-ments in the cohesion policy process has been marked enough to inspire new models of the Union as an exercise in 'multilevel governance' (Hooghe and Marks 2001). In these circumstances, the Commission's role is central but difficult: it must develop proposals that are acceptable to member governments as well as to the intended beneficiaries of the programmes. Thus, it must be careful to ensure that all get their 'fair' share.

The coordination method

New forms of policy coordination—between national policies and between national and EU policies—have recently emerged, and they differ in significant ways from the Community method. The coordination method relies on the sys-tematic comparison of national policies, with 'best practices' identified to facili-tate 'benchmarking', whereby national policies are periodically measured to see how close they come to matching the success of the most successful member state. The coordination method is now is used to coordinate national employment pol-icies and justice and home affairs policies, and thus it has extended the EU's reach in the realms of both market-cushioning and polity-building policies.

The coordination method features:

- The Commission as the facilitator of networks of national experts and, sometimes, independent scrutinizer of national policies.
- The involvement of independent experts as promoters of new policy ideas and techniques, who interact with national experts in what are sometimes called 'epistemic communities' (Haas 1999: see Box 7.1).
- The convening of high-level groups in the Council to compare national approaches and encourage peer review of national policies.
- Dialogue with specialist committees in the EP.

■ Policy outputs in the form of 'soft'—that is, non-binding—rules and policy recommendations.

Market-cushioning and polity-building

The Commission has sometimes encouraged member states to embrace the coordination method as a first step towards the eventual transfer of direct policy powers to the EU. This strategy worked in the case of environmental policy in the 1970s, which became a Community policy in 1987 (see Chapter 2). Similar efforts were made in the fields of research, and some aspects of education policy, with less dramatic transfers of policy competencies.

Recently, the coordination method has been used to extend policy cooperation to areas previously untouched by the EU. The European Council has established a series of processes and strategies named after the cities in which they were launched: Cardiff, Luxembourg, Cologne, and Lisbon (see Box 7.2). Most seek to promote the 'soft' convergence of national policies, without resort to new EU legislation, but with the aim of solving shared European socio-economic and employment problems, often using what has become known as the 'open method of coordination' (Hodson and Maher 2001: see Box 7.1). All touch very important policy areas, where international cooperation has traditionally been non-existent. The coordination method makes the EU framework relevant, but the main powers of decision-making continue to rest with member governments.

The coordination method is also used extensively in justice and home affairs, especially to address sensitive issues of internal security. Interestingly, this cooperation has led to the creation of new agencies, such as Europol (created in 1998), for EU-wide police cooperation. Here, as elsewhere, the coordination method sometimes leads to new and increasingly more integrated policy networks of national officials who previously had little contact with their counterparts in other EU member states.

The jury is still out on whether the coordination method really works. So far the results have been rather modest. When member governments bind themselves to action via 'soft' commitments, they are often less diligent in delivering than they are when they bind themselves legally. Supporters of the Community method have been quick to condemn the coordination method as a travesty of EU tradition. Yet, the reality is that EU member states increasingly seek to solve policy problems—especially arising from the effect of the EU's internal market on national policies such as pensions or unemployment—that they share, but which manifest themselves very differently in different member states. A single policy, even in the form of a directive, often makes little sense. Without new techniques such as the open method, it is questionable whether there would be any European policy cooperation at all on such questions.

Box 7.2 New 'processes' and 'strategies'

The European Council has fallen into the habit of agreeing new 'processes' and 'strategies' designed to achieve economic goals, but without resort to EU legislation. The most important ones are:

The Luxembourg Process (European employment strategy) aims to make labour markets more flexible and thus to boost employment. Its framework was introduced by the Amsterdam Treaty (1997) and the process launched by the Luxembourg European Council (1997). Giving birth to the 'open method' of policy cooperation, it has involved reporting of national employment data, peer review, agreement on annual employment guidelines, and country-specific recommendations. The process is largely voluntary and the greatest pressure that can be brought to bear on any member government is via a non-binding Council recommendation.

The Cardiff Process (product and capital market reform). Similar to the Luxembourg process, the Cardiff process aims at improving the functioning of product and capital markets through the voluntary coordination of national policies both with each other and with EU policies. Launched at the Cardiff European Council (1998), it requires each member state to submit national reports annually on their progress towards economic reform, and the Commission to report each year on the functioning of EU product and capital markets (the 'Cardiff Report'). From 2002 the process included an annual assessment of the quality of public services in each member state.

The Cologne Process (macroeconomic dialogue). Introduced by the Cologne European Council (1999), this process promotes the coordination of macroeconomic policies with a view to achieving non-inflationary growth and employment. All relevant actors, notably the Social Partners (employers and trades union associations), the ECB, as well as Council and Commission representatives meet twice a year for a confidential exchange of views on ways to promote better macroeconomic conditions.

The Lisbon Strategy (economic, social, and environmental renewal). The Lisbon strategy, launched in March 2000, is the most high profile of the new 'processes'. Its overall aim is to give the EU 'the most dynamic economy in the world' by 2010 through integrated EU and national actions in the economic, social, and environmental fields. A special European Council is now held each spring specifically to monitor progress on the Lisbon agenda. Yet, inevitably other issues (especially recent political events) end up being discussed. Advances in the first few years of the Lisbon process were generally patchy and slow.

The intergovernmental method

Throughout the history of the EU there have been examples of policy cooperation that have depended mainly on exchanges between national policy-makers, with little or no involvement by the EU institutions. The intergovernmental method has been most often employed in domains that touch very sensitive issues of state sovereignty, such as fiscal and foreign policy, where there may be benefits from cooperation but governments do not wish to see their national policies constrained too tightly. This method is characterized by:

- The active involvement of the European Council in setting the overall direction of policy.
- The predominance of the Council of Ministers or coalitions of member governments in consolidating cooperation.
- A limited or marginal role for the Commission.
- The exclusion of the European Parliament and the European Court of Justice.
- A central role for policy-specialized national officials, who over time become linked in new policy networks.
- Decision-making that can be quite opaque to national parliaments and the public.

Polity-building

At times EU member governments have been prepared to commit themselves to extensive mutual consultation, but have judged the full EU institutional framework to be premature, inappropriate, or unacceptable. In some cases—as in monetary policy—a system of intergovernmental consultation eventually was replaced by a collective, supranational policy regime. In other cases—including foreign, security, and defence policies—the intergovernmental method persists, although with the EU's institutions and rules increasingly prominent.

It might be tempting to dismiss the intergovernmental method as weak and unambitious. However, the treaties are scattered with examples where the cooperation has first taken place outside the treaty framework and encouraged confidence-building between national ministers and officials. Eventually, the intergovernmental method either fails to produce results or member governments learn to trust their opposite numbers in specific policy areas to the point where they become willing to cooperate in the EU sphere. Particularly sensitive areas—such as defence—may require a period of 'light' cooperation using informal, collective regimes before habits of cooperation become engrained enough for governments to embrace binding commitments. For example, one of the first steps towards a European Security and Defence Policy (ESDP) was the convening of an informal EU Council of defence ministers, interestingly under the Council Presidency of Austria—a militarily non-aligned state—in 1998.

Very different forms of intergovernmental cooperation exist even within the EU's treaty framework. EMU stands out as an example of a policy domain where confidence was built in a kind of consortium of key national policy-makers from central banks and financial ministries. Its largely successful record made it easier for subsequent decisions to be taken by twelve out of fifteen EU member governments to create a collective agency—the European Central Bank—to manage the euro. But the European System of Central Banks (ESCB), a powerful governing council with power to determine overall monetary policy and set interest rates, is effectively an intergovernmental consortium consisting of the heads of national central banks.

In justice and home affairs recurrent intergovernmental consultations, combined with the pressure of events (immigration and terrorism), have put the EU on the road to an increasing range of common measures. As we have seen, these pressures have also led parts of the justice and home affairs agenda to be subjected to the coordination method. But the enormous diversity (some would say confusion) of JHA policy is also illustrated by the fact that visa, immigration, and asylum policies are inching towards being incorporated into the first pillar, where the Community method applies.

In foreign, security, and defence policy we can also observe a gradual transition from the intergovernmental to the coordination method. More and more extensive consultation between national policy-makers has given rise to shared policy responses. One striking example is the proposal to create a European Rapid Reaction Force. It has brought defence ministers and military officials into the shaping of EU policy positions agreed under the banner of the Common Foreign and Security Policy (CFSP).

How far the intergovernmental method will take cooperation in foreign, security, and defence policies is a very open question. It is difficult to foresee the Commission ever having the monopoly it enjoys over proposing policies in the first pillar on questions of European defence. However, there is no question that the intergovernmental method has proven, over time, to be crucial in moves to build the EU into a more active, developed, unified polity.

Process and governance

We have examined three different variants of the EU's policy process, but for the most part left open a basic question: where does power lie? Who controls the policy process and determines outcomes when each is employed? Put in the language of one of the most vital questions in the study of politics generally (see Dahl 1961), who governs?

The EU policy process is distinctive. No state or other international organization makes policies through such a complex, transnational process in which politicians, officials, and interested groups from across a continent interact to shape—sometimes to prevent—shared policy outcomes (see Box 7.3). Whatever variant of the policy process is employed, the EU is a system of *governance* (see Chapter 8) but one without a government. Thus, there is very lively debate among analysts of the EU, mirrored in arguments between practitioners, as to who really governs.

. Here we suggest that most power lies with the EU's supranational institutions when the Community method is employed. Meanwhile, governance usually occurs through networks of policy-specialized, interdependent actors under the coordination method. Finally, it is the member governments themselves who govern collectively when the intergovernmental method is used.

The EU is a source of *supranational* governance in areas where it has created a new kind of politics by, in effect, transferring powers to a terrain where supranational institutions rule. Of course, the EU's member governments are always powerful, at every level and in every institution. Decisions of the European Court of Justice can dramatically determine outcomes. But it is above all bargaining between the EU's legislative institutions, between which powers are shared more than separated, that determines outcomes.

In theoretical terms, we can explain how this system has emerged over time by resort to neofunctionalism. Its concept of 'spill-over', according to which integration in one policy sphere (the internal market) begets more integration in others (EMU), helps explain why tentative experiments in purely intergovernmental cooperation have eventually led to more supranational governance. Meanwhile, institutionalist theories help us explain the behaviour of the main actors in supranational governance, which is shaped in important ways by engrained habits of cooperation, shared understandings, and the way that institutional structure determines politics.

The EU is a source of *networked* governance when it employs the coordination method. The increased use of this method encourages us to be somewhat agnostic about how far European integration has transformed or will transform European politics. To be sure, the EU's policy process reflects underlying changes in political and economic relationships across Europe, particularly ones arising from globalization and increasing interdependence between states, and between national and EU policies. But national and EU policy processes and institutions remain formally distinct from one another (even if they are very much linked in practice). The point is that, arguably, there exists no inexorable trend to more and more supranational governance. On this reading, new kinds of policy network are emerging which link together different kinds of actor: administrative and political, national and supranational, public and private. These networks act as bridges between

Box 7.3 COMPARED TO WHAT?

The EU and 'Other' Federations

Attempts to shed light on the EU by comparing its policy process or institutional structure to those of other political systems have been rare, and limited in their success. Most tend to assume that 'the government of the EU will become stronger and more intrusive, at least over the medium term' (McKay 2001: 143), thus transforming the EU into something like a federal 'state' analogous to Australia, Canada, Germany, or Switzerland. This assumption may seem dubious, especially in light of the recent proliferation of 'light' EU policy coordination arrangements. Yet, we do find parallel political debates in, say, the US and Europe about devolution, subsidiarity, citizenship, and how to solve problems of legitimacy (see Nicolaïdis and Howse 2001).

Moreover, the uniqueness of the EU only really shines through when we match its policy process up against those of other exercises in multilevel governance. Germany's constitution, or Basic Law, is analogous to the EU's Treaties in the many ways it seeks to promote consensus, such as by requiring super-majorities for dramatic moves such as impeaching the German Chancellor. Similarly, the Commission can be dismissed by the EP *only* as a collective and on the basis of a two-thirds vote of *all* of its members. Germany's political parties are powerful in the selection of leaders, policy-making, and patronage, as are the broad European party families—informally, at least—in the EU system.

Yet, such comparisons only go so far. The European Commission, which is neither purely 'government' nor 'administration', works on the basis of collective responsibility under a President whose powers over the college have increased in recent years. In contrast, German cabinet ministers are granted explicit, independent powers over their policy portfolios, with the Chancellor only charged with coordinating government policy. Some contend that the EU effectively has a bicameral legislature, especially under co-decision, with the Council acting as a sort of upper house representing the EU's member states. But others insist that the EU needs a 'second chamber' consisting of national parliamentarians on the model of Germany's upper house, or Bundesrat.

Maybe above all, the EU has not embraced federal-style rules for agreeing constitutional change. Germany's Basic Law may be amended only by a two-thirds majority vote of both the Bundesrat and its lower house, the Bundestag. EU member governments—not the EP or national parliaments—continue to monopolize power to amend the Union's Treaties (although national parliaments must ratify Treaty amendments). The Treaties themselves remain a set of agreements between governments, and not an agreement between a 'state' and its citizens, or what all federal states have: a constitution.

national, EU, and international institutions, and policies made at each of these levels. EU policy networks facilitate new patterns of policy-making in and around the EU institutions—defence is a prime example, with uniformed military officials now regular inhabitants of the Council of Ministers headquarters, where they would never have set foot a few years ago. But networked governance is also changing the way in which national institutions operate. Justice and home affairs ministries were traditionally some of the most parochial and inward-looking of all national ministries before the EU came along.

In particular, policy network analysis helps us make sense of new forms of multilevel governance. What seems clear is that members of Brussels-based networks, which are primarily focused on the EU policy process, now often overlap with networks of national and international experts and officials in other political capitals, who must know something about what happens in Brussels but are not active participants there. Meanwhile, the recent emergence of transnational networks of policy activists and entrepreneurs encourage exchanges and coordination between Brussels and other levels of governance, not least by making 'international resources available to new actors in domestic political and social struggles' (Keck and Sikkink 1998: 1). The creation of new European regulatory agencies, most of which rely heavily on expertise held at the national level, along with zero growth in the personnel and resources of the EU's own institutions, has led to pleas for normative thinking about how network governance *should* be organized in Europe (Metcalfe 2000).

Finally, the *intergovernmental* method finds member governments monopolizing both power to determine policy and power to decide how to organize cooperation. The ways in which the EU operates may complicate and moderate the way governments behave, but nonetheless it is they who call the shots. On this reading governments predominate partly because they hold the reins of legitimate elected power; they can choose when and whether to accept international rules, and even EU rules that are binding in principle. Ultimately, it is member governments, not the EU institutions, which decide treaty changes (with ratification by national parliaments and, in some cases, referendums).

It might be argued that pure intergovernmentalism rarely exists in the EU. Even where governments call the shots, such as in the European Council, the Commission President participates and the EP President always attends. But here it is important to distinguish between different kinds and magnitudes of EU decisions. 'History-making' decisions that change the European Union—its procedures, institutions, or remit—are usually intergovernmental decisions, in which the EU's supranational institutions have little role or influence (Peterson and Bomberg 1999: 10–16). To illustrate, the Commission itself bemoaned how it was marginalized—even bullied—at the Nice summit. Then again, it is hard to find examples where the Commission had tangible influence over choices about how to revise the Treaties at Maastricht or Amsterdam (Peterson 2002: 81). The big, transformative, 'treaty-amending sets of agreements that propel ... integration forward' have traditionally been quite purely intergovernmental decisions, and liberal intergovernmentalism offers compelling explanations for them (Moravcsik 1998: 1).

The EU policy pendulum

We have seen that there is considerable debate about whether European integration is effectively a one-way process towards an 'ever-closer Union', or not. In examining the EU's policy process, we can find evidence to support either of two opposing arguments: that the intergovernmental approach usually puts Europe on the path towards more supranationalism, *or* that the open method and other 'soft' forms of policy cooperation show that the 'Monnet method' (see Chapter 2) of fostering ever more integration has reached its limits and is now exhausted. Regardless of which argument we accept, it seems important to try to identify what determines choices about which policy process is applied to new or closer policy cooperation.

One of us has suggested the metaphor of a *pendulum* to convey both the sense of movement in the EU policy process and uncertainty about its outcomes (Wallace 2000*b*). The policy pendulum swings between the national political arenas of the participating member states and the European and global areas. On the one hand, the EU remains a collection of strong states in many policy sectors. On the other hand pressures to cooperate are often powerful and in some policy areas—such as pensions and health care—becoming more powerful.

Sometimes the forces of magnetism are so strong that agreements are made to address a policy dilemma at the international level: take international trade and the WTO. At other times the country-based forces of magnetism keep policy-making—such as on education—firmly in the purview of member states, even if the EU is involved at the margins (for example, through the Erasmus/Socrates schemes to promote student mobility). In some instances no magnetic field is strong enough to provide a firm resting-point for policy-making: debates continue as to where to locate policy powers—as in justice and home affairs—and the pendulum sways erratically and uncertainly. Sometimes national policy-makers choose a European forum *other* than the EU to address a particular problem—human rights questions are mainly the domain of the Council of Europe. But it is striking how much stronger the magnetism of the EU usually is compared to that of other regional organizations in Europe.

Our pendulum metaphor is only one of several ways of characterizing the push–pull between the national and the European levels. Another is to explain decisions about where to make policy as the product of *competition* between the national,

European, and the international arenas to provide effective results. For the EU, 'results' are crucially important because the EU arena gathers much of its legitimacy from the extent to which it can deliver outcomes that bring greater good to European citizens (see Chapter 8).

An alternative explanation for what seems like constant tinkering with the EU's policy process is that the nature of *issues* has changed. In large part because of globalization, today's governments face more 'wicked problems', or ones that are unusually complex and not amenable to public policy solutions, particularly not national ones (Rittel and Weber 1973). Sometimes no arena can deliver effective results, as is arguably illustrated by the case of aid to the developing world. But that does not stop efforts to make the process of making and delivering EU policy more coherent and efficient (see Chapter 10). In social and justice and home affairs policies, it often seems that neither national nor European institutions are capable of delivering coherent and effective policy outcomes. Policy responsibilities in these domains are not neatly assigned to either the member states or the EU, and instead oscillate between the two. In both instances there are actually Treaty provisions that prevent the EU from certain kinds of intervention. Nevertheless the EU has become increasingly involved in these areas, albeit mostly by developing 'soft' powers and networked governance.

A key task for any student of the EU is to determine what factors are likely to encourage policies to develop and to be sustained at the European, rather than at the national or international levels. Yet, we often find that even policies that have

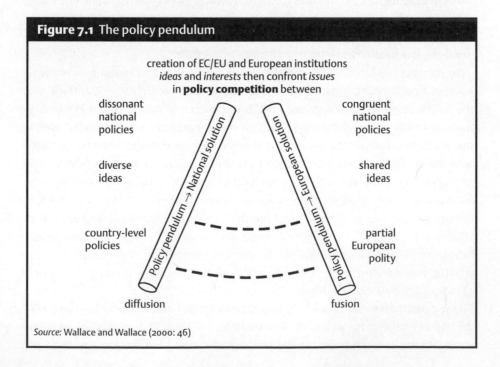

Figure 7.1 The policy pendulum

creation of EC/EU and European institutions
ideas and *interests* then confront *issues*
in **policy competition** between

dissonant national policies

diverse ideas

country-level policies

Policy pendulum → National solution

Policy pendulum → European solution

congruent national policies

shared ideas

partial European polity

diffusion   fusion

Source: Wallace and Wallace (2000: 46)

been sustained at the European level for long periods of time becoming subjects of new debates about process and method. In competition policy the main responsibility lies with the Commission, and thus the single market looks thoroughly Europeanized. However, competition policy is gradually shifting away from an approach centred on supranational governance to a process in which networks of national competition authorities will make more decisions. Agricultural policy has been managed on the European level for more than forty years, but recent years have seen calls for the renationalization of the CAP. In foreign policy, the debate seems never-ending about how the EU should be represented: the old 'troika' arrangement, grouping together the outgoing, current, and next Council Presidencies was replaced post-Amsterdam by a new troika consisting of the Commissioner for External Affairs, the 'High Representative' of the CFSP (see Chapter 10), and the Council Presidency. But few deny that the new arrangements still confuse and frustrate non-EU governments, especially when international events require prompt and coherent EU responses. One effect is to inspire calls within EU circles to scrap the rotating Presidency altogether. In all of these arenas we are witnessing change in the policy process.

The pendulum of European policy-making thus oscillates between the national and the European arenas, and sometimes between them and the international level. Choices have to be made about which level to assign policy responsibilities, and what process to adopt at whatever level is chosen. It is notable that we can observe a greater willingness to invest in EU-level policy-making at some times rather than at others: the single market gained credibility as a goal in a particular historical moment; so did EMU; and so, perhaps, will the evolving European defence policy. There is no doubt that the EU has become a leading forum for policy experimentation in Europe, with new policy experiments often embracing new and different types of process. The EU's capacity for improvization is often impressive.

Still, some of the most interesting, fundamental, and controversial questions about European integration concern how durable, expansive, and self-propagating the EU's policy process really is. Does new EU policy cooperation beget more, and eventually more supranational, policy cooperation? Or can we foresee the renationalization of some EU policies? Can the EU's policy process cope with the strains of enlargement? Risky as it is to try to answer these questions, they are unavoidable.

Conclusion

The EU penetrates the policy processes of its member states, and vice versa. The Union's policy process could be viewed as an amalgam of national policy processes, which in turn has 'Europeanized' policy-making at the national level (see

Chapter 4). A wide variety of players from the regional, national, and supra-national levels contribute to EU policy-making. Moreover, the same member states take part in many international and other European organizations, whose own policy processes penetrate their counterparts in Brussels.

We have distinguished between three different variants of the EU policy process. The Community method assigns a strong role to the EU institutions. The coordination method relies on repeated interactions between the member state administrations and Brussels bureaucrats. The intergovernmental method puts member governments in charge, but operating in a consortium.

Our emphasis has been on change more than continuity, both in terms of how each of these methods have been tweaked and adjusted over time, *and* how policy coordination in any given sector can slide from one method to another. The number and diversity of EU policy methods have expanded significantly in recent years. Getting a 'handle' on the EU's policy process is hard and not getting any easier.

The most important common denominator in all variants of the policy process, and the most timeless principle of EU governance, is the goal of seeking agreement, preferably by consensus. Whatever rules formally apply, major policy changes are almost never undertaken without the accord of all the member states and, to a lesser extent, the EU's institutions. Of course some variants of the policy process—particularly the Community method—provide stronger incentives to compromise. But the process from initiative to implementation is often long regardless of what method applies, and the players involved are typically many. The number will increase with enlargement (see Chapter 9). Somehow, the EU of today seems to get there in the end, and reach agreement when and where it is important that it should. The EU of tomorrow will see its time-honoured capacities for improvization and consensus-building tested as never before.

Discussion questions

1. Why does the EU need to make policies by so many different methods?

2. What are the most important ways in which the EU's main policy processes—the Community, coordination, and intergovernmental methods—differ from one another? What do they have in common?

3. Why have new and different forms of policy cooperation, such as the 'open method', been embraced at the EU level in recent years?

4. What challenges will enlargement pose for the EU's policy process?

Further reading

For an analysis of the EU's policy-making processes see Wallace and Wallace (2000) and Cram (1997). Peterson and Bomberg (1999) focus more broadly on *decision-making*. On the role of the EU's institutions in the policy process see Peterson and Shackleton (2002), Nugent (2001), Corbett et al. (2000), Dehousse (1998), and Hayes-Renshaw and Wallace (1997). For historical and conceptual overviews see Dinan (1999), Hix (1999), Moravcsik (1998), Milward (1992), Nugent (1999), and Scharpf (1999).

Corbett, R., Jacobs, F., and Shackleton, M. (2000), *The European Parliament*, 4th edn. (London: Catermill).

Cram, L. (1997), *Policy-Making in the European Union: Conceptual Lenses and the Integration Process* (London and New York: Routledge).

Dehousse, R. (1998), *The European Court of Justice* (Basingstoke and New York: Macmillan).

Dinan, D. (1999), *Ever Closer Union: An Introduction to European Integration*, 2nd edn. (Basingstoke and New York: Macmillan).

Hayes-Renshaw, F., and Wallace, H. (1997), *The Council of Ministers of the European Union* (Basingstoke and New York: Macmillan).

Hix, S. (1999), *The Political System of the European Union* (Basingstoke and New York: Macmillan).

Milward, A. S. (1992), *The European Rescue of the Nation-State* (Berkeley, CA, and London: University of California Press and Routledge).

Moravcsik, A. (1998), *The Choice of Europe: Social Purpose and State Power from Messina to Maastricht* (London and Ithaca, NY: UCL Press and Cornell University Press).

Nugent, N. (1999), *The Government and Politics of the European Union*, 4th edn. (London: Macmillan).

—— (2001), *The European Commission* (Basingstoke and New York: Palgrave).

Peterson, J., and Bomberg, E. (1999), *Decision-Making in the European Union* (Basingstoke and New York: Palgrave).

Peterson, J., and Shackleton, M. (eds.) (2002), *The Institutions of the European Union* (Oxford and New York: Oxford University Press).

Scharpf, F. (1999), *Governing in Europe: Effective and Democratic?* (Oxford: Oxford University Press).

Wallace, H., and Wallace, W. (2000), *Policy-Making in the European Union*, 4th edn. (Oxford and New York: Oxford University Press).

Web links

PreLex, a database on inter-institutional procedures, follows the major stages of the decision-making process between the Commission and the other institutions: **www.europa.eu.int/prelex/apcnet.cfm?CL=en**. On the different economic processes (Box 7.2) see the homepages of the Presidencies of the member states: **www.ue.eu.int/en/presid.htm**. For European Council conclusions see **www.europa.eu.int/council/off/conclu/**. To see how gender equality informs the making of all EU policies, see **www.europa.eu.int/comm/employment_social/equ_opp/index_en.htm**.

Chapter 8

Governance and Legitimacy

Lynn Dobson and Albert Weale

Contents

Overview

Governance—established patterns of rule without an overall ruler—is the concept which best captures the unique structure, evolution, and operations of the European Union. The EU has evolved beyond an ordinary association between independent states, but not to the extent that it has become a state in its own right. Some puzzles related to its political legitimacy thus arise. Above all, why should its citizens comply with EU laws, and recognize and accept as proper the political authority of the EU's political institutions and activities? Rather than seeking to explain why and how integration moves forward, or how EU actors interact, this chapter addresses the normative question of what the EU *ought* to be like. After introducing the concepts of legitimacy and governance we examine the way in which the system of EU governance has developed. We then ask whether it is right that it has evolved as it has. Finally, we explore options for giving the EU greater political legitimacy.

Introducing legitimacy and governance in the EU

The problem of legitimacy

To say that a governing system is legitimate is to say that it has the right to rule and make decisions. Is the EU a legitimate form of political authority? The question is complex because, as is often said, the EU is unlike any other political system in the world. Perhaps, for this reason, we should not expect it to conform to traditional norms of democracy. Yet concern about a *'democratic deficit'* (see Box 8.1) in the EU is widespread. Indeed, it has been said that if the EU itself applied to join the EU as a member, it would be rejected for being insufficiently democratic. If the EU is not democratic, yet is growing more important in political decision-making, can this be right? As we shall see, questions about legitimacy and democracy take us to the heart of political controversies surrounding the EU.

The idea of governance

The term *governance* is frequently used in discussions of the EU. Indeed, the EU is often said to be a system of governance. What does this mean? To answer this question, think first of *governments*. Governments are made up of teams of political representatives who are elected into office and take up ministerial positions

---

Box 8.1 Key concepts and terms

The **Charter of Fundamental Rights of the European Union** was adopted by the European Council at the Nice Summit in December 2000, but was not made legally binding. It seeks to strengthen and promote fundamental rights for all persons in the EU by setting out a series of rights such as freedom of speech and fair working conditions.

Democratic deficit refers broadly to the belief that the EU lacks sufficient democratic control. There is no EU government or opposition which can be held directly accountable for the EU's actions.

The **Monnet method** was named after the Jean Monnet, French civil servant and architect of the ECSC. The 'Monnet method' refers to integration proceeding incrementally and through small steps. Political objectives and debates (on, say, the future of Europe) are sidelined as cooperation focuses on seemingly uncontroversial issues such as common tariffs on coal and steel.

supported by the permanent bureaucracy that services them. The EU, unlike national political systems, has no government in this sense. Heads of State and Government, and ministers meet in Councils to agree laws and rules. The Commission, operating as the EU's civil service, has the task of drawing up and overseeing the detailed formulation of rules. But there is no one set of people we can point to as being accountable for what is decided in the EU, nor an opposition that can be elected in their place.

Although there is no EU government, law-making and political decision-making do occur. When people use the term governance they are indicating that this political activity goes on in a structured way. Governance, then, means 'established patterns of rule without an overall ruler'. Even though there is no government, the EU undertakes the sort of activity that governments traditionally have done. The EU is thus a system of governance without government.

Why has governance in this form arisen? Many aspects of life can no longer be effectively dealt with by national systems of government. The regulation of global markets, international finance, and humanitarian law could hardly be managed other than through international collaboration. Many threats to security or quality of life in society escape any kind of national control. Organized crime and terrorism often disregard borders, as do viruses, pollutants, and internet pornography. These threats can only be curtailed or regulated by going beyond the governing administration of any particular state territory.

The term governance is not limited to international cooperation. Within state boundaries, too, policy may be so complex that its successful formulation and execution demands interaction amongst a wide range of actors. For example, if it is to enjoy any prospect of policy success, a central government ministry must act in partnership with other levels of government, other public bodies, other associations in civil society, and the 'users' or consumers of the service or policy. Public administration seems increasingly to be made not by single executive agencies, but rather by networks (see Chapter 1) composed of people from a number of organizations, who are interlocked in working relationships oriented to common purposes. At the international level these networks take the form of transnational bodies and agencies and policy-makers meeting regularly to make important decisions. The concept of governance captures this complex mode of governing in the absence of the traditional hierarchical structures of government.

Putting these two features together—the need for international cooperation and the increasing use of partnership even by traditional governments—we can see why the EU has evolved into a system of governance. The main features of EU governance are explored next.

The development of EU governance

We have already noted that the EU is unlike any other system of governance in the world. What makes it unique? Part of the answer to this question lies in its past, and the manner in which it originated and developed. The EU is a product of what is sometimes called the '*Monnet method*' of integration (see Box 8.1). The method is named after Jean Monnet (see Chapter 2) who had a simple but important idea. Instead of trying to persuade European governments to merge together, he thought that they were more likely to cooperate if they concentrated on practical tasks. Instead of trying to combine armies, they should rationalize steel production. Instead of creating a European system of taxation, they should cooperate to support agricultural production. Steel or agricultural production were unlikely to attract particular controversy or citizen engagement. Integration under the Monnet method thus has tended to proceed with the 'permissive consensus' of public opinion (Lindberg and Scheingold 1970).

The second way in which the EU is unique relates to its future, and in particular to the way European integration deepens and widens, seldom stopping along the way. Consider, as an illustration, the EU's membership. It has enlarged from its original six members in the 1950s to fifteen members in 2002, is likely to have about twenty-five members within a few years after that, and may well have yet more in the future. The EU's external borders are constantly shifting, and the size and composition of its population changing likewise, but without a clear sense of when these changes will stop and where the boundaries will settle (see Chapter 9).

Besides the oddities of the EU's past and its projected future, its structure and workings have a number of unique features. One is its institutional complexity, especially by comparison with European nation-states. As outlined in Chapter 1, the EU is a system of multilevel governance: rules are made and policies decided upon and executed by different actors in many different bodies at different levels of organization. For example, an EU directive will require agreement from the Commission, the Council of Ministers, and the Parliament. It will usually be implemented by the member states. And its status may be challenged in the European Court of Justice. With this separation of powers, the EU is more like the complex US system than it is like a traditional European nation-state.

This complexity might not matter if the rules and laws for which the EU was responsible were technical matters of international agreement, like those, say, issued from the International Postal Union. However, the EU makes rules that affect the lives of EU citizens more deeply than is immediately obvious. In economic, social, legal, constitutional, and even external security policies, a substantial and significant shift in policy responsibility from the state to the EU has taken place. Most European citizens would be surprised and possibly even amazed to discover how much their lives and opportunities are shaped by what emerges from EU decision-making (see Chapter 6; Hooghe and Marks 2001).

A final distinctive feature, and the one relating most directly to the question of legitimacy, concerns democratic institutions. Because decision-making takes place through a unique system of governance, the EU does not have the traditional democratic features of its member states. In European nation-states, governments are elected or emerge from political parties competing with one another in elections. There are more or less clear and robust linkages between mass and elite politics. By contrast there is as yet no developed European party system with Europe-wide parties contesting elections. The EU thus lacks the traditional channels of democratic representation and accountability. Does this lack of democratic structures undermine its overall legitimacy? To answer this question we need to consider the idea of legitimacy in more detail.

Understanding legitimacy

Legitimate means 'rightful'. Political legitimacy 'involves the capacity of the system to engender and maintain the belief that the existing political institutions are the most appropriate ones for society' (Lipset 1963: 77). Thus, persons subject to the binding rules made by political authorities, or at least the overwhelming majority of them, must accept that the political institutions making those rules have a right to do so. Note that this judgement is quite different from a judgement about the merits of the rules themselves. What matters is that the institutions are thought to have the authority to make the rules.

All sorts of political systems have been deemed legitimate according to this test. Inhabitants of Japan have ascribed legitimacy to the emperor, and many Europeans before the nineteenth century to a monarch. In the contemporary democratic states of Europe citizens want the EU to be broadly liberal-democratic, although of course they might disagree as to what this means in detail.

If we turn to ideas in modern democratic theory, we can better understand questions about the EU's legitimacy. For a political regime to be legitimate, its citizens will need to be convinced about three things: its democracy, its performance, and its identity (see Beetham and Lord 1998). The democratic elements are sometimes considered 'inputs' into the system. That is, citizens need to be convinced that political authority is properly constituted and exercised. Its methods and procedures have to meet certain criteria such as legality, fairness, accountability, and compliance with specified democratic norms (such as elections). If these criteria are met the system has 'input legitimacy'.

Yet citizens also will expect the political system and its institutions to *perform* reasonably well. However chosen, a system will lose legitimacy if it cannot deliver basic needs such as sustenance or stability. We can consider this 'output' legitimacy. Thus to be legitimate, political authorities (such as governments) must pursue appropriate purposes *and* be sufficiently effective in that performance.

Finally, electors in a liberal-democratic polity must be assured not only that the system's institutions are 'right' and 'good', but also that they are 'theirs'. They are unlikely to countenance as legitimate rule by those who are not members of the polity, no matter how benevolent or rule-conforming. No amount of procedural probity or substantive success will make a political regime legitimate in the eyes of its citizens where the ruling elite is regarded as a foreign 'them' rather than as an 'us'. So questions of 'identity' between rulers and ruled are important for the legitimacy of political authority, too. This last element is often described as the 'congruence' criterion, and poses special problems for the institutions at EU level, as they are superimposed on many different and pre-existing national identities (see Box 8.2).

Why might EU institutions be thought to lack legitimacy when judged by these tests? The fact that policy is made internationally causes some problems of

Box 8.2 COMPARED TO WHAT?

Sources of legitimacy

Nation-State	European Union
procedures	
National governments are accountable to national parliaments. They act under the rule of law, and by majoritarian or consensual decision-making.	Member states and supranational bodies act in accordance with EU treaties and law; member states act by qualified majority or unanimous voting; accountability is dispersed and consensus highly valued.
performance	
National governments are expected to take responsibility for, and be effective across, a very wide range of policies pursued for the common good.	EU is expected to deliver peace and prosperity and the conditions in which member state objectives can be pursued.
identity	
Based on assumption of 'one people', self-governing with common history, destiny, values and culture; citizen allegiance is to national institutions.	Based not on 'one people' but on assumption of broad common destiny; multiple but compatible cultures; joint loyalties, but at variable strengths; partners in Union are states and peoples.

legitimacy, but is not in itself decisive. Everyone recognizes that where policy deals with problems that cut across national boundaries (climate change, trade) it is sensible to make policy at the level of international organizations. Rather, the problems arise from the way in which the EU handles its responsibilities. Put another way, those who see a crisis of political legitimacy in the EU point less to 'what' the EU does than to 'how' it does it. What is it about EU procedures that might be problematic? Let us look at each of the 'legitimacy criteria' in more detail to find out.

Procedural criteria: democracy

The EU still has a number of decision-making features that are difficult to reconcile with familiar democratic procedures. The first might be called its prevailing mode of 'rule by technocracy'. Both Jean Monnet and Walter Hallstein, who became an influential Commission President in the early 1960s, stressed the importance of making the High Authority of the European Coal and Steel Community independent of elected representatives. Nowadays, the technocratic bias of the EU is reinforced by much Council business being settled through negotiations between unelected officials in Coreper (see Chapter 3). The closed nature of its proceedings has allowed for efficient or consensual agreements amongst member states, but accountability, transparency, and representation have been its casualties.

   The incremental Monnet method has also meant that European integration is an open-ended process. There are no stated limits to the powers of the European Union, in contrast, say, to the US Constitution where the tenth amendment to the constitution explicitly limits the power of the federal government (see Walker 2000). The nearest equivalent to such demarcation is the principle of *subsidiarity* (see Box 1.1) first outlined in the 1992 Maastricht Treaty and further refined in a protocol to the 1997 Amsterdam Treaty. This principle provides that action by EU-level institutions is justifiable where (*a*) the objectives of the proposed action cannot be sufficiently achieved by member state action within those national frameworks; *and* (*b*) the objectives of the action can be better achieved by action at the EU level. Yet its meaning remains open to many different interpretations. Indeed, when subsidiarity was first being discussed, Jacques Delors, then President of the Commission, offered a large financial prize (still unclaimed!) to anybody who could define it adequately on one sheet of paper.

   With some exceptions (mostly the Nordic states), national executives in the Council of Ministers or the European Council have largely escaped scrutiny and control by domestic legislatures, with all the erosion of domestic accountability and transparency that suggests (see Williams 1991). The lack of parliamentary accountability applies not only at the level of national parliaments but also with respect to the European Parliament. In particular, the EU is involved in many areas

(Common Agricultural Policy, justice and home affairs, security policy) where the EP's role remains weak (see Chapter 3).

All of this is problematic because existing decision processes are often difficult for ordinary or even informed citizens to fathom. To be sure, considerable effort has been made to open up access to EU documents. As discussed in Chapter 5, consultation practices and lobbyists' access to decision-makers has become somewhat less ad hoc and arbitrary in recent years, and should be standardized further if the aims of the White Paper on Governance (discussed below) are met. However, much decision-making is still secretive, especially in Coreper, which brings together national civil servants and experts in a complicated array of committees and working groups. In the face of these procedures it is doubtful whether changes such as more consultation will do much to allay worries about democracy in the EU.

A more promising procedural reform is underway in the Parliament. In existing European democracies it is political parties that provide the principal link between citizens and the government. Parties compete with one another for a share of votes, and in doing so seek to offer popular programmes or policies. Currently the parties in the European Parliament are national parties, even though they associate in transnational federations and are organized into like-minded groupings in the Parliament. Their primary links are with national party structures, and their appeal is to national voters by way of national—and not EU—issues. Several proposed measures—including extra funding—may help to create political parties that are truly European in their membership and programmes, and provide those parties with incentives to respond to voters' needs and wishes on an EU-wide basis.

Attempts to secure popular consent for EU initiatives have hitherto been primarily through referendums held to ratify treaty revision (such as the 1992 referendums in Denmark and France to ratify the Maastricht Treaty or the 2001 and 2002 referendums in Ireland to ratify the Nice Treaty). But these results often reflect the popular standing of national governments more than a collective judgement about the acceptability of proposed institutional changes. Thus, less dramatic reform such as the strengthening of EU-wide parties may be a more effective and enduring way to increase procedural legitimacy. If more fully developed, European parties could provide a clearer link between individuals and political decision-making at the EU level. Such parties could encourage debate on European issues within an EU-wide electorate, rather than within separate national electorates.

Substantive criteria: performance

If we turn to the 'output' dimension of legitimacy, the EU has been very successful. For many, the avoidance of armed conflict, and increases in trade and prosperity engendered by the EU were sufficient to push to the background the matter of how democratic or otherwise legitimate the EU's operations were. However, the 1992 decision by Danish voters not to ratify the Maastricht Treaty acted as a wake-up call to EU political elites. Since then, the ability of the EU to 'deliver the goods' of peace and prosperity has been challenged for several reasons.

First, it has proved much easier to achieve what is called 'negative integration' than 'positive' integration (see Chapter 6). That is, it has been easier to create the conditions for the single market by *removing* barriers (different national standards, red tape at borders, hidden tariffs) than it has been to establish *positive* integration: actual common policies to deal with problems like transport or economic security. This lack of positive integration is problematic for legitimacy because the member states have over the last century developed as welfare states, and commitments to community and solidarity (in left, centre, and right-wing variants) are widespread and enduring among European electorates. Indeed, in the eyes of many Europeans, dealing with the problems that markets cannot solve is precisely what governments exist to do. If EU governance cannot achieve positive integration (common solutions to problems) alongside negative integration (removing obstacles to trade) many of its citizens will believe it is failing in one of its principal purposes.

The performance problem is compounded by two others springing from the nature of EU decision-making processes. The first is the notion of 'path dependency' introduced in Chapter 1: the EU's complex decision-making process makes it difficult to change established policies that have outlived their usefulness. For instance, at one time the Common Agricultural Policy gave farmers economic security and helped European governments promote rising living standards by ensuring food supplies. Over time, however, even CAP supporters would concede that the policy has become inefficient, wasteful, and environmentally damaging. Yet the complex and entrenched policy-making procedures surrounding CAP have rendered meaningful reforms extremely difficult to achieve.

Similarly, EU decision-making rules, with their requirement of consent from many actors, make it difficult to establish policies that are necessary. For example, many would argue the EU needs to establish a Europe-wide carbon/energy tax if it is to deal effectively with the problems of global climate change. But determined opposition from a very few governments (or even one) for such a proposal can stymie such a move. In short, despite its generally high output legitimacy, the EU sometimes cannot do the things it ought to do, and cannot undo the things it ought no longer to do.

Congruence criteria: identity

We have already said that a political system needs to foster a sense of identity if it is to be legitimate. This legitimacy is partly a matter of whether citizens view the common institutions as 'ours', and partly a matter of whether they believe there is an 'us' to be served by common institutions. EU integration has always been based on the idea of the ever closer union of the *peoples* of Europe. But a sense of a common civic identity among European peoples is difficult to grow where membership is so fluid—after all, nobody knows who will constitute the citizenry of the EU in ten or twenty years' time. Besides that, community is hard to foster where very marked social and economic disparities exist. The current enlargement of the EU will bring in up to a dozen countries having historical backgrounds and socio-economic profiles very different to those of existing EU members (see Chapter 9).

When it comes to citizens' identification with institutions, it is clear that a lot still needs to be done. The Maastricht Treaty made every citizen of an EU member state a 'citizen of the EU'. Yet this formal act has done little to instil a greater sense of identity or belonging (see Box 8.3). The EU's pooled sovereignty and shared decision-making practices do not allow citizens a sense of 'ownership' over particular policies, because EU policies are the result of a complex process of negotiation and bargaining amongst an array of actors. It is certainly not easy for citizens to discern with any precision what role their elected representatives have played in the formulation of those policies.

Add to this lack of identification the widespread ignorance and confusion about the EU's institutions and procedures, not helped by the EU's complexity and its plethora of bodies and rules. Citizens have little idea how to participate politically, nor why they should. At its worst, supranational governance is seen as remote, obscure, unresponsive, and performed by a secretive and unaccountable caste of technocrats and 'Eurocrats' whose values and lives seem very far removed from those of the ordinary voter. Much of this is unfair caricature, of course. The EU policy-making institutions are in many ways far more open than many of their national counterparts. But even if they are inaccurate, popular perceptions of a large gap between elites and masses in EU governance are not conducive to democratic legitimacy. If people feel they stand little chance of making their views count through democratic procedures they will soon stop bothering to try, and cease to take elections or parliaments seriously.

Meeting the individual requirements of democracy, performance, and identity can be tricky enough. But addressing them altogether is exceptionally difficult. For example, it has been persuasively argued by Dahl (1994: 28) that

In very small political systems a citizen may be able to participate extensively in decisions that do not matter much but cannot participate much in decisions that really matter a great deal; whereas very large systems may be able to cope with problems that matter more to a citizen, the opportunities for the citizen to participate in and greatly influence decisions are vastly reduced.

Supranational systems of governance like the EU thus pose a dilemma for their citizens, as gains in substantive (performative) legitimacy may be at the cost of losses in procedural (democratic) legitimacy, and vice versa.

Box 8.3 HOW IT REALLY WORKS

Citizenship

On Paper	*. . . .and in Practice*
Article 17	
Every person holding the nationality of a Member State shall be a citizen of the Union. Citizenship of the Union shall complement and not replace national citizenship.	Nearly 90 per cent of citizens feel attached to their country, while around 60 per cent feel attached to Europe *as well as* to their country. In every Member State, a majority is proud to be European. People who feel their identity is wholly or at least partly European are a majority in nine of the fifteen Member States.
Article 18	
Every citizen of the Union shall have the right to move and reside freely within the territory of the Member States.	Freedoms of movement—to look for work or study in any Member State—are the rights best known to citizens (82 per cent are aware of them), and are of most interest to citizens. But fewer than 2 per cent of EU citizens actually take advantage of these rights.
Article 19	
Every citizen of the Union residing in a Member State of which he is not a national shall have the right to vote and to stand as a candidate at municipal elections in the Member State in which he resides, under the same conditions as nationals of that state.	Only 25 per cent of citizens are aware of these rights. Fewer than 5 per cent of citizens living in another EU country are registered to vote in its local elections.
[The same applies for elections to the European Parliament.]	Voting turnout in European parliamentary elections suggests indifference. Only 49 per cent voted in the 1999 elections across the EU (and as low as 24 per cent in some Member States). Turnout by citizens in Member States of residency only was even lower—9 per cent.
Article 20	
Every citizen of the Union shall, in the territory of a third country in which [his Member State] is not represented, shall be entitled to protection by the diplomatic or consular authorities of any Member State, on the same conditions as the nationals of that Member State.	According to the Commission (2001c) the documents to implement this right 'are still not legally in force because certain Member States have failed to introduce the necessary legislation at national level'.

Box 8.3 *Continued . . .*

On Paper	*. . . .and in Practice*
Article 21	
Every citizen of the Union shall have the right to petition the European parliament . . . [and to] apply to the Ombudsman.	The number of petitions presented to the Parliament over the period 1997–2000 shows a declining trend (from 1311 to 958). On the other hand, the number of citizens complaining to the Ombudsman has increased every year since 1996.

Sources: Eurobarometer 47, Eurobarometer 54; European Commission/European Opinion Research Group Survey 'Young Europeans in 2001'; Treaty Establishing the European Community (consolidated); Commission (2001*f*), Commission (2002*c*).

Governance and legitimacy: alternative 'solutions'?

If the EU has a legitimacy problem, what are the solutions? How can its problems of democratic legitimacy be overcome? In this section we outline some of the answers put forward by analysts and practitioners.

A United States of Europe? Federalism and constitutionalism

One model of possible governance often implicit in people's minds is that of the United States. Siedentop (2000) has advocated for the EU an American-style constitutional settlement, grounded in a common set of underlying cultural values. Whilst comparisons to other systems of multilevel governance like the US may be helpful, let us simply draw attention to some very obvious differences between the two systems.

First, the US goes to a great deal of trouble to socialize each generation into the American creed. There is no comparable process in Europe, and it is exceedingly doubtful that Europeans would be receptive to it if there were. Efforts in the 1980s to promote popular identification with EU symbols and artefacts such as the flag, an annual Europe Day (9 May), an anthem, television channels, and the like, were met mostly with apathy or derision from supporters and detractors of the EU alike. Secondly, nation-state identity and powers remain strong in Europe, particularly in defence and foreign affairs. More pragmatically, the multiplicity of languages in

Europe makes it difficult for a common European party system to emerge. Thus the proper structural equivalent, if there is one, is not to a developed federal system but to something beyond the loose North American Free Trade Agreement yet short of the US federal system.

The idea of developing a US of Europe is flawed for other reasons. The EU is in many respects already a decentralized system with an informal constitution (the Treaties plus the *acquis communautaire*). An approach developed for another part of the world (and over 200 years ago at that) is unlikely to be able to address the specific needs of the EU in the twenty-first century (see Moravcsik 2001). Finally, very few Europeans want to be assimilated on the model of the American melting pot. Instead they want to remain as separate and diverse peoples, but peoples united in a multiplicity of ways around core values and projects they hold in common, such as a commitment to liberal democracy, respect for the rule of law, the promotion of human rights and a decent society, and welfare and prosperity. Citizens might well adjust to and pragmatically support a form of EU governance able to deliver those values, but a 'European patriotism' on the American model seems rather improbable, and most EU citizens would not consider it an attractive proposition.

So, a United States of Europe is not on the cards. But that does not mean that a strengthening of lower levels of government, or constitutional debate amongst the European public at large, is unlikely or undesirable. On the contrary, these developments are underway (see below). They should help to clarify and refine just what kind of EU polity its citizens want, and how it should work in tandem with their national and sub-national systems of governance to meet contemporary challenges.

Resisting EU governance

A quite different quest is to fight to preserve democracy at the level of the nation-state by resisting the shift of power *or* legitimacy to the EU level. Although it may seem paradoxical, from this point of view it is not desirable to eliminate the EU's democratic deficit, since a legitimate European Union would be a centralizing European Union. Making the Union's institutions appear the more 'rightful' creators of binding rules will be at the cost of making national institutions appear to be less appropriate sites of such rule-making. Member states are thus more likely to be able to preserve their own democracies if they can resist the pressure to democratize or empower the EU (see Gustavsson 1998). However, there are a number of problems with this view.

For a start, it is too late. The single market programme and the creation of economic and monetary union marked a decisive change in the way that European economies are governed. The EU is operating progressively more like one large economy than several separate economies, and political decision-making needs to reflect this fact. Scharpf (1999) has argued persuasively that the creation of the single market undermined the capacity of the member states to impose high welfare standards. Yet these welfare standards are an essential component in the legitimacy of European states in the post-Second World War era and remain highly valued by their citizens. In other words, democratic legitimacy at the level of member states has already been undermined by the liberalization of trade that the member states have desired and successfully pursued. Reversing the economic gains that have resulted from market integration would only further such 'de-legitimation'.

Further, reserving powers explicitly to the member-state level would probably require something explicit, perhaps along the lines of the tenth amendment to the US Constitution. But the vagueness of the subsidiarity principle makes this sort of precision difficult. Another possible EU equivalent to the tenth amendment might be a proposed catalogue of competences assigning policy responsibilities to specific levels of government. The idea is being discussed in the special Convention on the Future of Europe in 2002–3, but an explicit, uncontentious catalogue is obviously difficult to agree.

Promoting and improving EU governance

A third solution to the legitimacy problem relates to a more general promotion and improvement of EU governance. In July 2001 the European Commission published its White Paper on Governance with the aim of enhancing democracy in the EU by promoting new forms of governance (Commission 2001*b*). The Commission understands governance to mean the rules, processes and practices which determine how European powers are exercised. The norms (standards) it hopes to encourage in European governance are openness, participation, accountability, effectiveness, and coherence. Its goal is to strengthen the efficiency and overall quality of public management, and also to bring about the involvement of citizens to a greater extent in devising and putting into effect the decisions that concern them in their daily lives. The Commission's plans for good governance as set out in its White Paper included the standardization of practices of rule-making and implementation, and the establishment of norms allowing participation by more groups and citizens. As a result of these initiatives, the Commission believes, governance will become more inclusive, as well as more democratic, and the European public will become more effectively involved in public debates on matters of common concern. The White Paper acknowledges the growing need for greater public involvement, but critics claim the Paper's interpretation of both 'legitimacy' and governance' are too narrow. Nor does it address even nominally the question of how such aspirations might be met in the context of enlargement (see Box 8.4).

Box 8.4 The White Paper on European Governance: A Critique

The 2001 White Paper was the European Commission's attempt to improve governance in the EU. But several criticisms have been levelled at this effort. Four are summarized below.

1. The White Paper's view of 'the problem' is skewed.
It places too much emphasis on efficiency and effectiveness, and sees legitimacy as almost entirely a matter of performance.

2. Despite its stated aims, the White Paper does not and cannot address the problems of democracy in the EU.
Efficient governance cannot be a democratic substitute for parliamentary activity. There needs to be one space where matters can be publicly debated, the interactive effects of policies considered, and decisions coordinated.

3. Even within the sphere of policy-making performance, the Commission's plans will not necessarily boost democratic legitimacy.
Although the White Paper invites wide participation it is not clear who precisely will have access to policy-making forums. More attention needs to be paid to issues of power and equality between participating groups.

4. Overall, the White Paper's proposals would do more to strengthen the role of the Commission than to enhance democracy or legitimacy.
In the Paper, the Commission retains discretion over whom, when, and how to consult. Incorporating more actors into more extensive consultation procedures would also expand the Commission's management role.

Compiled from: Groupe gouvernance AJM (2001)*, Joerges, Meny, and Weiler (eds.) (2001).

* Groupe gouvernance AJM is a working group of academics brought together by the Commission to comment on the White Paper.

The Commission thus interprets the idea of better governance primarily as that of better management of public affairs and greater consultation of interested parties. But this specific initiative should be seen as a piece in the bigger jigsaw of current constitutional change in the EU. The matter of governance is closely linked to questions of political rule as well as to questions of executive management. Some of the changes to governance in this broader sense are already afoot or being actively debated by citizens, politicians, and officials. For instance, at the 2000 Nice European Council, EU heads of state and government adopted a non-binding Charter of Fundamental Rights which set out series of rights such as freedom of speech and voting rights (see Box 8.1) The European Council also announced plans for an Intergovernmental Conference to begin in 2004. The IGC was mandated to take on board suggestions emerging from the Convention on the 'Future of Europe', which began work in 2002 (see Chapter 11). More generally the heads of state and government at Nice called for a wider public debate on the EU's governance and future, and invited citizens and civil society actors to make their views known. Many European political leaders have themselves recently outlined their visions and aspirations for the future organization and workings of the EU. With perhaps twenty-seven rather than fifteen members, European governance will need significant streamlining (see Leonard 2000).

So, far from being a rather dull topic concerned with public administration or executive management, governance is crucial to the larger and pressing questions about the future of the EU. What kind of polity do its citizens want it to be? In particular, how democratic could it, or should it, become?

Conclusion

Analysing the EU as a system of governance enables us to see how its various parts interact: we can see more accurately how it really operates, how rules are really made, and who are really the main players in decision-making and policy-making. What it cannot tell us is whether this is how it ought to be. Nor can it help us identify what kinds of considerations and principles should guide our thinking and ground our propositions about how it ought to be. In particular, it does not enlighten us as to whether European citizens think the institutions of EU governance are the appropriate ones to generate binding rules throughout the EU across a swathe of policy areas, nor why citizens hold the views that they do, nor whether they are justified in holding them. To address these sorts of questions, we need to invoke the notion of legitimacy. Reflecting on the legitimacy of political authority allows us to evaluate the sources of popular acceptance of EU institutions.

What has become apparent is that the EU's substantive performance—bringing about peace and prosperity—was until recent times deemed sufficient to legitimate the EU. But substantive performance alone can no longer carry the burden. With the growing maturity of the EU, attention is increasingly directed at the ways those policies are shaped and decided. The perception that the EU reaches into 'every nook and cranny' of national life has provoked heightened interest in questions of political and cultural identity. Though its citizens would no doubt prefer better policy performance along with procedures that were more democratic, they may not be able to have their cake and eat it—not entirely. As we saw on page 165, trade-offs may have to be made between the EU's efficiency and effectiveness on the one hand, and its democracy on the other (Dahl 1994). Citizens will have to decide where the balance must be struck.

So is there a solution to the EU's legitimacy problems? The answer to this question is 'no', at least not if we think of a solution akin to the one that was discovered in Philadelphia in 1787. But perhaps that is just the wrong question. After all, the open-ended and open-textured nature of EU integration since its beginnings suggests a deep resistance to the imposition of solutions, blueprints, and quick fixes. Perhaps it would be more apt and fruitful to ask: what are the tasks we need to undertake in order to ask more useful and more interesting questions? If governance in the EU is to earn democratic legitimacy the overriding task, we conclude, is the greater clarification of the democratic values its citizens want to secure, and the balances they are willing to strike between those values.

Discussion questions

1. 'Power without responsibility'—is this an accurate assessment of governance without government?
2. Can a polity be democratic without being legitimate—or vice versa?
3. Do people need to believe they are 'one people' before they can be a citizenry? Discuss with reference to the EU.
4. What proposals would you offer to make the EU more democratic, or more legitimate?

Further reading

The volumes by Beetham and Lord (1998) and Hooghe and Marks (2001) are excellent treatments of governance. Siedentop's *Democracy in Europe* (2000) is a lively contribution to the debate, accessible to a lay readership, though for a balanced evaluation it should be read along with Moravcsik's review (2001). Useful collections across the range of governance, legitimacy, and citizenship are also provided by Hayward (ed.) (1995), Lehning and Weale (eds.) (1997), and Weale and Nentwich (eds.) (1998). Lord's *Democracy in the European Union* (1998) is a short but superb analysis of the issues. The books by Abromeit (1998) and Vibert (2001) are demanding but important contributions to current debates. For useful coverage of aspects of citizenship, see Bellamy and Warleigh (eds.) (2001). Leonard (2000) offers a collection of essays by leading political and academic figures on the 'future of Europe'.

Abromeit, H. (1998), *Democracy in Europe: Legitimising Politics in a Non-State Polity* (New York and Oxford: Berghahn Books).

Beetham, D., and Lord, C. (1998), *Legitimacy and the EU* (Harlow and New York: Addison Wesley Longman Ltd.).

Bellamy, R., and Warleigh, A. (eds.) (2001), *Citizenship and Governance in the European Union* (London and New York: Continuum).

Hayward, J. E. S. (ed.) (1995), *The Crisis of Representation in Europe* (London and Portland, Oregon: Frank Cass).

Hooghe, L., and Marks, G. (2001), *Multi-Level Governance and European Integration* (Lanham and Oxford: Rowman and Littlefield Publishers, Inc.).

Lehning, P., and Weale, A. (eds.) (1997), *Citizenship, Democracy and Justice in the New Europe* (London and New York: Routledge).

Leonard, M. (ed.) (2000), *The Future Shape of Europe* (London: The Foreign Policy Centre).

Lord, C. (1998), *Democracy in the European Union* (Sheffield: Sheffield Academic Press Ltd.).

Moravcsik, A. (2001), 'Despotism in Brussels? Misreading the European Union', *Foreign Affairs*, 80/3: 114–22.

Siedentop, L. (2000), *Democracy in Europe* (Middlesex: Allen Lane, the Penguin Press); (2001, New York: Columbia University Press).

Vibert, F. (2001), *Europe Simple Europe Strong: The Future of European Governance* (Oxford: Polity Press in association with Blackwell Publishers Ltd.; Malden, MA: Blackwell Publishers Inc.).

Weale, A., and Nentwich, M. (eds.) (1998), *Political Theory and the European Union: Legitimacy, Constitutional Choice and Citizenship* (London: Routledge/ECPR).

Web links

Several websites offer more detailed coverage of some of the issues raised in this chapter. The Commission's White Paper on Governance is found at **www.europe.eu.int/comm/**. An internet debate on the future of the EU is at **www.europa.eu.int/futurum**. The Commission's comprehensive European public opinion surveys are at **www.europa.eu.int/comm/dg10/epo**. You can also access Eurobarometer polls through this site. The Charter of Fundamental rights adopted at Nice can be found at: **www.europa.eu.int/comm/justice_home/index_en.html**.

Part IV

Current Issues and Trends

Chapter 9
EU Enlargement . . . And Then There Were 28?

Lykke Friis

Contents

Overview

When the Treaty of Rome was signed by the original six, few could have imagined how many additional countries would eventually 'knock on the EU's door'. That knocking has become almost deafening, and the EU's negotiation room has become crowded with applicants. Today, enlargement is at the heart of the EU's relations with the rest of Europe and will shape in profound ways the EU's ability to create a stable continent. This chapter explores the meaning and key dynamics of EU enlargement, how it works and with what effect. It argues that enlargement should not just be seen as a foreign policy tool; it will also largely determine what kind of Union will emerge in the coming years. Put another way, enlargement should be treated as a phenomenon intrinsic to the European integration process, and not just as an appendix to its overall development.

Introduction: understanding enlargement

When the framers of the early EU put the finishing touches to the Treaty of Rome, it was clear that the EU would not remain a 'closed shop' with a fixed number of customers. Open membership and changing borders are two characteristics that make the EU unique and underline the argument that the EU is an 'experiment in motion'. After all, it is very rare that states are equipped with an enlargement clause in their constitutions which invites neighbouring countries to join fully in their ventures. Yet that is what the EU's Treaties have. As can be seen from Box 9.1, the Amsterdam Treaty welcomes any 'European state' meeting certain criteria while leaving open the question of what constitutes a 'European state'. Perhaps intentionally, the Treaties leave the future borders of the Union unspecified.

The EU's growth has thus been incremental and organic. By 1995 nine countries had joined the original six to form the EU (see Box 4.1). Applicants have been guided by different motives. For some, membership was mainly an economic enterprise (UK and Denmark), whereas the political rewards of joining were more important for others (Greece, Spain, and Portugal). The first country to post its application was the UK in 1961. Due to French obstruction, however, it was only in 1973 that the UK, together with Denmark and Ireland, could hoist its flag outside the EU buildings (see Chapter 2). Enlargement to the north was followed by enlargement to the south, when Greece (1981), Spain, and Portugal (1986) were able to join. Three non-aligned countries, Sweden, Finland, and Austria, which had been prevented from joining during the Cold War, took advantage of the geopolitical changes after 1989 to gain membership in 1995. Before then they had

---

Box 9.1 Welcome! Enlargement and the EU Treaties

The Treaties stipulate certain principles that any would-be EU member must respect, but they also leave wide open the question of what constitutes a 'European' state.

Article 49 of the Amsterdam Treaty:
'Any European State which respects the principles set out in Article 6 (1) may apply to become a member of the Union . . . '.

Article 6 (1) of the Amsterdam Treaty:
'The Union is founded on the principles of liberty, democracy, respect for human rights and fundamental freedoms, and the rule of law, principles which are common to the Member States.'

feared that EU membership would compromise their neutrality and possibly antagonize Russia. As can be seen from Box 4.1, the end of the Cold War triggered a near avalanche of applications—mostly from former Warsaw Pact members. Since February 2000, the EU has been negotiating with a record-high number of twelve countries.

The core purpose of this chapter is to explore how this enlargement process works and how best to understand it. We start by asking the simple, but nevertheless thought-provoking question—what is enlargement? In the second section we analyse how enlargement negotiations take place in practice, from a country's application to the ratification phase. The third section analyses in more detail the EU's fifth enlargement round and its likely implications.

What is enlargement?

At first sight it is easy to answer the above question—enlargement refers to a new state joining the EU. However, if one tries to put one of the classical labels— foreign or domestic (internal) policy—on this process, it becomes far more intriguing. Is enlargement best understood as EU foreign or internal policy? On one hand enlargement is very much foreign policy if we define that broadly as the EU's actions towards non-members and the outside world. Understood in this way enlargement is a key foreign policy tool: accepting a new, potentially unstable democracy and shoring up its political and economic health can be the ultimate and most efficient foreign policy response from a Union seeking to secure its borders (see Chapter 10).

On the other hand, enlargement is shaped by and itself shapes internal policy in profound ways. Bringing in new countries requires the EU to reform various internal policies, practices, and institutions to accommodate newcomers. Enlargement in its own right is therefore a motor of integration. In that respect, it is problematic that the classical theoretical approaches to integration have largely ignored enlargement (see Chapter 1). As will be seen below, however, insights from the theories can be used to explain the enlargement phenomenon.

Any accession round has the potential to change the EU in at least three ways. First the accession of new members affects the EU's institutional structure. Any newcomer must be represented in the various institutions; for instance it will have to obtain a number of seats in the European Parliament and votes in the Council of Ministers. Such changes can easily influence the efficiency of the institutions as well as the balance between small and large member states. As a result, enlargement mandates institutional reform, and the inevitable political wrangling accompanying it.

Secondly, enlargement has the capacity to change the EU's policy agenda. Either existing policies (say environmental or cohesion policy) must be reformed to accommodate new members, or new policies may be developed to address the interests of the newcomers. For example, Greek accession added olive oil to the EU's common agricultural policy while Finnish and Swedish accession introduced the concept of arctic agriculture.

The final dimension of change concerns the EU's borders. Every time a newcomer joins, the EU is endowed with a new external border and hence new neighbours. The almost inevitable result is that the EU adapts its policy towards these new neighbours—possibly at the expense of existing relations with other countries. For instance, when the EU accepted Spain, Portugal, and Greece, it became far more active in the Mediterranean. Similarly, the accession of Finland was one of the reasons prompting the EU to deal more extensively with Russia in the 1990s.

Because accession rounds change the Union they also affect the vested interests of the present member states in the EU. This is the core reason why enlargement negotiations have generally been dramatic and lengthy (see Table 9.1). Any enlargement round automatically triggers a *renegotiation* of the old member states' 'cost-benefit balance sheets' of membership. To what extent, for instance, will eastern enlargement remove some of the central benefits of membership from Spain, Portugal, or Greece (recipient of cohesion funding) and France (agricultural funds)? Whether and how enlargement takes place very much depends on the ability of participants to strike a new balance between member states' interests in the EU.

Table 9.1 A lengthy affair: from application to membership

	Date of application	Duration of negotiations (months)	Date of membership	Total period between application and membership
United Kingdom[a]	10.5.67	19	1.1.73	5 years, 8 months
Denmark	11.5.67	19	1.1.73	5 years, 8 months
Ireland	11.5.67	19	1.1.73	5 years, 8 months
Greece	12.6.75	34	1.1.81	5 years, 6 months
Portugal	28.3.77	80	1.1.86	8 years, 9 months
Spain	28.7.77	76	1.1.86	8 years, 5 months
Austria	17.7.89	13	1.1.95	5 years, 3 months
Sweden	1.7.91	13	1.1.95	3 years, 4 months
Finland	18.3.92	13	1.1.95	2 years, 8 months

[a] UK's second application

The staircase to membership: application to accession

Steps 1–4: first moves

One practical way to understand the enlargement process is to imagine a 'staircase to membership' (see Figure 9.1). Both the EU and applicant state need to climb seven steps for enlargement to occur. The first (*step 1*) is the most obvious: any movement up the stairs depends on an application for membership which must be sent to the Council of Ministers. At this initial step, the Council mainly acts as a

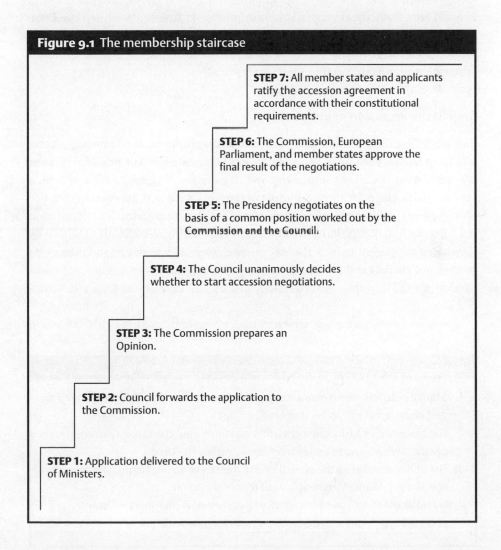

Figure 9.1 The membership staircase

STEP 7: All member states and applicants ratify the accession agreement in accordance with their constitutional requirements.

STEP 6: The Commission, European Parliament, and member states approve the final result of the negotiations.

STEP 5: The Presidency negotiates on the basis of a common position worked out by the Commission and the Council.

STEP 4: The Council unanimously decides whether to start accession negotiations.

STEP 3: The Commission prepares an Opinion.

STEP 2: Council forwards the application to the Commission.

STEP 1: Application delivered to the Council of Ministers.

letterbox. As soon as it has received the application it forwards it to the European Commission (*step 2*). The only exception to this rule was in 1986, when the Council without further ado, turned down the application of Morocco.

The role of the Commission is to prepare an opinion which examines whether the applicant is fit to start accession negotiations (*step 3*). For example, the applicant must meet the EU's basic membership criteria as agreed at the 1993 Copenhagen European Council. These include the requirement that the applicant be a stable democracy and feature an economy able to survive within the single market (see Box 9.2). The Commission's Opinion is then sent to the Council which decides on the basis of unanimity whether the EU should invite the applicant into the negotiation room (*step 4*). With the exception of Greek accession, the Council has always followed the Opinion of the Commission. (In the Greek case the Council, keen to encourage the democratic reform process in Greece, overruled the Commission's 'verdict' that the country was not fully ready to start accession negotiations.) If all member states agree to open negotiations, the EU and the applicant (also called a *candidate country*) climb to *step 5*.

Step 5: the accession negotiations

Step 5 is where the true nitty-gritty negotiations begin. To proceed, the negotiators will have to deal with nearly 80,000 pages of EU legislation. For practical reasons the legislation is divided into thirty-one negotiation 'chapters', each of which covers a particular policy area. Some of the chapters (such as those covering science and research) will cause few problems, since the relevant amount of EU legislation is rather limited or uncontroversial. Other chapters, conversely, are likely to be concluded or 'closed' only at the last minute since they touch upon core vested interests of current and aspirant member states. Agricultural subsidies and structural funds fall into this 'heavyweight' category and involve the toughest battles (see Box 9.3).

Accession negotiations are characterized by several features. First, although

---

Box 9.2 The Copenhagen Criteria—rules for EU membership

1. Stability of institutions guaranteeing democracy, the rule of law, human rights, and respect for and protection of minorities.
2. The existence of a functioning market economy, and the capacity to cope with competitive pressures and market forces within the Union.
3. The ability to take on the obligations of membership, including adherence to the aims of political, economic, and monetary union.
4. The EU itself must have the capacity to absorb new members without endangering the momentum of European integration.

Box 9.3 Negotiation battles

Drawing on the world of boxing, we can divide negotiations chapters into various 'weight' classifications based on the potential difficulty involved in their resolution.

Flyweight

(chapters which can be closed quickly)

- Science and research
- Education and training
- Small and medium-sized companies
- Industry
- Statistics

Lightweight

(chapters that have potential for conflict)

- Telecommunications
- Foreign and security policy
- Consumer and health policy
- EMU
- Financial control
- Culture and audiovisual policy
- Customs union
- External relations
- Fisheries

Heavyweight

(chapters that can cause severe problems)

- Free movements of goods
- Environment
- Free movements of persons
- Free movements of services
- Company law
- Competition
- Taxation
- Social policy and employment
- Energy
- Transport

Super Heavyweight

(chapters that can only be closed in the 'end game')

- Regional policy
- Agriculture
- Justice and home affairs
- Free movements of capital
- Finance and budget
- Institutions
- Others

---

the Commission draws up the negotiation mandates for the member states, the intergovernmental emphasis of the enlargement process is clear. The EU's chief negotiator is not the Commission (as it would be in, say, trade negotiations with third countries) but rather the Council Presidency. Indeed, enlargement negotiations are qualitatively different from any other negotiations the EU conducts with non-members. As Avery (1995: 1) puts it:

They [accession negotiations] are not about future relations between 'us and them', but rather about relations between the 'future us'. It is this process of the external becoming internal which gives accession negotiations such extraordinary interest.

A second feature of accession negotiation is its dual character. By this we mean member states have to negotiate internally; they must agree a mandate which sums up what they can offer the applicant. Then they must negotiate externally. On the basis of the internally agreed mandate, the EU as a whole must negotiate with each applicant individually. Some of the toughest negotiations (not least over budgetary questions) may occur even before the EU enters formal negotiations with applicant states.

A third feature of any accession negotiation is that it is asymmetrical. This is mainly because the applicant is in the position of a *demandeur*: it wants to join an already existing club and is often keener to join than the EU is to have it. Moreover, the EU has a far better overview and knowledge of the negotiation chapters than the applicant. Finally, the EU is empowered with the last word on an applicant's 'fitness' for membership. To use a sporting analogy, the EU's position in the negotiation 'game' is enviable: it is not only a player and a referee, but is also allowed to play all its matches at home (see also Grabbe 1998). Hence, the EU has been able to establish most of the ground rules, such as the stipulation that applicants must adopt the EU's entire *acquis* or set of treaties and legislation. The applicant might obtain breathing spaces (or transition phases) before it has to apply the EU rules, but permanent derogations or opt-outs are ruled out from the beginning.

Although the asymmetry of accession negotiation leads to tough bargaining conditions set by the EU, there are limits to how tough the EU can be. First of all, a breakdown in the negotiations with Central and Eastern Europe might quickly give the impression that the EU had 'failed' the new democracies in the East. An organization that has presented itself as a champion for democracy and peace in Europe would try to avoid such an outcome. Secondly, excessively tough negotiating behaviour could lead to requests for renegotiation of entry terms once the newcomer has joined. To a certain extent, this is what happened in the mid-1970s, when the UK insisted on a renegotiation of its membership terms (see Dinan 1999).

A final characteristic is the importance of compromise and package deals. Enlargement negotiations are almost always concluded with a package deal, with the EU and the applicant state swapping concessions across chapters ('I'll give in on agriculture if you give in on environment'). Moreover, although accession negotiations are officially conducted with each applicant individually, it is especially in this 'end game' phase that the EU has a clear tactical interest in tying the various negotiations together (see Box 9.4).

Steps 6 and 7: reaching the top

Once the Council Presidency has concluded the negotiations successfully, several EU institutions must approve the result (*step 6*). Approval is needed first from the Commission which has to prepare another opinion—this time on the overall accession treaty. The second institution is the European Parliament which under the assent procedure has the power to block enlargement. If it turns down an accession treaty, enlargement cannot go ahead. If the Parliament gives its go-ahead, the Council (in what is basically a formal decision) has to approve the

Box 9.4 HOW IT REALLY WORKS

Bilateral negotiations and group dynamics

Formally, accession negotiations are conducted bilaterally. The EU negotiates with one applicant at a time and each is treated according to its own merits. Analysing past enlargement rounds, however, suggests otherwise. With the exception of Greece, all rounds of accession have taken place in waves and all have been influenced by group dynamics. The reasons are both practical and tactical.

First, the EU tends to take in new members in groups or 'waves' because it makes practical sense to do so. Enlargement implies that the newcomer will have to be represented in the EU's institutions and included in the EU's budget. It is simply in the interest of the EU to bring in countries together as a means of avoiding a constant process of internal reform that enlargement requires. Similarly, it is easier to deal with groups of countries that either share the same political and geographical background or have close economic relations. A good example of the former is the Portuguese and Spanish accession. Although Portugal was prepared before Spain, it had to wait until Spain was ready. An example of close economic relations between applicants is Norway which, due to its close economic ties with Austria, Sweden, and Finland, was eased into the accession process at record speed (although it did not join with the others in 1995).

A second reason for the group dynamic is tactical. The EU can use internal competition between the applicants to put pressure on specific applicants. For instance the Commission publishes accession negotiation league tables, charting which applicant has closed negotiations in which area. This pressuring tactic is especially efficient in the 'end game', when the EU can play on the applicant's fear of being left behind in the queue.

Group dynamics have already played a significant role in the fifth enlargement round. By 2002, speculation focused on whether the most 'EU-fit' applicants, such as Hungary, Slovenia, and Estonia would be asked to wait for the far larger (and hence more complicated applicant) Poland. Or was the EU—precisely because of the group dynamic—heading towards a 'big bang' where ten applicants would join at the same time? In any event, the idea that each candidate is judged strictly on its own particular merits is illusory. Group dynamics also determine who gets in and when.

accession treaty. Once this is done, the candidate countries are invited to a brief ceremony where the accession treaties are signed.

The final step on the membership staircase is ratification (*step 7*). All member states and applicant states must ratify the treaties before accession can take place. With the exception of France in 1972, EU member states have thus far formally ratified accession by means of a vote in their national parliaments. However, depending on national constitutional requirements and the sensitivity of the membership question, applicant states may also hold a referendum on the issue. As can be seen from Table 9.2, such referenda were held in Ireland, Denmark, Austria, Sweden, Finland, and Norway. In the UK a referendum was not held on the original accession treaty, but on the membership terms in 1975. No applicant has so far suffered the ignominy of being pushed down the stairs by the EU in this final phase. The Norwegian electorate, however, has twice pushed its own government off the stairs by rejecting membership in the national referendum.

In the fifth enlargement round most applicant states planned to hold referenda on membership. Although polls showed a majority in favour of membership in all applicant states, support for enlargement began to shrink as negotiations tackled the difficult 'heavyweight' issues (see Eurobarometer 2001). Similarly, in the existing fifteen member states, general public support for enlargement hovered at around 50 per cent in 2002 but dipped when issues of jobs and agriculture were mentioned (Eurobarometer 2002*b*).

Table 9.2 Referenda on EU membership

Referendum in Candidate Country

Candidate	Date	For	Against	Turnout	Result
Ireland	10 May 1972	83.1%	16.9%	70.9%	YES
Norway	24–5 Sept 1972	46.7%	53.3%	79.2%	NO
Denmark	2 Oct 1972	63.4%	36.6%	90.1%	YES
United Kingdom[a]	5 June 1975	67.2%	32.8%	64.0%	YES
Greece	no referendum				
Portugal	no referendum				
Spain	no referendum				
Austria	12 June 1994	66.6%	33.4%	81.3%	YES
Finland	25 June 1994	56.9%	43.1%	74.0%	YES
Sweden	13 Nov 1994	52.8%	47.2%	83.3%	YES
Norway	27–8 Nov 1994	47.8%	52.2%	89.0%	NO

Referendum in a member state on allowing others to join:

France[b]	23 April 1972	68.3%	31.7%	60.2%	YES

[a] Referendum on renegotiated membership terms.
[b] Allowed United Kingdom, Denmark, and Ireland to join.

The EU's fifth enlargement round

Foreign policy dimension

Until 1989 enlargement was an important but circumscribed foreign policy tool for the EU. After all, due to the Cold War, there was a clear limit to how many countries could join. This situation changed dramatically after 1989. Even so, in the immediate period following the collapse of the Berlin Wall, the EU was not particularly interested in adding new countries to its membership list. Indeed, the EU spent quite a bit of time trying to fend off applications by offering alternatives to membership. Chief amongst these alternatives was the European Economic Area, a free trade area linking the EU with non-EU West European states (see Box 2.4). Another alternative to immediate membership was a series of political and trade association agreements (called 'Europe Agreements') with several Central and Eastern European countries. The core reason for these stalling tactics was that the fall of Berlin Wall had reopened the all-important German (unification) question. For most member states it was important first to address this question—which included 'enlargement' of the EU to include the former East Germany—before the EU could move towards further enlargement.

In addition, many countries were afraid that a massive enlargement could undermine the integrative achievements and depth of the Union. The beginning of the 1990s was thus characterized by a robust debate on whether integration should be deepened or widened—or both. Another argument against swift enlargement was the uncertainty about the cost: how much would enlargement actually cost and which of the member states would have to pick up the largest part of the bill?

Relatively quickly, however, member states came to the conclusion that enlargement was the only tool that stood a credible chance of stabilizing Central and Eastern Europe. If the EU did not export stability, it ran the risk of importing instability, for instance in the form of immigration or crime. Politically, it was also difficult for an organization which throughout the Cold War had presented itself as a club for democracy and peace to then turn down the new democracies now that membership was finally a realistic option. Finally, economic promise—in the form of increased trade and investment flows between East and West—also favoured enlargement.

At the European Council in Copenhagen in June 1993 the EU offered the prospect of membership to all Central and Eastern European countries which had (or were about to) conclude the special association or Europe Agreements mentioned above. Several years later, at the 1997 European Council in Luxembourg, EU leaders agreed to open negotiations with the countries which were deemed most prepared for membership at the time: Cyprus, the Czech Republic, Estonia, Hungary, Poland, and Slovenia. The remaining applicants, which were quickly dubbed the 'second wavers' (Slovakia, Lithuania, Latvia, Bulgaria, and Romania), were asked to deepen their reform efforts before negotiations could begin.

Having extended the prospect of membership to twelve new countries, many politicians (and scholars) thought that growth in membership had peaked. In 1999 this evaluation was proven wrong. In June, after the bloody conflict in Kosovo which had led to NATO intervention, the EU extended the promise of member-ship to five countries of South-Eastern Europe: the Former Yugoslav Republic of Macedonia, Albania, Croatia, Bosnia Herzegovina, and the Federal Republic of Yugoslavia. This expansion underlined how the EU uses enlargement as a means to export stability.

The EU's decision to consider membership of countries from South-Eastern Europe had immediate effects on its wider enlargement policy. First it alarmed countries in the so-called 'second wave'. Countries like Bulgaria—not as prepared as Hungary but well ahead of others—were worried they would be relegated to the 'third division' of accession and forced to wait for a country like Albania to meet the entry criteria. Precisely to remove such concerns, the EU decided at the Helsinki European Council in 1999 to open negotiations with the second wavers. At this Council meeting, it was also decided that Turkey should obtain the special status of 'accession candidate'. Turkey was not, however, invited to accession negotiations since it has not fulfilled the Copenhagen criteria regarding human rights and respect for minorities.

Expanding the list of 'invitees' was politically understandable. Most govern-ments in the region have used the promise of EU membership as the light at the end of a tunnel full of painful economic and political reform. But the promises are also problematic; major blockages in the enlargement process could well lead to major disappointment, and possibly instability, in the wider European region.

The EU hesitated to specify when the next wave of enlargement would take place. At the Gothenburg European Council in June 2001, the Heads of State and Government stated that 'the objective is that [the candidate countries] should participate in European Parliament elections of 2004 as Members'. Since countries have always joined on the 1st of January, this statement could imply that member-ship will take place in January 2004. Whenever the precise date, it is fair to assume that European stability and the success of the EU's foreign policy will very much depend on enlargement.

Internal policy dimension

Enlargement will also influence the future internal character and identity of the EU. What is special about this fifth enlargement is that member states have decided to reform the EU *before* accession (see Box 9.2, number 4). Prior to Eastern enlargement, institutional reform and a streamlining of the EU's policies have almost always been postponed until after accession has taken place (see Preston 1997). This preparation is one reason why EU enlargement to the East has been slow compared to NATO enlargement (see Box 9.5).

Enlargement to the East has prompted three different sets of internal reform. First, it has prompted institutional change. The IGC leading up to the Amsterdam Treaty was the first ever to be dedicated to preparation for enlargement. But so devilish were the institutional reforms needed that the Treaty largely failed to fulfil its purpose of completing them (see Chapter 4). Three issues were particularly problematic. The first concerned the European Commission: could each state still have a Commissioner once EU membership exceeded fifteen or twenty? The second issue concerned the voting weights in the Council of Ministers. Could the EU still maintain a system in which small states were over-represented in votes (in terms of population) when a whole queue of small states were about to join? Or would this not lead to a situation in which a group of countries, representing only a minority of the EU's total population, could vote down a group which had the backing of governments representing a majority of the EU's population? The third issue concerned the introduction of more qualified majority voting. The core concern here was that an EU of twenty-seven or twenty-eight which maintained the unanimity rule on core policy areas would quickly be deadlocked.

Since the member states were not able to overcome these issues in Amsterdam, a new attempt had to be made in Nice in December 2000. As explained in Chapter 4, some progress was made in Nice: the size of the Commission was streamlined; a new system of voting weights was agreed upon; and several policy areas (if not the most crucial ones) were moved to qualified majority voting. Yet several member states questioned whether the Treaty of Nice was really sufficient to ensure a well-functioning Union of twenty-eight. A major exponent of this view was Germany's foreign minister Joschka Fischer, who, even before the Nice Treaty was signed in 2001, argued that additional reform was required in order to avoid paralysis (Fischer 2000). The Treaty of Nice thus was not to be the last word on institutional change. A new IGC in 2004 was planned to examine the balance of power between the various institutions and try to achieve a clearer division of competencies between the EU, its member states and the regions. To be sure, these questions did not arise only because of enlargement, but they were certainly accentuated by the prospect of accession.

The second area of internal reform prompted by enlargement concerns EU policies. The accession of countries which are relatively poor and dependent upon agriculture will profoundly affect two major policies in particular: agriculture and cohesion policy (see also Table 4.3). On average, agriculture represents 20 per cent of total employment in Central and Eastern Europe, more than four times as much as in the EU (Commission 2001c). If all farmers were to receive the level of

Box 9.5 COMPARED TO WHAT?

EU and NATO enlargement

With the fall of the Berlin Wall it was generally believed that the EU would be the first major institution to enlarge to the East. This belief was (among other reasons) linked to the general perception that Russia would resist NATO enlargement, but accept EU enlargement. Yet NATO was the first to enlarge to the East, adding Hungary, Poland, and the Czech Republic in 1999. Several factors explain this difference in speed.

First, NATO is an alliance with an undisputed leader, the US, which can push enlargement forward. The EU is not endowed with such a clear leader and any enlargement must meet the unanimous approval of all its member states. Secondly, NATO deals with a limited set of issues (defence and security), whereas the EU is engaged in nearly as many issues as the governments of its member states. EU accession negotiations must cover a vast range of policies from veterinary standards to EMU. In effect, virtually all sectors within an applicant state will have to undergo intense preparations for membership, and many of these sectors—such as trade, agriculture, or environment—can prove far more complex than the restricted, if sensitive, realms of security and defence dealt with by NATO.

To be sure, NATO membership in the 1990s does now require applicant states to achieve certain political and economic goals, such as a commitment to the rule of law, human rights, and social justice. But these criteria are more flexible than either the Copenhagen criteria or *acquis* which all EU hopefuls are required to adopt.

Finally, unlike NATO, it is not possible for the EU to accept countries without first undergoing massive reform of certain policies, especially agricultural and cohesion policy. To illustrate the point, were the EU to accept Poland without reforming the common agricultural policy the EU's budget could explode. A former German minister of defence summed up this point as follows: 'You can join NATO with old tanks, but you cannot join the EU with ancient agriculture' (*Frankfurter Allgemeine Zeitung*, 15 October 1999). Similarly, EU decision-makers all concede that EU enlargement requires institutional change, whereas such radical internal reform has not been deemed necessary in the case of NATO enlargement. Thus despite external checks on NATO enlargement (mainly in the form of Russian unease) it has proved easier—or at least quicker—than EU enlargement.

agricultural subsidies received by existing member states, the EU budget would skyrocket. Similarly, cohesion policy will be heavily affected. If existing eligibility criteria for structural funds were applied, virtually all regions in Central and Eastern Europe would be eligible. The result would be a phenomenal increase in the structural funds budget as well as howls of protest from current recipients (see Chapter 6).

Member states thus agreed in the late 1990s to embark upon policy reform well before accession. This forward planning was once again a novelty in the EU's enlargement history. But the reform process, carried out under the label of 'Agenda 2000', was neither smooth nor painless. The French farm lobby made clear it would not give up its traditional subsidies without a fight, nor would Spain willingly relinquish its generous structural funds. The negotiations were further complicated by the fact that the core net contributor to the EU budget, Germany, had 'shut the cash box' after unification, and argued vehemently against any increase in the EU's budget.

The reform package of Agenda 2000 was drawn up at the Berlin European Council in March 1999. Although it did contain limited reform of the EU's agricultural policy and structural funds, it once again revealed a clear tension between the member states' wish to allow in new members while protecting their vested interests. For instance, leaders at the Berlin European Council agreed that Central and Eastern European farmers would not immediately be able to obtain the same direct payments from the EU as would their colleagues in the current member states. Additionally, the cohesion costs for enlargement were curbed by the decision that a member state's total receipts from the EU's structural and cohesion funds should not exceed 4 per cent of their GDP. However, the leaders knew the Berlin agreement would not be the last word on policy reform and they pencilled in a later date to revisit the compromises made. The next round of agricultural and budget reform will once again determine the future of the Union's policies: will the EU still have agriculture as one of its core policies? What kind of solidarity (in terms of structural funds) can be achieved in a Union of twenty-seven or twenty-eight—especially given the reluctance of current member states to pay more into the EU budget?

The third set of reforms prompted by enlargement concerns borders. The new round of accession will present the EU with a whole range of new neighbours, such as Ukraine and Belorus. Accepting four countries that border either Russia itself or its enclave of Kaliningrad (Poland, Lithuania, Estonia, and Latvia) requires the EU to strengthen its policies towards Russia. In the late 1990s the Schengen Agreement (see Box 2.2) which facilitates cooperation on border control, was incorporated into the Amsterdam Treaty. Because new members must adopt all treaty provisions, a guarantee to exercise effective border control—to avoid, for example, a substantial influx of illegal immigrants from further east—is now a condition of EU membership. For the new members this requirement will prove tricky, especially for a country like Poland. Maintaining its strong regional relationship (for instance in terms of barter trade) with a country like Ukraine will be difficult once Ukrainian citizens are asked to queue at the common border and obtain a visa (see the *Economist* 19 May 2001).

Indeed, the EU has not really managed to develop a strong, creative relationship with its neighbours that could relieve this feeling of being shut out and condemned to live on the 'wrong side of the EU border'. The pressure on the EU is only increased by the fact that countries like Egypt and Morocco will work very hard (with the support of, at least, Spain, France, and Portugal) to avoid the status of being the EU's 'forgotten periphery'. More profoundly these reforms have raised the question never addressed in the Treaties: where, precisely does Europe end and its external neighbours begin?

In sum, the changes prompted by enlargement will have a major impact upon the future shape and identity of the Union. Will the EU start to 'unpack' membership, that is, offer a partial membership, which is so far not in the Treaties? If not, how will it respond effectively towards its new neighbours? The core purpose of enlargement is to create more, not less stability. On one hand, increasing the number of countries inside the club is one way to ensure stability amongst an ever wider circle. On the other hand, simply shifting the EU's borders to countries which are far more unstable than those presently in the queue might only generate new kinds of stability problems. In short, this round of enlargement leads the EU into uncharted territory.

Conclusion

This chapter has presented the key features of the enlargement process, how it works and with what effects. It has suggested that a number of participants shape this process. Member states' interests are paramount, especially at the negotiation stage. But a focus on member states and intergovernmental bargaining alone underestimates the role played by the EU's institutions. A close look at the 'staircase' reveals the crucial role played by the EU's institutions at different steps up the ladder. More importantly, as new institutionalists would remind us, this chapter has shown how EU institutions act as carriers of norms and principles which themselves influence member states' preferences. Witness the constant emphasis in European Council declarations (especially during the Cold War) that the main purpose of the EU was to strengthen democracy and peace throughout Europe. Once the Berlin Wall tumbled down it was difficult for enlargement-sceptical countries to argue convincingly against Eastern enlargement, whatever their specific national interests. In this respect enlargement can only be understood as a process by combining intergovernmental and new institutionalist thinking.

This chapter's core argument, however, is that enlargement is best understood as *both* EU domestic and foreign policy. It will largely determine what kind of Union will materialize in the coming years *and* how stable the European continent will become. Put another way, enlargement shapes the entire process of European integration. Understanding integration means viewing enlargement not just 'as an episode, or succession of episodes, [but] rather as a phenomenon somehow intrinsic to the integration process itself' (Wallace 2000*a*: 150).

Finally this chapter has raised questions regarding the possible implications of the current round of enlargement. To what extent will the member states honour the whole avalanche of promises given to potential members in the last ten years? More generally, are the member states heading towards an 'ever closer union' or just an 'ever larger Union'? Which would lead to a more stable continent? The answers to these questions can only be found by studying the EU's enlargement policy not as an isolated event but as a fundamental part of the EU's future identity and operation.

Discussion questions

1. Why, more than ten years after the fall of the Berlin Wall, had the EU still not accepted any country from Central and Eastern Europe as a member?

2. 'Accession negotiations are basically just a case of "take-it-or-leave it" for the applicant state.' Do you agree?

3. Considering the member states' vested interests in the present system, why doesn't the EU just put enlargement on a backburner?

4. In what ways will Eastern enlargement determine the future of the EU?

Further reading

In recent years the literature on enlargement has become quite voluminous. For the EU's previous rounds of enlargement and attempts to compare them see Michalski and Wallace (1992), Preston (1997), and Redmond and Rosenthal (1998). For an overview of the EU's present enlargement policy, see Sedelmeier and Wallace (2000), Friis and Murphy (2000), Mayhew (2000), and Grabbe (2001). For the impact of enlargement on the EU's institutions and policies see Kerremanns (1998) and Josling (1998). The link between foreign policy and enlargement is covered in K. E. Smith (1998) and Amato and Batt (1998). For attempts to comprehend enlargement theoretically, see Schimmelfennig (1999) and Fierke and Wiener (1999).

Amato, G., and Batt, J. (1999), *The Long-Term Implications of EU Enlargement: The Nature of the New Border* (Florence: European University Institute).

Grabbe, H. (2001), 'Profiting from Enlargement', *Center for European Reform*, CER-pamphlet June 2001.

Fierke, K., and Wiener, A. (1999), 'Constructing Institutional Interest: EU and Nato Enlargement', *Journal of European Public Policy* 6/5: 721–42.

Friis, L., and Murphy, A. (2000), 'Eastern Enlargement—A Complex Juggle', in M. G. Cowles and M. Smith (eds.), *Risks, Reforms, Resistance or Revival: The State of the European Union* (Oxford: Oxford University Press): 186–204.

Josling, T. (1998), 'Can the CAP Survive Enlargement to the East?', in J. Redmond and G. G. Rosenthal (eds.), *The Expanding European Union—Past, Present, Future* (London: Lynne Rienner Publishers): 17–40.

Kerremanns, D. (1998), 'The Political and Institutional Consequences of Widening: Capacity and Control in an Enlarged Council', in P.-H. Laurent and M. Maresceau (eds.), *The State of the European Union*, vol. 4: *Deepening and Widening* (Boulder, CO: Lynne Rienner): 87–109.

Mayhew, A. (2000), 'Enlargement of the European Union', *Sussex European Institute*, SEI-Working Paper 39.

Preston, C. (1997), *Enlargement and Integration in the European Union* (London: Routledge).

Redmond, J., and Rosenthal, G. (eds.) (1998), *The Expanding European Union. Past, Present and Future* (Boulder, CO: Lynne Rienner).

Sedelmeier, U., and Wallace, H. (2000), 'Eastern Enlargement—Strategy or Second Thoughts?', in H. Wallace and W. Wallace (eds.), *Policy-Making in the European Union* (Oxford: Oxford University Press): 425–60.

Schimmelfennig, F. (2001), 'The Community Trap: Liberal Norms, Rhetorical Action, and Eastern Enlargement of the European Union', *International Organization* 55/1:47–80.

Smith, K. E. (1999), *The Making of EU Foreign Policy: The Case of Eastern Europe* (London: Macmillan).

Web links

For an update on recent developments in the enlargement negotiations (including developments in the applicant countries) see **www.euractiv.com/**.

The Commission's official website (including official documents and speeches on enlargement) can be found on **www.europa.eu.int/comm/enlargement/index.htm**.

For overviews and analyses of specific member states' enlargement policy, see **www.tepsa.be/html/online-publications.html** (Enlargement/Agenda 2000-Watch).

Chapter 10
The EU as a Global Actor

John Peterson and Michael E. Smith

Contents

Overview

One of the most interesting and surprising effects of European integration has been the emergence of the EU as a global power. European foreign policy is a composite product of a variety of policy-making systems. On most economic issues, the EU is able to speak with a single voice. It tends to have more difficulty showing solidarity on environmental or aid policy, but is very powerful when it does. The Union's foreign policy aspirations now touch on areas of 'high politics': it claims to have a Common Foreign and Security Policy and has begun work on a European Security and Defence Policy. But distinctly national policies persist and policy coherence remains elusive. The expanding role of the EU in foreign policy raises new questions about who does—or should—speak for Europe, as well as what the European Union stands for in international politics.

Introducing European foreign policy

The founders of what became the European Union had little or no ambition to create a new kind of international power. In fact, the original European Economic Community was given no external powers beyond authority to represent its member states in international trade negotiations. Vesting the EEC with this authority was hardly radical, given that a common market could not, by definition, exist without a common external tariff and trade policy.

The European Union has developed into a global power, a development that was almost unimaginable in the 1950s. Virtually no topic of foreign policy is now off limits to it. Yet, the EU is a strange and confusing kind of power, especially since distinctive *national* foreign policies endure in Europe and show few signs of disappearing. Consequently, the notion of 'European foreign policy', comprising *all* of what the EU and its member states do in world politics, has gained prominence (see Hill 1998; Soetendorp 1999; Nuttall 2000; White 2001). There is no doubt that the share conducted by the EU has increased steadily. For example, equipping itself with the euro has made the EU a major international monetary power. Enlargement has been one of the most effective EU foreign policy tools, encouraging far-reaching and mostly desirable changes in the Union's backyard (see Chapter 9). Despite charges to the contrary, the EU reacted swiftly and (mostly) as one to the terrorist attacks of 11 September 2001 on the United States (see Box 10.4).

Development

The EU has grown into an international power for two basic reasons. First, even the Union's largest states are medium-sized powers compared to, say, the US or China. All European states, especially smaller ones, seek to use the EU as a 'multiplier' of their power and influence in international politics. According to a logic known as the 'politics of scale', the whole—the EU speaking and acting as one—is more powerful than the sum of it parts, or member states acting individually. This logic has been very much self-styled by the EU, as no other regional organization has ever aspired to have a foreign policy (Ginsberg 2001).

Second, the Union has transformed its international role through its own policy initiatives. Its international weight has increased each time it has enlarged. Meanwhile, it has accumulated new foreign policy tools, beginning with aid programmes for Africa in 1963 and culminating (perhaps) with a European Security and Defence Policy (see Appendix I). The policy that has done the most to empower the EU internationally has been creating the world's largest single capitalist market.

Key features

The emergence of the EU as a global actor has been impressive. Still, European foreign policy is hindered by a series of gaps that often prevent outcomes from matching ambitions. One is the gap between task expansion, which has been considerable, and the integration of authority, which has been strictly limited. To illustrate the point, the total number of European diplomatic staff worldwide (EU plus national officials) is more than 40,000 diplomats in 1,500 missions. Yet, no single minister or government can give orders to this huge collection of officials. No one would ever claim that the US—with 15,000 staff in 300 missions—is weaker in global politics because it is so outnumbered (Everts 2002: 26). A basic problem for the EU is that it has never given a clear answer to Henry Kissinger's legendary (and apparently apocryphal) question: 'What one telephone number do I call when I want to speak to "Europe"?' (Wallace and Wallace 2000: xx). Severe tensions persist between member states and the main EU institutions about 'who speaks for Europe'.

Another gap exists between the EU's unity on international economic issues, which is often impressive, and its frequent disunity on more political issues. On matters of 'low politics' involving economics or welfare, the EU usually speaks with more or less a single voice. External trade policy is made via the Community method of decision-making, which delegates considerable power to the Union's institutions. Thanks largely to a series of path-breaking judgements by the European Court of Justice, the Community has considerable authority in environmental diplomacy and development policy. The birth of the euro promises, in time, an integrated EU presence in international monetary diplomacy.

In contrast, the Union often fails to speak with one voice on matters of 'high politics', which touch most directly on national sovereignty, prestige, or vital interests. The EU's Common Foreign and Security Policy (CFSP), created by the Maastricht Treaty in the early 1990s, is meant to cover 'all aspects of foreign and security policy'. However, there exists no common EU foreign policy in the sense of one that replaces or eliminates national policies. Rather, European foreign policy is a product of three distinct but interdependent systems of decision-making (White 2001):

- a national system of foreign policies;
- a Community system focused on economic policy (and based within the first pillar in the EU's tri-pillar structure); and
- an EU system centred on the CFSP (or second pillar).

Overlap between these systems is considerable (see Table 10.1). 'Europe' is the world's largest foreign aid donor, but only when the contributions of the Union and its individual member states are added together (see Box 10.2). Just because EU

Table 10.1 European foreign policy: three systems

System	Key characteristic	Pillar (or Treaty base)	Primary actors	Policy example
National	Loose (or no) coordination	Outside EU's structures	National ministers and ministries	war in Afghanistan
Overlap	*Some coordination of national and EU efforts*	*Pillar 1 with nuances (i.e. in annexes to Treaty; no funds from Community budget)*	*National ministers and ministries, Commission*	*Lomé convention*
Community	EU usually speaks with single voice	Pillar 1	Commission and Council	Commercial (trade); environmental policy
Overlap	*Turf battles*	*Pillars 1 and 2*	*Council and Commission*	*economic sanctions policy*
EU	'common, not single' policy	Pillar 2	Council General Secretariat; High Representative; national ministers and ministries	CFSP, ESDP

environmental policy is made via the Community method does not mean that it is always clear who speaks for Europe in international environmental diplomacy. For instance, the EU delegation at the 2001 Bonn summit, at which the Kyoto Protocol on global warming was kept alive, included representatives of *all* the EU's member states and major institutions. Television pictures of the all-night negotiations showed a senior European Parliament official and the Spanish Environment Minister looking on not from seats allocated to the EU, but from the only seats available: ones formally reserved for Fiji.

Many students of international politics believe that the line dividing high from low politics has blurred in a post-Cold War world. Trade disputes between the EU and US or the Union's designation of Russia as a 'market economy' can become matters of high politics. Meanwhile, the EU has begun work on a defense policy: the ultimate expression of high politics. Thus the gap between high and low politics has closed in the EU. But two other gaps remain wide.

One is between the EU's economic power and its political weight. It endures not least because the Community system remains far more efficient and decisive than the CFSP system. Regardless, it remains difficult to envisage member states ever delegating much power to decide life and death questions, such as whether to use military force, to the Union's institutions.

The final gap is between the world's expectations of the EU and its capacity to meet them (Hill 1998). In the early days of the post-Cold War period, European foreign policy-makers often oversold the Union's ability to act quickly or decisively in international affairs. A famous example was the claim by Luxembourg's Foreign Minister, Jacques Poos, that an EU-brokered ceasefire at the outset of the Yugoslavian civil war (which fell apart within hours) marked 'the hour of Europe, not the hour of the Americans'. Thereafter, far more pains were taken to play down the EU's ability to wield its international power rapidly or resolutely. But the EU still struggles to meet the expectations of its foreign partners.

The national 'system' of foreign policies

Distinctive national foreign policies certainly have not disappeared from Europe, even if the EU has become a more important reference point for them. There is no denying that all EU states attempt to put their own national stamp on European foreign policy. France uses the EU to try to enhance its own foreign policy leadership of a Europe that is autonomous from the United States. Germany has wrapped its post-war foreign policy in a European cloak in order to rehabilitate itself as a foreign power. The UK views the EU as useful for organizing pragmatic cooperation on a case-by-case basis. Small states rely on the EU to have a voice in policy debates usually dominated by large states. Neutral European states find the EU provides them with a forum for security cooperation without requiring them to sign on to a mutual defence pact. But no EU member state would deny that it has its own, individual, *national* foreign policy.

Here, we only sketch the contours of a very complex system of national foreign policies (see Hill 1996; Manners and Whitman 2000), but note that the system is remarkable in at least three respects:

- its endurance;
- its continued centrality as a source of European foreign policy; and
- how it reflects the distinctive logic of foreign policy coordination.

The last point is crucial. The logic governing the coordination of national foreign policies differs fundamentally from the logic of market integration. Integrating markets mostly involves 'negative' integration, or sweeping away old barriers to trade, instead of constructing new common policies and structures. Separate national policies can be tolerated as long as they do not impede free trade. Market integration typically has clear goals, such as zero tariffs or opening up specific product markets. Progress can usually be measured and pursued according to clear timetables.

In contrast, a truly common foreign policy (analogous to, say, the Common Agricultural Policy) requires 'positive' integration: creating new institutions and structures to replace national ones. If all states do not toe the line when the EU condemns a human rights violation or imposes an arms embargo, then the Union cannot be said to have a policy at all. Foreign policy coordination is mostly immune to specific goals or timetables. To illustrate, compare the two main policy projects of the Maastricht Treaty (Smith 1997). Monetary union had a clear goal—the euro—and a timetable for achieving it, as well as clear criteria for measuring progress. The CFSP was given no clear goal, let alone any timetable or criteria for achieving it.

Defenders of Europe's system of foreign policy coordination, such as Chris Patten (2001), Commissioner for External Affairs, usually concede that Europe lacks a *single* foreign policy. However, they insist that the EU has a *common* foreign policy, through which EU member states and institutions act in common. Each plays to its strengths and contributes to a (more or less) common cause. Increasingly, all respect common EU policies and procedures.

Critics counter-claim that the 2001 war in Afghanistan was just one case amongst many showing that Germany, France, and the UK still count for much more than the Union's smaller states on matters of high politics. Indeed, each of the EU's largest states often count for more than the EU itself. However much the Community and EU systems have been strengthened in recent years, nation-states remain primary sources of European foreign policy, and are likely to remain so.

The Community system

The Community system for foreign policy-making consists of three main elements:

- external trade policy;
- aid and development policy; and
- actions to 'externalize' the internal market.

Commercial (trade) policy

The European Union is a major trading power, accounting for about 40 per cent of all global trade if intra-EU trade is included. The EU is often a purveyor of neoliberal values, particularly following its drive to 'free' the internal market in the 1980s. Yet, all trading blocs discriminate against outsiders. More than half of all EU trade is internal trade, crossing European borders within a market that is meant to be borderless. EU member states are often accused of acting like a club in which it is agreed that each will take in the other's 'high cost washing', or products that are lower in quality or higher in price than goods produced outside Europe, ostensibly to protect European jobs. One recent study found that discrimination against non-EU producers, because it stunts competition, was costing the EU between 6 and 7 per cent of its Gross Domestic Product each year, or the equivalent of the annual economic output of Spain (IIE 2000).

If the EU seems a schizophrenic trading power, it is because it blends very different national traditions of political economy. Generally, its southern member states are far less imbued with neoliberal values than those in the north. In particular, French opposition to free trade in so-called cultural products—such as films and television programmes—has delayed the extension of the Community method to trade in services, a fast-growing category of trade. A 'cultural exception' enshrined in the 2001 Treaty of Nice keeps all trade deals which touch upon cultural products subject to veto by any member state.

Sometimes, it is more difficult for the EU to agree internally than for the Union to agree deals with its non-EU trading partners. The power of the Commission in external trade policy is easy to overestimate (see Box 10.1). However, the EU does a

---

Box 10.1 HOW IT REALLY WORKS

Commercial (trade) policy

Trade policy appears to be the most integrated of all EU external policies. Case law and the Treaty establishing the European Community Treaty (not the separate 'Treaty on European Union') state clearly that the Commission negotiates for the EU as a whole. There exists no Council of Trade Ministers. The EP has only the right to be consulted, although its assent is required for any international agreement that establishes international institutions or has important budgetary implications, such as 'association agreements' including the EU's customs union with Turkey. Legally, the Commission's dominance is clear. Still, the Commission must watch its back. Member governments typically defend their own economic interests robustly at all stages of the process: when defining the Commission's mandate for negotiations, during the negotiations themselves, and when the Council ratifies draft deals. At the last stage, the Treaty says that the Council can decide by qualified majority votes. In practice, important external trade measures almost never pass without unanimity. Thus, tensions between intergovernmentalism and supranationalism exist at the heart of the Community system as well as in the second pillar, even though the EU has a more solid record of achievement in external trade policy than in any other area of foreign policy.

remarkably good job of reconciling Europe's differences on trade. When the EU *can* agree, international negotiations become far more efficient. There is capacity in the Community system for shaming reluctant states into accepting agreements that serve general EU foreign policy aims, or even simply out-voting them. For example, the Commissioner for external trade (and Frenchman), Pascal Lamy, piloted a initiative in 2001 that gave the world's poorest countries duty-free access to the EU's markets for 'everything but arms', which France opposed but essentially was forced to accept. The deal was criticized for not doing enough to promote third world development. But the EU generally claims that it offers the world's poorest countries a better deal than do most industrialized countries.

Aid and development

Besides presiding over the world's largest capitalist market, the EU (together with its member states) is the world's leading donor of development aid (see Box 10.2). These two sources of international power are increasingly combined, along with other policy instruments, in preferential trade agreements such as the Union's free trade agreements with Mexico or South Africa, or political cooperation agreements to promote democracy or human rights using the CFSP. The EU's relations with its most important neighbours—Turkey, Russia, and the Central and East European states—are usually conducted through package deals involving trade, aid, and political dialogue. Increasingly, the EU seeks region-to-region agreements such as the EuroMed partnership with the countries of the Mediter-ranean, and the Lomé convention, a trade and aid accord between the EU and 77 African, Caribbean, and Pacific (ACP) states. In the process, European foreign policy has become more coherent, as such package deals require links between different systems for making European foreign policy. For example, most aid

---

Box 10.2 COMPARED TO WHAT?

The EU as an aid donor

By the early twenty-first century, total global spending on development aid was worth about €55 billion per year. The EU and its member states accounted for more than half of the total—over €30 billion—with the EU itself spending just over €5 billion. For purposes of comparison, the US spent about €11 billion on foreign aid, with more than half going to two countries alone: Egypt and Israel (the latter a 'developed country'). Japan spent about €15 billion. Perhaps the most revealing yardstick for comparison was aid spending as a percentage of total GNP: Europe's total was 0.33 per cent, Japan's was 0.27 per cent, while the USA's was only 0.10 per cent (down from 0.58 per cent in the mid-1960s).

to the ACP states is distributed via the European Development Fund (EDF), which member states finance directly and which is not part of the EU's general budget.

The EU's aid policy has faced new and serious challenges in recent years. First, evidence that EU aid programmes are simply not working has prompted 'donor fatigue'. The new wisdom—reflected in World Trade Organization (WTO) rules (Forwood 2001)—is that poorer countries need 'trade not aid'. Trade with developed countries is seen as helping poorer countries to grow from within, while aid is often wasted, especially through corruption. Yet, the world's poorest countries, most of them African, continue to insist that they need large injections of aid, and remain wary of the EU's preference for creating free trade areas with and amongst ACP states.

Second, the EU has been forced to reconsider its relationship with Central and Eastern Europe. One result in the early 1990s was a series of comprehensive 'Europe Agreements', modeled on existing EU pacts with Arab states (the Euro–Arab Dialogue), Central American states (the San José accords), and the Association of South-East Asian Nations. The Europe Agreements were viewed by many as a way for the EU to delay its enlargement (see Chapter 9). But the Agreements were innovative in their combination of political dialogue with Central and East European states on CFSP issues—such as non-proliferation of weapons or ex-Yugoslavia—with trade and cooperation agreements, again linking the Community and EU systems.

The Europe Agreements also facilitated the delivery of *all* Western economic aid, including that from non-EU sources, to Central and Eastern Europe, thus boosting the Union's foreign policy role in post-Cold War Europe. The EU contribution was mostly through two new and massive aid programmes: PHARE (originally an abbreviation for 'Poland and Hungary: Aid for the Reconstruction of Europe', but also the French word for lighthouse) and TACIS ('Technical Assistance to the Commonwealth of Independent States', or the former Soviet Union). Spending on these programmes averaged over €1 billion per year during the 1990s. Combined with sharply increased levels of aid to the Mediterranean and the Balkans, and even Asia and Latin America, the effect was to make the EU a truly global aid donor, while provoking fears that it was more concerned with its standing in global politics than with helping the world's poorest (mostly African) states escape from their grinding poverty (see Table 10.2).

By the early twenty-first century, the EU increasingly deployed trade instruments and political dialogue, rather than aid, to promote development. Yet, large transfers of aid continued to flow to the Lomé countries (more than €14 billion for 1996–2000), as well as Central and Eastern Europe (€6.7 billion for 1995–9), the Mediterranean (€4.7 billion for the same period), and—increasingly—the Balkans (€4.65 in Community aid for 2000–6, with nearly as much contributed from national European sources). The Union also remained the world's largest donor of

Table 10.2 Regional distribution of EU aid (as % of all EU donor aid)					
	1987	1988	1990	1995	1998
ACP (including S. Africa)	68.7	69.4	42.8	37.1	43.6
Asia	6.7	5.4	9.8	9.5	9.0
Latin America	4.0	3.8	6.8	6.6	7.1
Mediterranean	3.9	7.4	11.9	11.8	20.0
Central and East Europe	0.1	—	21.0	19.7	9.0
Former USSR	—	—	0.2	11.2	3.6

humanitarian aid through the European Community Humanitarian Office (ECHO), located within the Commission. It announced the largest contribution of any donor to humanitarian aid in Afghanistan within days of the start of the war there in 2001.

Yet the EU's good deeds are often marred by bad 'plumbing'. ECHO was slammed for its lax spending controls by the Committee of Independent Experts whose 1999 report sparked the mass resignation of the Santer Commission. Commissioner Patten made reform of the EU's development programmes a personal crusade, and EU aid delivery certainly became more efficient under his watch. But the Commission (2002a) had far to go before it escaped charges that it was the 'worst development agency in the world' (see Short 2000).

External impact of 'internal' policies

In a sense, the European Union has no internal policies. Nearly everything the EU does has external effects. When the Union negotiates internal agreements on fishing rights or agricultural subsidies, the implications for, say, fishermen in Iceland or farmers in California, can be immediate and direct.

A general rule of thumb, based on a landmark European Court decision (see Weiler 1999: 171–83), is that where the EU has legislated internally, an external policy competency is transferred to it automatically. The Community has taken this route several times in environmental policy, to the point where it now participates in several international environmental agreements through the first pillar, even if multiple voices often speak for Europe (see Box 10.3). Similarly, the creation of the euro has led to rivalries between different versions of the Council, the Commission, and the European Central Bank about who speaks for the EU in monetary diplomacy.

Where internal lines of authority are clear, the EU can be a strong and decisive negotiator. The Commission has become a powerful, global policeman for vetting mergers between large firms. When the Union seeks bilateral economic agreements, such as the 1997 Transatlantic Economic Partnership with the US

Box 10.3 COMPARED TO WHAT?

The EU and US at The Hague summit

The Hague summit on global warming in late 2000 was not a happy moment for the EU. After marathon negotiations, the EU was tantalizingly close to an agreement with the (outgoing) US administration under Bill Clinton. Suddenly, however, the Union's internal unity collapsed and so did a summit deal. The US Undersecretary of State for Global Affairs, Frank Loy, blamed the result on the 'pathologies of EU decision-making'. One problem was that the Deputy British Prime Minister, John Prescott, became the Union's primary interlocutor with the Americans, much to the dismay of the French Environment Minister, Dominique Voynet, who was chairing the EU Environment Council under the French Presidency (and later called Prescott 'an inveterate macho'). Four EU environment ministers, including Voynet and her German opposite number (but certainly not Prescott), were members of Green parties. According to one US participant, key European negotiators could thus 'go for broke, posture, and not mind dramatically losing because their constituents would still love them' (interview, 8 February 2002).

But other factors, not all internal to the EU, contributed to the collapse of the summit. Most EU environment ministers enjoyed portfolios that were far more robust—giving them far more autonomy—than that of their American counterpart. Thus the US had to go through as much (if not more) internal negotiation as the EU before it could define its position, which then could be shifted only marginally before any chance of a deal was gone. Finally, in this case, as is usual in international negotiations, American negotiators had to be seen to be tough with the EU and other major players to keep the support of the US Congress. Yet, the EU itself seemed to need to show its toughness with the Americans before it could agree its own internal environmental policy deals. The follow-up to The Hague summit saw EU states go to extraordinary lengths, with George W. Bush now in the White House and the US effectively out of the negotiations, to strike a deal on cutting emissions. The environment Commissioner, Margot Wallström, insisted: 'We can go home and look our children in the eyes. Something has changed in the balance of power between the United States and the EU' (*European Voice*, 26 July 2002).

(Pollack and Shaffer 2001), the Commission is the obvious and really only authority that can negotiate for the Union as a whole.

Given its market of over 375 million consumers, and the large number of regulations needed to make it truly 'single', the Union's most important international task may be externalizing the internal market: that is, reconciling the rules which govern it with rules governing global trade. The EU sometimes does the job badly, agreeing messy compromises on issues such as data protection or genetically modified foods which enrage its trading partners. External considerations can be a low priority when the Union legislates, and effectively treated as someone else's problem. Most of the time, the internal market has offered non-EU producers better or similar terms of access than they were offered before the internal market existed. But while the number of disputes with the EU's trading partners is relatively small, most are still bitterly fought.

A final task involves reconciling the EU's internal policies in Justice and Home Affairs (JHA) with its external obligations. What are often called 'soft' security issues, such as immigration, transnational crime, and drug trafficking, rose to the top of the European policy agenda as Eastern enlargement drew nearer, and especially after the terrorist attacks of 11 September 2001. To the surprise of many, the EU managed to agree ambitious agreements on a common definition of terrorism and a European arrest warrant.

European cooperation in this domain is rooted primarily in two intergovernmental frameworks created outside the then European Community: the 1976 Trevi framework to fight terrorism and drug trafficking and the 1985 Schengen Agreement on border controls. Thanks mainly to German influence, these two domains were linked and brought into the EU under the Maastricht Treaty. However, JHA cooperation had little impact on European foreign policy during most of the 1990s, as only a handful of specific actions could be agreed within the third pillar. Progress was hampered by weak institutions and the tendency of JHA officials, unlike diplomats, to guard jealously their domestic legal cultures and resist creating new, 'European' ones. As a partial solution, the 1997 Amsterdam Treaty mandated that policy on border controls, immigration, asylum, visas, as well as judicial cooperation, could gradually become subject to EC rules and procedures, with the possibility of introducing qualified majority voting within five years. Still, slap-dash institutional compromises such as absorbing the Schengen Agreement into the EU's treaties, but with opt-outs for the UK, Denmark, and Ireland, suggest that JHA policy will continue to straddle the Community and EU systems, and remain something of an institutional mess, as member states continue to disagree about how to organize and prioritize JHA issues.

The EU system

The gap between the Union's growing economic power and its limited political clout was a source of increasing frustration in the 1990s. One response was the creation of a distinct *EU system* of making foreign policy, although according to no clear plan. With the second pillar and the CFSP at its centre, it overlapped with but did not replace the Community system. Over time, it incorporated a nascent European Security and Defence Policy (ESDP), thus raising new questions about precisely what kind of global actor the EU was becoming.

The Common Foreign and Security Policy

The EU's present ambitions on matters of high politics have their origins in the 1960s. After the French rejection of the European Defence Community guaranteed the ascendancy of NATO in defence matters, the Community turned its attention to foreign policy, not least because of American disregard for European preferences in Vietnam and the Middle East. In 1970, a loose intergovernmental framework, European Political Cooperation (EPC), was created to try to give collective expression to the foreign policy interests of EC member states. Linked to the Community, but independent of it, EPC was dominated by national foreign ministers and ministries. The Commission was little more than an invited guest, with no right to propose or vote. Member governments identified where their national interests overlapped, without any pretension to a 'common' foreign policy. Still, EPC fostered consensus on difficult issues such as the Arab–Israeli conflict (through the Euro–Arab Dialogue) and relations with the Soviet bloc (through what became the Organization for Security and Cooperation in Europe, or OSCE). EPC also helped the Community burnish its reputation as a defender of human rights by becoming the vehicle for its collective condemnation of South Africa's *apartheid* system. The EPC's primary tools were diplomatic *démarches* and declarations, but its relationship with the EC became increasingly organic through the use of economic aid or sanctions, such as against Argentina during the Falklands War.

Over the course of twenty years, EPC showed that foreign policy coordination was not only possible but had the potential to make Europe a 'civilian power'. That is, the EC could be seen to uphold multilateralism, liberalism, and human rights as basic values, and instinctively to seek peaceful, diplomatic solutions to international conflict instead of military ones (Peterson 1996: 163–5). European Political Cooperation was given treaty status and formally linked to the activities of the Community in the 1986 Single European Act.

Within a few years, the EPC was exposed as inadequate in the face of the geopolitical earthquakes that shook Europe. With the Maastricht negotiations still focused on monetary union, the idea of strengthening foreign policy cooperation as part of plans for creating a 'political union' was given impetus by the dramatic transitions in Central and Eastern Europe, the Gulf War, the attempted coup against Mikhail Gorbachev (and subsequent collapse of the Soviet Union), and the brewing civil war in Yugoslavia. Thus, negotiators at Maastricht grafted two new policy domains (CFSP and JHA) onto the existing Treaty of Rome, resulting in the European Union's three-pillar structure.

The CFSP upgraded the role of the Commission, giving it the right—shared with member governments—to initiate proposals. The CFSP even allowed for limited qualified majority voting, although it was always clear that most second-pillar actions would require unanimity. Compliance mechanisms in the CFSP were not as strong as those in the first pillar, with the European Court of Justice mostly excluded. The Common Foreign and Security Policy (like JHA policy) remained largely intergovernmental, even if links to the Community system were gradually strengthened (see Box 10.4).

After the CFSP was launched, the habits of intensive exchanges established

---

Box 10.4 HOW IT REALLY WORKS

Making CFSP decisions

Provisions in the Maastricht Treaty for qualified majority voting (QMV) on foreign policy seemed to mark a major change from European Political Cooperation. However, QMV has only very rarely been used in the second (or third) pillar. One problem is that rules governing when QMV may be used are far more complex than in the first pillar, and allow any member state to block even a proposal to decide by qualified majority. Moreover, several states remain allergic to the idea of using majority voting to 'supranationalize' the CFSP. For example, the CFSP produced a number of unanimously-agreed actions in the Balkans, which then required further decisions on implementation (such as on funding humanitarian aid) which some states, together with the Commission, suggested should be taken by QMV. In every case at least one state, usually the UK, refused to allow the use of QMV to avoid setting a precedent. Thus, the EU system of foreign policy-making (in both its second- and third-pillar manifestations) mostly operates on the basis of consensus.

Still, each time the EU is faced with an international crisis, it tends to act more quickly, coherently, and decisively than it did in response to the *last* crisis. For example, following the terrorist attacks against the US on 11 September 2001, the EU agreed a raft of statements or decisions within ten days. These included separate statements by the Commission President, Romano Prodi, and EU heads of state or government; a joint statement by Prodi with the EP's President, the High Representative for the CFSP, and the EU heads of state or government; a statement by an extraordinary meeting of Foreign Affairs ministers; a statement and specific measures by extraordinary Transport and Justice and Home Affairs Councils; and conclusions and specific measures by an extraordinary European Council. The EU's relatively unified policy response and the terrorist threat in general both seemed likely to lend momentum to the integration of European foreign policy.

within EPC meant that member governments were able to agree a considerable number of common positions and joint actions, the CFSP's two major policy instruments, even if both remained ill-defined (see Nuttall 2000: 184–8). Specific measures, which sometimes went well beyond the usual EPC declarations and *démarches*, included:

- support for humanitarian aid (1993), administration (1994) and democratic elections (1995 and 1997) in Bosnia;
- 'Stability Pacts' to stabilize borders in Central and Eastern Europe (1993);
- support for democracy in South Africa (1993), Russia (1993), and Zaire/Congo (1996); and
- aid for crisis management in the Great Lakes region of Africa (1996).

Nevertheless, critics scorned the CFSP's inability to deal with more complex or urgent security issues, above all the wars in ex-Yugoslavia but also a Graeco-Turkish dispute over islands in the Aegean (1997) and the refugee crisis which followed Albania's economic collapse (1997). The EU was somewhat better at *saying* things in foreign policy than it had been under EPC. But it seemed only marginally more capable of actually *doing* things.

The CFSP was considered ripe for reform when the Treaty of Amsterdam was negotiated in 1997. This time, the majority voting controversy was mostly avoided by creating a new doctrine of 'flexibility', also known as constructive abstention or enhanced cooperation. Under any name, this doctrine allows member states to opt out of certain CFSP actions (particularly those involving defence) as an alternative to vetoing them. Thus, coalitions of the willing can proceed with joint actions even if some member governments find themselves unable or unwilling to participate.

The Amsterdam Treaty's main second-pillar innovation was the creation of a new High Representative for the CFSP (who is also the Secretary-General of the Council). The High Representative was designed to help give the EU a single voice and the CFSP a single face. After his appointment in 1999, former NATO Secretary General Javier Solana was quite successful in convincing both the media and other institutional actors to consider him the EU's foreign policy 'chief'. Solana was particularly prominent in the Union's diplomatic efforts, in close cooperation with NATO, to head off civil war in Macedonia in 2001. However, the EU continued to be represented externally—as it was in diplomatic visits to Pakistan, Iran, Egypt, Saudi Arabia, and Syria after 11 September 2001—by its 'troika', with Solana joined by the Foreign Minister of the state holding the Council Presidency and the European Commissioner for External Affairs. In other cases, such as the Group of Eight summits, special formulas for representation involved a confusing mix of Commission and national officials. Europe thus continued to show multiple faces even when it managed to speak with a single voice.

A European Security and Defence Policy?

Given the CFSP's mixed record, it might seem paradoxical to extend the EU foreign policy system into the realms of defence and security. Most EU states have long accepted the supremacy of NATO on defence matters. Attempts led by France to make the exclusively European defence alliance, the Western European Union (WEU), an 'integral part of the development of the Union', as stated in the Maastricht Treaty, came to little. Yet, in recent years the EU has taken small but decisive steps towards creating a European Security and Defence Policy (ESDP).

The crisis in Kosovo marked a turning point. Again, the EU appeared timid and weak as it had earlier in Bosnia. NATO was the dominant force in pushing both crises towards resolution, and the US military contribution in both cases dwarfed those of Europe. Thus, the EU made firmer Treaty commitments to security cooperation, first in Amsterdam but especially at Nice. In particular, the so-called Petersberg tasks—humanitarian and rescue missions, peacekeeping, and crisis management, including 'peacemaking'—were marked out as basic EU foreign policy goals. The Union also set in motion its own merger with the WEU. A new Political and Security Committee of senior national officials was created and designated the 'linchpin of European security and defence policy and of the CFSP'. Plans were agreed to create an EU Rapid Reaction Force of 60,000 troops, to be operational by the end of 2002.

Sceptics noted that the EU already possessed such forces, including a multi-national 'Eurocorps' among others. It had always been able to draw upon the resources of the WEU. The problem was that Europe's militaries were weak, underfunded, and lacked basic necessities. Military spending in most EU states declined sharply after the Cold War, leaving the US to extend its lead in the so-called 'revolution in military affairs'. Meanwhile, the relationship of the ESDP to NATO remained unresolved. The American administration under George W. Bush continued to demand greater burden-sharing from the Europeans while also repeating its mantra of 'three no's': no decoupling of the US from Europe; no duplication of American forces by the EU; and no discrimination against the US, including in arms purchases.

In the construction of an ESDP, as in European foreign policy generally, formal treaty reforms often matter less than informal learning by doing. When it committed itself to an ESDP, the Union still had yet to take on an independent military operation. However, the Bush administration's desire to pull US forces out of Bosnia and Kosovo, especially in light of its focus on the war on terrorism, made the prospect of Europe going it alone in Balkans peacekeeping and policing a real prospect. The emerging gap between the EU's defence policy ambitions and actions, or its internal capabilities and external expectations, looked familiar to students of European foreign policy.

Theorizing the EU as a global actor

The expansion of the EU's foreign policy role has mostly confounded international relations theorists. Many find it difficult to abandon two assumptions: first, that power in international politics is a zero-sum commodity; and, second, that states are 'unitary-rational actors' and thus all alliances are temporary. Starting with these assumptions, it is almost impossible to avoid underrating the EU's achievements in foreign and security policy (see Mearsheimer 2001).

In contrast, the emergence of the EU as a global actor seems less anomalous to theorists concerned with international interdependence or globalization. Scholars in these camps assume that the intensification of human activities across state borders, such as trade, capital movements, or immigration, presents states in a region both with shared opportunities—an expanded market—and shared risks, such as international terrorism. To realize the benefits of cross-border exchange, while managing the risks, states turn to regional cooperation. Thus, European states have reconstituted certain areas of their sovereign authority at the EU level to help them manage the interdependence that binds them together. They have not *abandoned* their sovereignty; they have pooled it in response to evidence that they are more powerful acting together—in foreign policy as in other realms— than alone. In Europe more than elsewhere, power is not viewed as a zero-sum commodity (Keohane and Nye 2001).

Yet, why some external policy areas (such as trade policy) have been so much more amenable to EU policy cooperation than others (defence) remains a puzzle. Intergovernmentalist theories claim to solve it (Moravcsik 1998). Derived from liberal theories of international politics, intergovernmentalism views govern- ments as responsive above all to powerful, domestic economic pressures. When governments agree economic policy deals that benefit 'their' economic interest groups, they seek to lock in those gains by giving the EU's institutions strong powers of enforcement. In contrast, governments face far weaker pressures to delegate strong powers over foreign or defence policy to the EU's institutions.

However, once governments delegate powers to the EU's institutions, these powers can 'spill over' into related but separate policy domains in ways that can- not be predicted or controlled. This dynamic is central to neofunctionalist explan- ations of European integration (Burley and Mattli 1993; Haas 2001). Thus, while the CFSP remains largely intergovernmental in structure, EU states decided after Maastricht to fund it using the EU budget, rather than through national contribu- tions, thus making it subject to the politics of the EU budget-making process. Neofunctionalists would see the ESDP as the product of spill-over from the CFSP.

Institutionalist and network theories can also help explain why the EU's external activities have expanded (see Peterson and Bomberg 1999: 228–51). They start from different assumptions, but agree that practical norms of cooperation are established through social interactions and networks, which may qualify or even override the cost–benefit calculations of self-interested governments. The EU is actually a set of complex networks, organized around specific policy domains. It almost naturally produces habits and customs that eventually mature into rules of behaviour, some of which may become institutionalized. For example, the habits established after two decades of foreign policy exchanges within EPC led to the CFSP. The EU often creates new roles or organizations—such as the High Representative or the Political and Security Committee—which develop their own interests, missions, and activities and escape close intergovernmental control. Institutionalists tend to agree that international cooperation is far more complex and unpredictable than is often appreciated by governments, or international relations theorists.

Conclusion

The idea that the EU should take the lead in expressing European power internationally has become something like a mainstream view. In 2000, when the British Prime Minister, Tony Blair, urged that the EU should become a 'superpower but not a superstate', he provoked little controversy outside of his own country. The EU has come a long way from humble origins in foreign policy. But it remains an odd global power, which often seems to have an overabundance of foreign policy process that produces relatively little in terms of policy output.

More generally, the EU remains troubled by dilemmas that arise from its new international duties. One concerns the diffusion of authority. A coherent European foreign policy logically requires coordination of actions across national, Community, and EU systems of foreign policy-making. European foreign policy has become more coherent in recent years, but the Union's three-pillar structure explicitly seeks to separate the economic from the political in foreign policy. Arguably, since the EU lacks any government that can ensure coherence across its multiple systems, pillars, and policies, '[t]he European Union does not have a foreign policy in the accepted sense' (Allen 1998: 42). This problem seems unlikely to become less acute in an enlarged EU of thirty or more member states.

A second dilemma arises from the external implications of the creation of a 'citizen's Europe'. As the EU moves towards completely free internal movement of its citizens, it inevitably must police its external borders to deter organized crime, terrorism, and illegal immigration. Policies on immigration, asylum, customs, and policing affect citizens in fundamental ways, even defining who enjoys the right of EU citizenship itself. European policy-makers like to claim that what the EU stands for in international politics, above all, is respect for human rights (Alston 1999).

Yet, policing borders inevitably involves coercion, discrimination, and sharp distinctions between citizens and non-citizens. The goals of reducing barriers to internal economic integration and maintaining barriers to external economic migration are, at best, difficult to reconcile. At worst, they are contradictory.

Third, the EU cannot realize its external ambitions without agreeing a division of labour with a range of other international organizations, including the United Nations, NATO, the OSCE, the WTO, and others. One of the fundamental lessons of the Balkan wars of the 1990s was that coordination between multilateral institutions remains weak or ineffective. The EU instinctively seeks to strengthen multilateralism, but in doing so risks further constraining its ability to act forcefully and independently in foreign policy.

A final dilemma for the Union arises from its need to recast its relationship with the United States, and move from Cold War dependence to something like a partnership of equals. The Union is now determined to equip itself with a military capability without encouraging American disengagement from Europe. The emphasis of the ESDP is firmly on the Petersberg tasks, so as to preserve the EU's cultivated image as a 'civilian power'. But this emphasis also raises the specter of a future Atlantic alliance that is militarily unable to act *together* as an alliance, as opposed to one in which the US does the fighting and the EU keeps the post-war peace. This division of labour is widely viewed as a long-term recipe for atrophy of the alliance.

In sum, the EU has grown into an economic superpower, equipped with a single currency, and a major source of European foreign policy. Its Common Foreign and Security Policy has, slowly, begun to deserve that label. Yet the EU remains an often uncertain and hesitant global power. It will no doubt continue to frustrate its partners, but sometimes show surprising unity, and fascinate—probably as much as it confounds—future students of international politics.

Discussion questions

1. Define 'European foreign policy'. Why has this term become common currency amongst students of international politics?

2. Why has cooperation in foreign policy been so much more difficult to organize at the EU level than economic cooperation?

3. Explain why the most effective way for the EU to promote development in the less-developed world is increasingly seen as 'trade not aid'.

4. Can the EU remain a 'civilian power' if it also becomes a military power?

Further reading

The literature on European foreign policy has expanded considerably in recent years but it tends to become outdated rather quickly. Useful recent overviews include White (2001), Ginsberg (2001), Nuttall (2000), and Peterson and Sjursen (1998). Less challenging but still useful texts are Bretherton and Vogler (1999), Soetendorp (1999), and Piening (1997). An excellent historical overview is Nuttall (1992). On the notion of the EU as a 'civilian power', see Whitman (1998) and Cederman (2000), while a good introduction to debates about ESDP is Howorth (2001). In a sign of the durability of national foreign policies, some of the best literature on European foreign policy is focused on the contribution made by individual EU member states: see in particular Manners and Whitman (2000) and Hill (1996).

Bretherton, C., and Vogler, J. (1999), *The European Union as a Global Actor* (London and New York: Routledge).

Cederman, L.-E. (ed.) (2000), *Constructing Europe's Identity: The External Dimension* (Boulder. CO: Lynne Rienner).

Ginsberg, R. (2001), *The European Union in International Politics: Baptism by Fire* (Boulder, CO, and Oxford: Rowman and Littlefield).

Hill, C. (ed.) (1996), *The Actors in Europe's Foreign Policy* (London and New York: Routledge).

Howorth, J. (2001), 'European Defence and the Changing Politics of the European Union: Hanging Together or Hanging Separately?', *Journal of Common Market Studies* 39/4: 765–89.

Manners, I., and Whitman, R. G. (2000), *The Foreign Policies of European Union Member States* (Manchester and New York: Manchester University Press).

Nuttall, S. (1992), *European Political Cooperation* (Oxford and New York: Clarendon Press).

—— (2000), *European Foreign Policy* (Oxford and New York: Oxford University Press).

Peterson, J., and Sjursen, H. (eds.) (1998), *A Common Foreign Policy for Europe? Competing Visions of the CFSP* (London: Routledge).

Piening, C. (1997), *Global Europe: the EU in World Affairs* (Boulder, CO: Lynne Rienner).

Soetendorp, B. (1999), *Foreign Policy in the European Union* (London and New York: Longman).

White, B. (2001), *Understanding European Foreign Policy* (Basingstoke and New York: Palgrave).

Whitman, R. G. (1998), *From Civilian Power to Superpower? The International Identity of the European Union* (Basingstoke and New York: Palgrave).

Web links

The best places to start researching EU external policy are the specific policy areas of the EU, each of which has its own website:

External relations (general): **www.europa.eu.int/pol/ext/index_en.htm**.
Foreign and security policy: **www.europa.eu.int/pol/cfsp/index_en.htm**.
Humanitarian aid: **www.europa.eu.int/pol/hum/index_en.htm**.

Justice/home affairs: **www.europa.eu.int/pol/justice/index_en.htm**.
Trade: **www.europa.eu.int/pol/comm/index_en.htm**.
Development: **www.europa.eu.int/po/index_en.htm**.

The Commission's site—**www.europa.eu.int/comm/index_en.htm**—has general information about EU foreign policies. On the EU's relationship with the US, see **www.eurunion.org** and **www.useu.be**. Weblinks on the EU's other important relationships include ones devoted to the Lomé convention (**www.acpsec.org**), EU-Canadian relations (**www.canada-europe.org**), and the Union's relationship with Latin America (**www.recalnet.org**).

Chapter 11
Conclusion

John Peterson, Elizabeth Bomberg, and Alexander Stubb

Contents

Overview

The EU is exceptional and, in important respects, unique. It is also a very complex system, and there are few analytical 'bottom lines' about how it works. Nevertheless, here we revisit key themes that effectively guide understanding of the EU, before returning to the question: how can we best *explain* the EU and how it works? We review leading theoretical approaches, and specifically identify what each approach claims is most important to explain about the EU, and why. Finally, the chapter speculates on 'where do we go from here'? Does knowing 'how the EU works' give us clues about how it might work in the future?

Introduction

This book has offered a *basic* introduction to how the European Union works. A vast literature has emerged in recent years to satisfy those who wish to know more. A lot of it may seem confusing or obfuscatory to the curious non-expert. We—together with our authors—have tried to do better and be clearer. For example, we have tried to show that the EU is not so exceptional that it resists all comparisons.

Yet, it does not take much study of the EU before one is struck (or becomes frustrated) by how complex and ever-shifting it seems to be. Most of our 'compared to what' exercises have ended up drawing contrasts—some quite sharp—between politics and policy-making in Brussels and these same processes elsewhere. There are very few analytical 'bottom lines' about how the European Union works, except that it works quite differently from any other system for deciding who gets what, when, and how.

Three themes

That is not to say that, at first, all that seems solid about the EU melts into air when it is examined closely. We have offered (Chapter 1) three general themes as guides to understanding how the EU works. The first is experimentation and change. The European Union refuses to stand still: about the only thing that can be safely predicted about its future is that it will *never* remain unchanged for long. Second, EU governance is an exercise in sharing power between states and institutions, and seeking consensus across different levels of governance. Getting to 'yes' in a system with so many diverse stakeholders often requires resort to informal methods of reaching agreement, about which the EU's Treaties and official publications are silent. Third and finally, the gap between the EU's policy scope and its capacity—between what it *tries* to do and what it is *equipped* to do—has widened. The EU has been a remarkable success in many respects, but its future success is by no means assured. We briefly revisit each of these themes below.

Experimentation and change

Every chapter in this book, each from a different angle, has painted a picture of constant evolution and change. No one, unless a staunch intergovernmentalist, denies that the European Union has developed into more than an 'ordinary' international organization. However, its development has not been guided by any master plan. Rather, it has evolved through messy compromises struck after complex political bargaining between member states (Chapters 2 and 4), institutions (Chapter 3), and organized interests (Chapter 5).

One consequence is that when the EU changes, it usually changes incrementally. Radical reform proposals naturally tend to be scaled back in the direction of modesty in a system with so many different kinds of interest to satisfy. It is not hard to find cases where policies (the Common Fisheries Policy) or institutions (the Economic and Social Committee) are in desperate need of reform or simply past their sell-by dates.

However, apparently unexceptional acts of fine-tuning, such as slightly increasing the EP's power or sending an encouraging political signal to an applicant state, can sometimes gather momentum like a snowball rolling down a hill. Moreover, the EU's potential for wrenching and fundamental change, as illustrated by the launch of single currency or dramatic decisions by the European Court of Justice (ECJ), cannot be denied. Perhaps because the EU is such a young political system, it is sometimes surprisingly easy to change its structure or remit.

The more general point is that the EU is a fundamentally 'experimental union' (Laffan et al. 2000). Few argue that it always works like a smooth, well-oiled machine. Equally, almost no one denies that it is remarkably successful in coaxing cooperative, collective action out of sovereign states that regularly, almost routinely, went to war with each other a few generations ago. Increasingly, the Union is seen as a model or laboratory worthy, in some respects, of mimicry by other regional organizations in other parts of the world (see Box 2.4; Telo 2001; Keohane 2002).

Sharing power and seeking consensus

A second theme that cannot be avoided in studying the EU is that power is distributed widely—between states, institutions, and organized interests. At the same time, consensus and compromise are highly valued. Enormous efforts are often required to strike agreements that are acceptable to all who have a slice of power to determine outcomes. Just being able to agree is often viewed as an achievement in itself. Once sealed, EU agreements are almost always portrayed as positive sum—that is, bringing greater good to a greater number of citizens than did the previous policy. Of course, nearly every policy creates losers as well as winners. But the perceived need to preserve support for the Brussels system means that heroic attempts are usually made to avoid creating *clear* losers.

It follows that coming to grips with 'how the EU works' does not (just) mean mastering the Treaties. The formal powers of institutions and member states, and formal rules of policy-making, are not unimportant. They just do not come close to telling the whole story, since *informal* understandings and norms are crucial in determining outcomes. Most of our investigations of 'how it really works' have accentuated the importance of unwritten rules that have emerged over time and through practice, almost organically—as opposed to being mandated in formal or legal terms—and then been learned and internalized by EU policy-makers. For example, it is widely accepted in Brussels that formal votes in the Council should be avoided whenever possible. The idea that consensus should be the ultimate aim, and that long negotiations and manifold compromises are an acceptable price to pay for it, is powerfully engrained. Never, to our knowledge, has a proposal ever been passed by the Council by a qualified majority vote (QMV) when it has been opposed by two large member states (Peterson and Bomberg 1999: 54). These norms often matter far more than what the Treaties say about which state has how many votes, what constitutes a qualified majority, or where QMV applies and where it does not.

Moreover, the EU is a uniquely multilevel system of governance. Even the most decentralized, federal nation-states—such as Germany or the US or Switzerland—have a government and an opposition. The European Union has neither. As such, it often suffers (not least in foreign policy) from a lack of leadership. Rarely does one institution or member state, or alliance thereof, offer consistent or decisive political direction. Instead, grand bargains to agree quasi-constitutional change, as well as many more mundane agreements, result from a unique kind of power-sharing across levels of governance, as well as between EU institutions and member states. It is this diversity and mix of actors—regional, national, and supranational, public and private—the wide dispersal of power between them, and the need always to try to increase the number of 'winners' that render the European Union absolutely unique.

Scope and capacity

Third and finally, we have suggested that the EU's scope—both in terms of policy remit and constituent states—has grown much faster than its capacity to manage its affairs. Chapter 6 outlined the uneven yet unmistakable expansion of EU policy responsibilities. Chapter 9 focused on why, and with what consequences, the EU has continued to enlarge its membership. Chapter 10 showed how the EU has evolved, almost by stealth, into a global power. With no agreed upon 'end goal', the EU has taken on new tasks and members, but without a concomitant increase in capacity, or tools and resources to perform its designated tasks. Chapter 3 highlighted the institutional limits of EU. Can the Commission, equivalent in size to the administration of a medium-sized European city, manage an ever larger and more ambitious Union? Can one Parliament adequately represent more than 480 million citizens? Can twenty-seven or more ministers sit around the Council table and have a meaningful negotiation?

Crucially, as Chapter 8 made clear, the EU's political and geographic scope has increased without explicit support from its citizens. This gap between scope and capacity (institutional and political) raises broader questions about the EU's future. It seems risky to assume that the European Union can continue to take on ever more tasks and member states, while retaining its status as the most successful experiment in international cooperation in modern history.

Explaining the EU

While seeking above all to *describe* how the EU works, this book has also introduced—and tried to demystify—debates about what are the most important forces driving EU politics. Just as there is no consensus on the desirability of European integration, there is no consensus about what is most important about it. Social scientists disagree about what it is about the EU that is most important to *explain*. The position they take on this question usually reflects their own approach to understanding the EU: as an international organization (IO)? As a polity in its own right? Or as a source of public policies?

We have seen how theory can help us frame interesting questions, and help us determine what evidence is needed to answer them. If it is accepted that the European Union is exceptionally complex, then it stands to reason that there can be no one 'best' theory of EU politics. What the Commission President, Jacques Delors, once called an 'unidentified political object' is a little bit like other IOs such as NATO or the United Nations, a little bit like federal states including Germany and Canada, and a little bit like the other leading system for generating legally binding international rules, the WTO. But it closely resembles none of them. It makes sense in the circumstances to approach the EU with a well-stocked tool-kit of theoretical approaches, and to be clear about what each singles out as most important in determining how it really works.

International relations approaches

International relations (IR) scholars bring important insights to the study of the EU. They can always be relied upon to ask hard, stimulating questions about the nature of power in international politics, and the extent to which cooperation is possible or durable in the absence of any 'international government'. In seeking answers to these questions, students of IR add distinctive value—in two principal ways—to debates about the nature and significance of European integration.

First, approaching the EU as a 'system within a system'—a regional alliance in the wider scheme of global politics—encourages us to determine why European states have chosen to pool a large share of their sovereignty. For *neofunctionalists*, the answer lies in the way that the choices open to states become narrower after they decide to free trade and thus to increase their economic interdependence.

Functionalist pressures arise for further integration. EU institutions, in alliance with interest groups, guide and encourage 'spill-over' of cooperation in one sphere (the internal market) to new spheres (environmental policy). States remain powerful but they must share power with EU institutions and non-institutional actors in Brussels, as well as those in national and regional political capitals. In particular, EU member states cannot defy the ECJ, which has nurtured close alliances with national courts and often pushed European integration forward (Burley and Mattli 1993; Weiler 1999). For neofunctionalists, what is most important to explain about EU politics is how and why European integration moves inexorably forward. There are crucial differences between EU member states and ordinary nation-states in international politics, to the extent that European integration is largely irreversible.

Intergovernmentalists disagree. For them, member states remain free to choose how the EU should work (Moravcsik 1998). The Union is built on a series of bargains between its member states, which are self-interested and rational in pursuing EU outcomes that serve their economic interests. Of course, conflict may arise in bargaining between states, whose preferences are never identical. But, ultimately, the status quo changes only when acceptable compromises are struck between national interests—especially those of its largest states. The EU's institutions are relatively weak in the face of the power of its member states, which can determine precisely how much authority they wish to delegate to the Commission, Parliament, and Court to enforce and police intergovernmental bargains. For intergovernmentalists, what is most important to explain about the EU is how national interests are reconciled in intergovernmental bargains. European states are 'ordinary' states, whose national interests happen to be compatible often enough to produce unusually institutionalized cooperation. But only because member governments want it that way, and they could change their minds in future. European integrations remains reversible, and always will be.

A comparative politics approach

Scholars interested in comparing politics in different national systems have been relatively late in coming to the study of the EU. However, as the Union's policy remit has expanded, many comparativists have found themselves unable to understand their subjects—at least in Europe—without knowing how the EU works.

In particular, *new institutionalists*, whose work has become influential in the study of comparative politics as well as across the social sciences, have developed fresh, insightful analyses of how the EU works. Institutionalists view the EU as a system where cooperation is now normal and accepted. Policy-makers in Brussels have become used to working in a system where power is shared, in particular between its major institutions. Bargaining in the making of day-to-day, 'ordinary' EU policy is as much between institutions as it is between governments, in contrast to bargaining—primarily intergovernmental—in episodic rounds of Treaty reform. A key determinant of actual policy outcomes is the extent to which 'path dependency' has become institutionalized and radical policy change is precluded.

Institutionalists share important assumptions with neofunctionalists, particularly about the need to view European integration as a continuous process (see Pierson 1996). But institutionalists tend to study the Union as a political system in itself, analogous to national systems, as opposed to a system of international relations. For them, what is crucial to explain about EU politics is how its institutions develop their own agendas and priorities, and thus load the EU system in favour of certain outcomes over others. The European Union is extraordinary, above all because it has such extraordinary institutions.

A public policy approach

Studying EU politics without studying what it produces—actual policies—is like studying a factory while ignoring the product it manufactures. We have seen that most EU policies are regulatory policies, many of them highly technical. We have also seen how resource-poor EU's institutions are, and how reliant they are on expertise and resources held beyond Brussels and/or by non-public actors. Advocates of *policy network* analysis insist that EU policy outcomes are shaped and moulded in important ways by informal bargaining, much of which takes place outside the formal institutions or policy process (see Rosamond 2000: 123–5). By the time that ministers vote in the Council or MEPs vote in plenary, legislative proposals usually have been picked over and scrutinized line-by-line by a huge range of officials and, usually, lobbyists. Often, the proposal bears little or no relationship to what it looked like in its first draft. Those who must actually execute or respect EU legislation—national ministries, local authorities, private firms—tend to concur that the devil in EU legislation is in the details. Policy network analysis assumes that policy details are agreed in a world far removed from the political world of ministers and MEPs.

Moreover, the EU is distinctive in its lack of hierarchy: it has no government to impose a policy agenda, so policy stakeholders bargain over what the agenda should be. No one actor is in charge, so they must work together and exchange resources—legitimacy, money, expertise—to realize their goals. That said, the relative power of different types of actor varies enormously between policy sectors: the Commission has independent power in competition policy but is weak in foreign or defence policy; the Parliament co-decides internal market policy but has little or no role in justice and home affairs; the European pharmaceuticals industry basically regulates itself while the automobile industry is being revolutionized by EU decisions.

For policy network analysts, what is most important to explain about the EU is its policies and who determines them. An understanding of policy outcomes requires investigating how sectoral networks are structured: are their memberships stable or volatile, are they tightly or loosely integrated, and how are resources distributed within them? The EU is, in effect, a series of different and diverse subsystems for making different kinds of policy. What is common across the full range of EU activities is interdependence between actors: even those with the most formidable formal powers—the member states and EU institutions—are highly dependent on one another, and indeed on actors that have no formal power at all.

There is no one approach with a monopoly of wisdom on EU politics. All shed important light on key features of how the EU works. All downplay, if not ignore, factors that we can see are important—or can be in the right circumstances—in determining who gets what from the European Union. A first step in making sense of the EU is deciding what it is about this unidentified political object that is most important to explain.

Where do we go from here?

When we ponder where the European Union may be headed, we have to remember where it has been. For nearly two decades, the Union has always been either preparing, negotiating, or ratifying a new treaty: see Appendix I. In the fifteen years after 1985, the EU modified its basic treaties four times. The next treaty change is already in the pipeline. No Western nation-state has made four major changes to its constitution, including hundreds of amendments, within the span of fifteen years. By way of comparison, the US Constitution has been subject to less than thirty amendments over 200 years.

Agreeing to reform the EU's institutions, disagreeing on the details, and then agreeing to try to agree again in a future intergovernmental conference (IGC) has become routine. Meanwhile, the EU's policy remit has expanded, and its membership, too. The Treaty of Nice (2001) marked an attempt to reform the EU's institutions to prepare the Union for enlargement. Its success in doing so was, to be charitable, limited. Valery Giscard d'Estaing, the chair of the so-called Convention on the Future of Europe (see below), was blunt in explaining why:

It was not a European debate [at Nice]. If you look at what the Heads of Government said when they came back to their national capitals, they didn't say, 'We improved the European system'. Not at all. They said that we gained this and that for our country . . . everyone was fighting for nationalistic results (quoted in Weiler 2002).

This narrow focus on national goals, as opposed to the 'European system', means that institutional development has not kept pace with changes in the EU's policy remit and membership. It is thus questionable whether ten or more new member states can be taken on board without the system seizing up like a motor that loses all its oil. So, where do we go from here?

Debating the future of Europe

Debating the future of the Union has become a popular sport among European political leaders. Kicked off by German Foreign Minister Joschka Fischer in May 2000, virtually all heads of state and government, of both member and candidate states, have outlined their vision for the future of the EU (see Leonard 2000). The politicians' version of the Eurovision song contest has produced a rather artificial debate. For example, Fischer's call for an explicitly federal EU came in the midst of the Nice negotiations, in which Germany did not support radical reform.

Nonetheless, a wide-ranging debate on the future of the Union is a legacy of the Nice Treaty. Keeping to the IGC tradition of 'I'll quit smoking tomorrow' (read: 'we'll agree *real* reforms next time') the heads of state and government decided to convene a new IGC in 2004 to deal with the constitutional issues which were not on the Nice agenda. These issues included:

■ *Simplification of the treaties*—particularly, splitting off from the current Treaties a short, clear statement of fundamental principles of EU governance.

■ *The role of national parliaments*—involving them more closely, in some form.

■ *The delimitation of competences*—defining more precisely where the line is drawn between the EU's powers and those of its member states.

■ *Legally binding fundamental rights*—specifically, the idea of incorporating the Charter of Fundamental Rights agreed at Nice into the Treaties.

These issues might not seem 'sexy'. But they cannot be discussed without provoking a wider debate about the very nature of the European project. Should the EU, for example, have a constitution? If so, what kind of constitution? Who should decide?

To launch a debate on these (and other) questions, EU leaders agreed to create a grandly-titled 'Convention on the Future of Europe', which began work in February 2002. The Convention was made up of representatives from the national governments (including those of applicant states), national parliaments, the European Parliament, the Commission, and the public. On one hand, the Convention was a radical departure for the EU. Previous IGCs were prepared by 'Groups of Wise Men' or a 'Reflection Group'. The former propagated the collective, usually nostalgic visions of former (old and exclusively male) statesmen. The latter were effectively monopolized by EU governments. This time, arguably, the 'top-down' approach had been discarded in favour of the 'bottom-up' approach of a Convention, in which all meetings were held in public, a refreshing change to traditional negotiations behind closed doors.

On the other hand, the first opinion polls after the convening of the Convention suggested that nearly two-thirds of EU citizens were entirely unaware that it was taking place. Less than one-third of those polled in France, where support for EU membership had fallen to its lowest levels since the early 1970s, were aware that the Convention was being chaired by Giscard d'Estaing, a former French President (Eurobarometer 2002*b*). Regardless of what the Convention produced, member governments remained 'masters of the Treaty' (Wessels 2001), again keeping for themselves a monopoly on power to decide the actual results of the 2004 IGC.

A whole new way of building Europe? Or business as usual? It remains unclear whether the Convention can rally Europe—defined in the broadest sense—behind a clear vision of how the EU should change. Arguably, it is plowing fertile ground, with nearly two-thirds of citizens in favour of an EU constitution (Eurobarometer 2002*b*). In any case, debates about the EU's future are wider and more inclusive now than they have ever been before.

How *will* it work?

Somewhat bravely, with some experience of two IGCs (see Stubb 2002), we conclude with a few thoughts—we will not call them 'predictions'—about the changes ahead in 2004 and beyond. We have seen that there is no shortage of controversy concerning what is most important in determining how the EU really works. Be that as it may, it is useful to resort to simplified models—three in particular—of how the EU *should* work to stimulate thinking about different potential futures. These models are by no means mutually exclusive. On the contrary, the European Union has always been a hybrid of the:

1. *Intergovernmental*;
2. *Federal*; and
3. *Community*.

An *intergovernmental* outcome to the 2004 IGC would mean a repatriation of competences, a weakening of the institutional triangle between the Commission, the Council and the European Parliament, and a return to unanimous decision-making—with many decisions taken outside the current institutional framework. Some moves might be made to deepen cooperation between a self-selected sub-set of member states under the (so far, unused) provisions for enhanced cooperation, or 'flexibility' (see Box 4.1; Stubb 2000; 2002). The effect might be to encourage other states to 'catch up' and seek to join new cooperative policy arrangements in ways that eventually further European integration. But such moves might also lead to rule by cabals, especially of larger member states, that lack transparency and act to divide the EU politically.

A more intergovernmental EU of the future is a possibility. Ultimately, however, it is unlikely to be the outcome of the 2004 IGC. The experience of the Nice negotiations and the need for efficiency in an enlarged Union have produced a new appreciation of methods of power-sharing that have worked in the past. It may seem contradictory, but two views were widely-held in Europe in the run-up to 2004. One was that the EU *really* needed institutional reform this time, not least because it would be so hard to agree future reforms in a Union of twenty-seven or more member states. The second was: if it ain't broke, why fix it—especially given all the uncertainty that comes along with ten new member states?

A more *federal* Europe post-2004 might mean a clearer division of competences, a European constitution with a set of fundamental rights and an institutional structure, perhaps with a bicameral parliament and an elected government. Arguably, a federal structure could be more transparent and democratic. Power-sharing in most federal regimes is governed by the subsidiarity principle, with powers formally divided in a way that brings government as close to the citizen as possible.

Put simply, member governments and their publics remain unwilling to take a quantum leap to a federal state. Many of the hallmarks of a federal state—a large central budget funded through direct taxation or giving the power of constitutional amendment to the legislatures or legislators of the constituent states (as opposed to their governments)—are unimaginable. There is no united political movement or *demos* pushing for a European federation. To be sure, as the history of the European Union shows, there can be federalism without a federation. The euro and European Central Bank are nothing if not federative elements. Thus, we find another apparent contradiction: the idea of a 'federal Europe'—a nightmare to Eurosceptics—is both a utopian pipe-dream and a practical reality in some areas of policy. But a 'United States of Europe' (see Chapter 8), if it ever arrives, will not arrive in 2004.

The final, *community* model of the future is a mix between the previous two. More than either of them, it favours continuity in European integration and is sceptical of radical change. The community model embraces a largely functional path of integration, and accepts that the EU does not yet (and may never) operate in policy areas such as health care and most forms of taxation. It accepts that the 'Community method' of decision-making, with powers shared between the EU's institutions, is inappropriate (at least initially) for some areas where European cooperation makes sense, including defence and border controls. But the community model values power-sharing for its own sake. It thus favours strengthening the current institutional triangle between the Commission, Council, and EP—with the ECJ adjudicating disputes between them.

A basic assumption underpinning this model is that the EU—warts and all—has worked to the further the greater good of European citizens. But form should follow function, not *vice versa* as in the federal vision. The community model represents a path that has been followed from the earliest beginnings of European integration in the 1950s. It may well live on in the EU of the future simply because, in the past, it has worked: most say reasonably and some say remarkably, even if a minority says not at all.

Conclusion

The reality of European integration is naturally more complex than the simple models that we have just outlined. To illustrate the point, the UK under the Blair government has offered proposals combining all three models. First, Blair supported the creation of a second chamber of national parliamentarians, an idea also supported by some federalists. Second, his government signalled a willingness to abandon the UK's national veto over asylum policy and subject it to the Community method. Third, Blair led calls for EU governments to appoint a new super-President of the Council, who would become the most powerful person in the EU, thus apparently putting the UK in the vanguard of the staunchest intergovernmentalists (see Straw 2002). Yet the idea was rejected as a step too far towards a United States of Europe by Jacques Delors, who was commonly labelled a federalist in the European press but cautioned on this occasion, 'let us not go faster than the music' (*European Voice*, 4 July 2002).

The EU has always been a combination of the three models. It is more than an 'ordinary' international organization, but less than a state. It is likely always to be a multilevel system in which the supranational, national, and regional co-exist. It is a unique and original way of organizing cooperation between states, whose governments (if not always their citizens) genuinely see themselves as members of a political 'union'.

The EU of the future will probably remain an experimental system, always in flux, with plenty of scope to be reformed and with competing ideas about how to do it. It will continue to be, above all, an exercise in seeking consensus and trying to achieve unity, where that makes sense, out of enormous diversity. As such, how it *really* works will never match one vision of how it *should* work.

Appendix I: Chronology of European Integration*

1945 May	End of World War II in Europe
1946 Sept.	Churchill's 'United States of Europe' speech
1947 Jun.	Marshall Plan announced
	Organization for European Economic Cooperation established
1949 Apr.	North Atlantic Treaty signed in Washington
1950 May	Schuman Declaration
1951 Apr.	Treaty establishing the ECSC signed in Paris
1952 May	Treaty establishing the European Defence Community (EDC) signed in Europe
Aug.	European Coal and Steel Community launched in Luxembourg
1954 Aug.	French parliament rejects the EDC
Oct.	Western European Union (WEU) established
1955 May	Germany and Italy join NATO
Jun.	EC foreign ministers meet in Messina to relaunch European integration
1956 May	Meeting in Venice, EC foreign ministers recommend establishing the European Economic Community (EEC) and the European Atomic Energy Community (Euratom)
1957 Mar.	Treaties establishing the EC and Euratom signed in Rome
1958 Jan.	Launch of the EC and Euratom
1961 Jul.	The UK, Denmark, and Ireland apply to join the EC
1962 Jan.	Agreement reached on the Common Agricultural Policy
1963 Jan.	French President Charles de Gaulle vetoes the UK's application; de Gaulle and German Chancellor Konrad Adenauer sign Elysée Treaty;
Jul.	Signing of Yaoundé Convention between EEC and 18 African states
1964 May	EEC sends single delegation to Kennedy Round negotiations on tariff reduction in General Agreement on Tariffs and Trade (GATT)
1965 Jul.	Empty Chair Crisis begins
1966 Jan.	Empty Chair Crisis ends with Luxembourg Compromise
1967 May	The UK, Denmark, Ireland, and Norway again apply for EC membership
Jul.	The executive bodies of the ECSC, EC, and Euratom merge into a Commission
Nov.	De Gaulle again vetoes the UK's application
1968 Jul.	The customs union is completed eighteen months ahead of schedule
1969 Apr.	De Gaulle resigns
Jul.	The UK revives its membership application

* Compiled by Desmond Dinan

1970 Oct.	Council agrees to create European Political Cooperation (EPC) mechanism; Luxembourg's Prime Minister Pierre Werner presents a plan for Economic and Monetary Union (EMU)
1972 Oct.	Meeting in Paris, EC heads of state and government agree to deepen European integration
1973 Jan.	The UK, Denmark, and Ireland join the EC
Oct.	Following the Middle East War, Arab oil producers quadruple the price of oil and send the international economy into recession
1975 Feb.	Lomé Convention (superseding Yaoundé Convention) agreed between EEC and forty-six African, Caribbean, and Pacific (ACP) states
Mar.	EC heads of state and government inaugurate the European Council (regular summit meetings)
Jun.	In a referendum in the UK, a large majority endorses continued EC membership
Jul.	Member states sign a treaty strengthening the budgetary powers of the European Parliament and establishing the Court of Auditors
1978 Jul.	Meeting in Bremen, the European Council decides to establish the European Monetary System (EMS), precursor to EMU
1979 Mar.	Member states launch the EMS
Jun.	First direct elections to the European Parliament
1981 Jan.	Greece joins the EC
1985 Jun.	The Commission publishes its White Paper on completing the single market
1986 Jan.	Portugal and Spain join the EC
Feb.	EC foreign ministers sign the Single European Act (SEA)
1987 Jul.	The SEA enters into force
1988 Jun.	EC and Comecon (East European trading bloc) recognize each other for first time
1989 Apr.	The Delors Committee presents its report on EMU
Nov.	The Berlin Wall comes down
1990 Oct.	Germany is reunited
1991 Dec.	Meeting in Maastricht, the European Council concludes the intergovernmental conferences on political union and EMU
1992 Feb.	EC foreign ministers sign the Maastricht Treaty
Jun.	Danish voters reject the Maastricht Treaty
1993 May	Danish voters approve the Maastricht Treaty, with special provisions for Denmark
Jun.	Copenhagen European Council endorses eastern enlargement
Nov.	The Maastricht Treaty enters into force; the European Union (EU) comes into being
1994 Apr.	Hungary and Poland apply to join EU
1995 Jan.	Austria, Finland, and Sweden join the EU
1995–6	Eight additional Central and Eastern European countries apply to join the EU

1997 Jun.   European Council agrees Amsterdam Treaty, which creates post of High
Representative for the CFSP, the European Council

Oct.   EU foreign ministers sign the Amsterdam Treaty

1998 Mar.   The EU begins accession negotiations with five Central and Eastern European
countries, plus Cyprus

UK and France agree St Malo Declaration on European defence

Jun.   The European Central Bank is launched in Frankfurt

1999 Jan.   The third stage of EMU begins with the launch of the euro and the pursuit of a
common monetary policy by eleven member states

Mar.   The Commission resigns following the submission of a report of an
independent investigating committee; the Berlin European Council concludes
the Agenda 2000 negotiations

May   The Amsterdam Treaty enters into force

Dec.   The European Council signals 'irreversibility' of eastern enlargement;
recognizes Turkey as a candidate for EU Membership

2000 Feb.   The EU begins accession negotiations with the five other Central and Eastern
European applicant countries, plus Malta

Dec.   Meeting in Nice, the European Council concludes the intergovernmental
conference on institutional reform

2001 Feb.   EU foreign ministers sign the Nice Treaty

Jun.   Irish voters reject the Nice Treaty

2002 Jan.   Euro notes and coins enter into circulation

Feb.   Convention on the 'Future of Europe' opens

Jun.   European Council of Seville reforms Council of Ministers

Oct.   Irish voters approve Nice Treaty

Appendix II: Glossary*

A number of the terms below are defined and elaborated in more detail in the Concept boxes of each of the chapters. Where this is the case, the Box number is provided.

An extremely useful encyclopaedia, which includes longer and more detailed entries than we can provide here, is: Desmond Dinan (ed.) (2000), *Encyclopedia of the European Union* (Basingstoke and New York: Palgrave), updated edition.

The EU also has its own official EU glossary which can be found at: **www.europa.eu.int/scadplus/leg/en/cig/g4000.htm**.

acquis communautaire (Box 4.1) Refers to the rights and obligations arising from the entire body of European laws, including all the treaties, regulations, and directives passed by the European institutions as well as judgements laid down by the Court of Justice.

cabinet The group of staff and advisers that make up the private offices of senior EU figures, such as Commissioners and the High Representative for the CFSP. Each Commissioner has six members in his/her *cabinet*.

Charter of Fundamental Rights (Box 8.1) Adopted by the Council at the Nice Summit in December 2000 but not made legally binding at the time, the Charter seeks to strengthen and promote the fundamental rights of EU citizens such as freedom of speech and fair working conditions. Its legal status will be discussed at the 2004 IGC.

cohesion policy Introduced after the first enlargement in 1973, its aim has been to reduce inequality between regions and compensate for the costs of economic integration. Its main tools have been the *structural funds* for poor or declining regions, and the *Cohesion Fund* for the poorest member states.

Comitology (Box 7.1) The web of committees made up primarily of national officials and experts, and chaired by the Commission, which oversees the implementation of EU legislation.

Common Foreign and Security Policy (CFSP) Created by the Maastricht Treaty, the CFSP in theory 'covers all areas of foreign and security policy' and includes provisions for majority voting. In practice, the CFSP is a work in progress: an evolving framework for intergovernmental cooperation and the coordination of national foreign policies, which is decided almost entirely by consensus. The Secretary-General of the Council is also the 'High Representative' for the CFSP.

Community method Usually employed where common EU policies replace national policies (such as competition or agricultural policy), the Community method is a form of

* Glossary was compiled with the assistance of Ned Staple, University of Edinburgh

supranational policy-making in which the Union's institutions share and wield considerable power. Usually contrasted with *intergovernmental* methods of policy-making.

Coreper (The Committee of Permanent Representatives) The most important preparatory committee of the Council, Coreper is a French acronym for the collected heads of the Permanent Representation (EU ambassadors) which, confusingly, is called 'Coreper II'. Deputy ambassadors, which handle more technical portfolios, meet in 'Coreper I' (see also **'Perm Reps'**).

democratic deficit (Box 8.1) Refers broadly to the belief that the EU lacks sufficient democratic control.

direct effect First established in the 1963 *van Gend en Loos* case, the doctrine has become a major principle of Community law. Under direct effect Community law applies directly to individuals (not just states) and national courts must enforce it.

directive The most common instrument for major EU legislation. Usually directives specify the goals of a policy but leave the means to be decided by member governments themselves.

Directorates General (DGs) The primary administrative units within the Commission, comparable to national ministries or Departments. There are about 20 DGs, each focusing on a specific area of policy such as competition or trade.

Elysée Treaty (1963) A treaty of friendship signed between Germany and France signalling greater political cooperation.

Europe Agreements Signed in the early 1990s, these special cooperation agreements between the EU and Central and East European countries aspiring to EU membership were viewed as a first step towards accession. The agreements cover economic cooperation, cultural exchanges, and some foreign policy coordination.

European Defence Community (EDC) A French-inspired and American-backed proposal, modelled on the Schuman Plan, for a European army. Tabled in 1950, EDC was a solution to the problem of rearming post-war West Germany, but it collapsed following its rejection by (ironically) the French National Assembly in 1954.

European Political Cooperation (EPC) The precursor to the Common Foreign and Security Policy (CFSP), what became known as EPC was launched in 1970 as a way for member states to coordinate their foreign policies and speak (and, less often, act) together when national policies overlapped.

European Security and Defence Policy (ESDP) The effort to give the EU a defence capability, particularly through the creation of a *Rapid Reaction Force* by 2002, which groups together national militaries to focus on the Petersberg tasks, including humanitarian aid, crisis management, and peacekeeping.

Europeanization (Box 4.1) Term used to describe the impact of the EU on member states' sovereignty, democracy, identity, national institutions, and systems of public policy making, as well as the impact of member states on the development of the Union.

Europol The European Police Office designed to improve the effectiveness with which national police forces across the EU cooperate across national borders.

federalism (Box 6.1) A political system which features the sharing of power and sovereignty between levels of government, usually between central or federal level, and sub-state (state, provincial, *Länder*) level.

free trade area (Box 2.4) An area in which restrictive trading measures are removed and goods can travel freely between signatory states. These states retain authority to establish their own tariff levels and quotas for third countries.

GDP (gross domestic product) An index of the total value of all goods and services produced by a country, not counting overseas operations.

GNP (gross national product) An index of the total value of all goods and services produced by a country, including overseas trade. Most common measure of a country's material wealth.

globalization (Box 1.4) The process by which the world becomes increasingly inter-connected and interdependent because of increasing flows of trade, ideas, people, and capital, which cross political borders.

governance (Box 1.4) An established pattern of rule in the absence of an overall ruler. The term is usefully applied to the EU, because of its lack of an identifiable government.

IGCs (Intergovernmental Conferences) Intergovernmental conferences bring together representatives of member states to hammer out amendments to the Treaties, or other history-making decisions such as enlargement.

integration (see Box 1.4) As applied to politics, a process whereby sovereign states relin-quish (or pool) national sovereignty to maximize their collective power and interests.

integration, negative Integration through market-building and the removal of obstacles to trade. Less ambitious than positive integration.

integration, positive Integration through the creation of common policies, which effect-ively replace national ones, and usually deal with cross-border problems.

intergovernmentalism (Box 1.4) Process or condition whereby decisions are reached by specifically defined cooperation between or among governments. Consensus is usually the decision rule and sovereignty is not directly undermined.

internal market More than a free trade area, an internal market signifies the free trade of goods, services, people and capital. Also known as the single market.

legitimacy The right to rule and make political decisions. More generally, the idea that 'the existing political institutions are the most appropriate ones for society' (Lipset 1963).

liberal intergovernmentalism A theory of European integration which assumes that the most important decisions in the development of the EU reflect the preferences of national governments rather than supranational organizations.

Monnet method (Box 8.1) Named after Jean Monnet, French civil servant and architect of the ECSC, the 'Monnet method' refers to integration proceeding incrementally and through small functional steps.

multilevel governance (Box 1.4) A term denoting a system of overlapping and shared powers between actors on the regional, national, and supranational (sometimes international) levels.

neofunctionalism A theory of European integration which assumes that economic integration in certain sectors will provoke further integration in other sectors. Economic integration can, in turn, lead to political integration and the formation of integrated supranational institutions.

new institutionalism As applied to the EU, a theoretical approach that suggests institutions, including rules, norms, and informal practices, can mould behaviour of policy-makers (including national officials) in ways that governments neither plan nor control.

path dependency The idea (developed especially by new institutionalists) that once a particular or policy path or course of action is taken, it is extremely difficult to turn back because of the 'sunk costs' (time and resources already invested). Used to explain why even those policies that have outlived their usefulness sometimes remained unreformed.

'Perm Reps' Eurospeak for the Permanent Representatives (EU ambassador) and the Permanent Representations (similar to embassies) of each member state. Together the 'Perm Reps' from each of the member states make up Coreper.

pillars A shorthand term for describing the 'Greek temple' architecture created by the Maastricht Treaty, with the first pillar (the pre-existing European Community) and the second (foreign and security policy) and third (justice and home affairs) pillars together constituting the 'European Union'.

policy networks Clusters of actors, each of whom has an interest or stake in a given policy sector and the capacity to help determine policy success or failure. Scholars applying this notion argue that policy outcomes are determined in important ways by the structure of networks that exist in given policy sectors.

Qualified Majority Voting (QMV) (Box 2.2) Refers to the most commonly used voting method in the Council of Ministers. Under QMV large member states have more votes than small ones and specified numbers of votes constitute 'qualified majorities' or 'blocking minorities'.

Schengen Agreement (Box 2.2) An agreement stipulating the gradual abolition of controls at borders. Thirteen EU member states are now signatories (Ireland and the UK have partially opted out) as well as Norway and Iceland. Incorporated into the EU under the Amsteram Treaty.

Schuman plan (Box 2.3) A plan by the French Foreign Minister, Robert Schuman, in 1950 to combine the coal and steel industries of Germany and France, thus making war between them impossible. It eventually became the basis for the European Coal and Steel Community, launched by the Treaty of Paris (also in 1950).

sovereignty (Box 1.4) The ultimate political authority over people and territory.

supranationalism (see Box 1.4) Literally, 'above states or nations', supranational decisions are made by processes or institutions which are largely independent of national governments. The term is usually contrasted with *intergovernmentalism*.

subsidiarity (Box 1.4) The idea that action should be taken at the level of government which is best able to achieve policy goals, but as close to the citizens as possible.

'third countries' Refers to non-EU countries, often in context of trade relations.

tours de table (see Box 4.1) A device to sound out positions in the Council of Ministers by taking a 'tour around the table' and allowing each delegation to make a statement on a given subject.

transparency The process of making official documents and decision-making processes more open and accessible to the public.

Western European Union Established in 1954 as an intergovernmental defence alliance comprising the UK and the EEC Six. Later grew to 10 member states (with Austria, Denmark, Finland, Ireland, and Sweden as observers) before effectively being incorporated into the EU itself in 2002.

References

Abromeit, H. (1998), *Democracy in Europe: Legitimising Politics in a Non-State Polity* (New York and Oxford: Berghahn Books).

Amato, G., and Batt, J. (1999), *The Long-Term Implications of EU Enlargement: The Nature of the New Border* (Florence: European University Institute).

Allen, D. (1998), ' "Who speaks for Europe?" The Search for an Effective and Coherent External Policy', in J. Peterson and H. Sjursen (eds.), *A Common Foreign Policy for Europe? Competing Visions of the CFSP* (London and New York: Routledge).

Alston, P. (ed.) (1999), *The EU and Human Rights* (Oxford: Oxford University Press).

Andersen, S., and Eliassen, K. (eds.) (2001), *Making Policy in Europe*, 2nd edn. (London: Sage).

Armstrong, K., and Bulmer, S. (1998), *The Governance of the Single European Market* (Manchester: Manchester University Press).

Aspinwall, M. (1998), 'Collective Attraction—the New Political Game in Brussels', in J. Greenwood and M. Aspinwall (eds.), *Collective Action in the European Union* (London: Routledge).

Avery, G. (1995), 'The Commission's Perspective on the EFTA Accession Negotiations', *SEI Working Paper* (12) (Sussex University, European Institute).

Azzi, G. (2000), 'The Slow March of European Legislation: The Implementation of Directives', in K. Neunreither and A. Wiener (eds.), *European Integration after Amsterdam: Institutional Dynamics and Prospects for Democracy* (Oxford: Oxford University Press): 52–67.

Beetham, D., and Lord, C. (1998), *Legitimacy and the EU* (Harlow and New York: Addison Wesley Longman Ltd.).

Bellamy, R., and Warleigh, A. (eds.) (2001), *Citizenship and Governance in the European Union* (London and New York: Continuum).

Benelux 2001, *Memorandum on the Future of Europe* **www.europa.eu.int/futurum/documents/other/oth200601_en.htm**.

Bomberg, E. (1998), *Green Parties and Politics in the European Union* (London: Routledge).

Booker, C. (1996), 'Europe and Regulation: The New Totalitarianism', in M. Holmes (ed.), *The Eurosceptical Reader* (New York: St. Martin's Press): 186–204.

—— and North, R. (eds.) (1996), *The Castle of Lies: Why Britain Must Get Out of Europe* (London: Duckworth).

Bradley, K. (2002), 'The European Court of Justice', in Peterson and Shackleton (2002: 118–40).

Bretherton, C., and Vogler, J. (1999), *The European Union as a Global Actor* (London and New York: Routledge).

Bulmer, S. (1984), 'Domestic Politics and EC Policy-Making', *Journal of Common Market Studies* 21/4: 349–63.

—— (1998), 'New Institutionalism and the Governance of the Single European Market', *Journal of European Public Policy* 5/3: 365–86.

—— and Lequesne, C. (forthcoming), *The Member States of the European Union* (Oxford and New York: Oxford University Press).

Burley, A.-M., and Mattli, W. (1993), 'Europe Before the Court', *International Organization* 47/1: 41–76.

Caporaso, J. (1996), 'The European Union and Forms of State: Westphalian, Regulatory or Post-Modern?', *Journal of Common Market Studies* 34/1: 29–52.

—— (2001), 'The Europeanization of Gender Equality Policy and Domestic Structural Change', in Green Cowles, Caporaso, and Risse (2001: 21–43).

Cederman, L.-E. (ed.) (2000), *Constructing Europe's Identity: The External Dimension* (Boulder, CO: Lynne Rienner).

Claeys, P-H., Gobin, C., Smets, I., and Winand, P. (eds.) (1998), *Lobbying, Pluralism and European Integration* (Brussels: European Interuniversity Press).

Commission (1993), *Commission Communication: An Open and Structured Dialogue between the Commission and Special Interest Groups*, OJC 63 final, Brussels, 2.12.93.

Commission (2001a), *Discussion Paper: The Commission and Non-Governmental Organisations: Building a Stronger Partnership*, COM (2000) 11 final, Brussels 18. 01.2001, available on **www.europa.eu.int/comm./secretariat_general/sgc/ong/en/communication.pdf**.

—— (2001b), *European Governance: A White Paper*, COM (2001) 428 final, Brussels 25.7.2001.

—— (2001c), *European Union and Enlargement: Fact Sheet*, Directorate-General for Agriculture, available at: **www.europa.eu.int/comm/agriculture/index_en.htm**.

—— (2001d), *The Institutions and Bodies of the European Union—Who's Who in the European Union— What Difference Will the Treaty of Nice Make? A Guide for European Citizens* (Luxembourg: Commission) (ch. 3, table).

—— (2001e), 'Interim Report from the Commission to the Stockholm European Council: Improving and Simplifying the Regulatory Environment' COM (2001) 130 final, Brussels, 7.3.2001.

—— (2001f), *Report from the Commission: Third Report from the Commission on Citizenship of the Union*, COM (2001) 506 final, Brussels 7.9.2001.

—— (2002a), *External aid programmes: financial trends 1989–2001* (Brussels: EuropeAid Cooperation Office) February.

—— (2002b), *General Budget of the European Union for the Financial Year 2002. The Figures* (Luxembourg: Commission).

—— (2002c), *Report from the Commission to the European Parliament and the Council on the application of Directive 94/80/EC on the right to vote and to stand as a candidate in municipal elections*, COM (2002) 260 final, Brussels, 30.05.2002.

Committee of the Regions (2001), *Répertoire: Associations/Bureaux de représentation régional et communale à Bruxelles*, Brussels, Nov. 2001.

Corbett, R., Jacobs, F., and Shackleton, M. (2000), *The European Parliament*, 4th edn. (London: Cartermill).

Court of Auditors (2001), *Annual Report concerning the financial year 2000*, Nov. 2001.

Cowles, M. G. (1996), 'The EU Committee of AmCham: the Powerful Voice of American firms in Brussels', *Journal of European Public Policy* 3/3: 339–58.

Cram, L. (1997), *Policy-Making in the European Union: Conceptual Lenses and the Integration Process* (London and New York: Routledge).

—— (2001), 'Integration and Policy Processes in the European Union', in S. Bromley (ed.), *Governing the European Union* (London: Sage): 143–64.

—— Dinan, D., and Nugent, N. (eds.) (1999), *Developments in the European Union* (Basingstoke and New York: Palgrave).

Dahl, R. A. (1961), *Who Governs? Democracy and Power in an American City* (New Haven: Yale University Press).

—— (1994), 'A Democratic Dilemma: System Effectiveness versus Citizen Participation', *Political Science Quarterly* 109/1: 23–34.

Dehousse, R. (1998), *The European Court of Justice* (London: Macmillan).

Dinan, D. (1999), *Ever Closer Union: An Introduction to European Integration*, 2nd edn. (Boulder, CO: Lynne Rienner Publishers and Basingstoke: Palgrave).

Dimitrova, A., and Steunenberg, B. (2000), 'The Search for Convergence of National Policies in the European Union: An Impossible Quest?', *European Union Politics* 1/2: 201–26.

Duchêne, F. (1994), *Jean Monnet: The First Statesman of Interdependence* (New York: Norton).

Earnshaw, D., and Wood, J. (1999), 'The European Parliament and Biotechnology Patenting: Harbinger of the Future?', *Journal of Commercial Biotechnology* 5/4: 294–307.

Egan, M. P. (2001), *Constructing a European Market: Standards, Regulation, and Governance* (Oxford and New York: Oxford University Press).

Eichengreen, B., and Frieden, J. A. (eds.) (2001), *The Political Economy of European Monetary Unification* (Boulder, CO: Westview Press).

EU Committee of the American Chamber of Commerce in Belgium (2002), *Guide to the European Parliament 2002–2004* (Brussels: EU Committee) (April).

Eurobarometer (2001), 'Candidate countries Eurobarometer', Autumn 2001, no 56. Available at: **www.europa.eu.int/comm/public_opinion/cceb/aceb20011_summary.pdf**.

Eurobarometer (2002a), 'Eurobarometer Special Survey 56.3: Getting Information on Europe, the enlargement of the EU, and support for European integration'. Available at: **www.europa.eu.int/comm/public_opinion/archives/eb/eb56_3/esumm_eu15.pdf**.

Eurobarometer (2002b) *Standard Eurobarometer 57* (Brussels: European Commission), June 2002. Available at **www.europa.eu.int/comm/public_opinion/archives/eb/eb57/eb57_en.htm** (ch. 11).

European–American Business Council (2001) *The United States and Europe: Jobs, Investment and Trade*, 7th edn. (Washington, DC: European–American Business Council).

European Monetary Institute (1999), *Press Release, 'The euro banknotes and the partially sighted'*, 14 Feb 99. **www.ecb.int/emi/press/press05e.htm**.

Eurostat (2002), available at: **www.europa.eu.int/comm/eurostat/Public/datashop/**.

Everts, S. (2002), *Shaping a Credible EU Foreign Policy* (London: Centre for European Reform).

Falkner, G. (2000), 'How Pervasive are Euro-Politics? Effects of EU Membership on a New Member State', *Journal of Common Market Studies* 38/2: 223–50.

—— Muller, W., Edwe, M., Hiller, K., Steiner, G., and Trattnigg, R. (1999), 'The Impact of EU Membership on Policy Networks in Austria: Creeping Change beneath the Surface', *Journal of European Public Policy* 6/3: 496–516.

Fawcett, L., and Hurrell, A. (eds.) (1996), *Regionalism in World Politics: Regional Organization and International Order* (Oxford and New York: Oxford University Press).

Fierke, K., and Wiener, A. (1999), 'Constructing Institutional Interest: EU and Nato Enlargement', *Journal of Public Policy Studies* 6/5: 721–42.

Fischer, J. (2000), 'From Confederacy to Federation—Thoughts on the finality of European integration', **www.auswaertiges-amt.de/6_archiv/2/r/r000512b.htm**.

Flora, P. (1999), *State Formation, Nation Building and Mass Politics: The Theory of Stein Rokkan* (Oxford: Oxford University Press).

Forwood, G. (2001), 'The Road to Cotonou: Negotiating a Successor to Lomè', *Journal of Common Market Studies* 39/3: 423–42.

Friis, L., and Murphy, A. (2000), 'Eastern Enlargement—A Complex Juggle', in M. Green Cowles and M. Smith (eds.), *Risks, Reforms, Resistance or Revival: The State of the European Union* (Oxford: Oxford University Press): 186–204.

Galloway, D. (2001), *The Treaty of Nice and Beyond: Realities and Illusions of Power in the EU*, UACES Contemporary European Studies Series (London: Continuum).

George, S. (1996), *Politics and Policy in the European Union* (Oxford: Oxford University Press).

—— (1998), *An Awkward Partner: Britain in the European Community*, 3rd edn. (Oxford and New York: Oxford University Press).

Gillingham, J. (1991), *Coal, Steel and the Rebirth of Europe, 1945–1955* (Cambridge: Cambridge University Press).

Ginsberg, R. (2001), *The European Union in International Politics: Baptism by Fire* (Boulder, CO: and Oxford: Rowman and Littlefield).

Glarbo, K. (2001), 'Reconstructing a Common European Foreign Policy', in T. Christiansen, K. E. Jorgensen, and A. Weiner (eds.), *The Social Construction of Europe* (London and Thousand Oaks, CA: Sage): 22–31.

Grabbe, H. (1998), 'A Partnership for Accession? The Implications for EU Conditionality for the Central and Eastern European Applicants', *Robert Schuman Centre Working Paper*, No. 12 (Florence: European University Institute).

—— (2001), 'Profiting from Enlargement', *Centre for European Reform*, CER-pamphlet June 2001.

Gray, O. (1998), 'The Structure of Interest Group Representation in the EU: Some Observations of a Practitioner', in Claeys et al. (1998: 281–301).

Gray, M., and Stubb, A. (2001), 'The Nice Treaty: Negotiating a Poisoned Chalice?', in G. Edwards and G. Wiessala (eds.), *The Annual Review of the EU 2000/2001 (Journal of Common Market Studies)*: 5–24.

Green Cowles, M., Caporaso, J., and Risse, T. (eds.) (2000), *Transforming Europe: Europeanization and Domestic Change* (Ithaca, NY: Cornell University Press).

Greenwood, J. (1997), *Representing Interests in the European Union* (London: Macmillan Press).

Groupe gouvernance AJM (2001), *Contributions sur la gouvernance*, Commission of the European Communities Secretariat General (Débat public sur l'Avenir de l'Europe) at **www.europa.eu.int/futurum/documents/press/jmgouv01.pdf**.

Gustavsson, S. (1998), 'Defending the Democratic Deficit', in A. Weale and M. Nentwich (eds.), *Political Theory and the European Union: Legitimacy, Constitutional Choice and Citizenship* (London: Routledge/ECPR): 63–81.

Haas, E. (1958), *The Uniting of Europe: Political, Social, and Economic Forces, 1950–7* (Stanford, CA: Stanford University Press).

——(1964), *Beyond the Nation-State: Functionalism and International Organization* (Stanford, CA: Stanford University Press).

—— (2001) 'Does Constructivism Subsume Neo-functionalism?', in T. Christiansen, K. E. Jorgensen, and A. Weiner (eds.), *The Social Construction of Europe* (London and Thousand Oaks, CA: Sage).

Haas, P. M. (1999), 'Compliance with EU Directives: Insights from International Relations and Comparative Politics', *Journal of European Public Policy* 5/1: 17–37.

Hayes-Renshaw, F. (1999), 'The European Council and the Council of Ministers', in Cram et al. (1999: 23–43).

—— and Wallace, H. (1997), *The Council of Ministers* (Basingstoke and New York: Palgrave).

Hayward, J. (ed.) (1995), *The Crisis of Representation in Europe* (London: Frank Cass).

Hill, C. (ed.) (1983), *National Foreign Policies and European Political Cooperation* (London: George Allen & Unwin).

—— (ed.) (1996), *The Actors in Europe's Foreign Policy* (London and New York: Routledge).

—— (1998), 'Closing the capabilities-expectations gap?', in J. Peterson and H. Sjursen (eds.), *A*

Common Foreign Policy for Europe? Competing Visions of the CFSP (London and New York: Routledge): 18–38.

Hix, S. (1999), *The Political System of the European Union* (Basingstoke and New York: Palgrave).

Hodson, D., and Maher, I. (2001), 'The Open Method as a New Mode of Governance', *Journal of Common Market Studies* 39/4: 719–46.

Hoffmann, S. (1966), 'Obstinate or Obsolete: the fate of the Nation State and the case of Western Europe', *Daedalus* 95/3: 862–915 (reprinted in S. Hoffmann (1995) *The European Sisyphus: Essays on Europe 1964–1994* (Boulder, CO, and Oxford: Westview Press)).

—— (1995), *The European Sisyphus: Essays on Europe 1964–1994* (London and Boulder, CO: Westview).

Holmes, M. (ed.) (2001), *The Eurosceptical Reader 2* (Basingstoke and New York: Palgrave).

Hooghe, L. (ed.) (1996), *Cohesion Policy and European Integration: Building Multi-Level Governance* (Oxford: Oxford University Press).

—— (2001), *The European Commission and the Integration of Europe* (Cambridge: Cambridge University Press).

—— and Marks, G. (2001), *Multi-Level Governance and European Integration* (Lanham, MD:, and Oxford: Rowman and Littlefield Publishers, Inc.).

Howorth, J. (2001), 'European Defence and the Changing Politics of the European Union: Hanging Together or Hanging Separately?', *Journal of Common Market Studies* 39/4: 765–89.

IIE (Institute for International Economics) (2000), *Measuring the costs of economic protection in Europe* (Washington, DC: Institute for International Economics), available at: **http://www.iie.com**

Jeffrey, C. (2002), 'Social and Regional Interests: ESC and Committee of the Regions', in Peterson and Shackleton (2002: 326–46).

Joerges, C., Mény, Y., and Weiler, J. H. H. (eds.) (2000), *What Kind of a Constituion for What Kind of Polity?* (Florence: European University Institute).

—— —— —— (eds.) (2001), *Mountain or Molehill? A Critical Appraisal of the Commission White Paper on Governance*, Working Papers, Jean Monnet Program, Harvard University, at **www.jeanmonnetprogram.org/papers/01/010601.html**.

Jorgensen, K. E. (2002), 'Making the CFSP Work', in Peterson and Shackleton (2002: 186–209).

Josling, T. (1998), 'Can the CAP Survive Enlargement to the East?', in J. Redmond and G. G. Rosenthal (eds.), *The Expanding European Union—Past, Present, Future* (Boulder, CO, and London: Lynne Rienner Publishers), 17–40.

Keating, M., and Jones, B. (1985), *Regions in the European Community* (Oxford: Clarendon Press).

Keck, M. E., and Sikkink, K. (1998), *Activists Beyond Borders: Advocacy Networks in International Politics* (Ithaca, NY, and London: Cornell University Press).

Keohane, R. O. (2002), 'Ironies of Sovereignty: the European Union and World Order', *Journal of Common Market Studies* 40(4): forthcoming.

Keohane, R. O., and Nye Jr., J. S. (2001), *Power and Interdependence* (New York: Addison-Wesley Longman).

Kerremanns, D. (1998), 'The Political and Institutional Consequences of Widening; Capacity and Control in an Enlarged Council', in P.-H. Laurent and M. Maresceau (eds.), *The State of the European Union*, vol. 4: *Deepening and Widening* (Boulder, CO: Lynne Rienner): 87–109.

Krasner, S. (1984), 'Approaches to the State', *Comparative Politics* 16/2: 223–46.

Krueger, A. (1997), 'Free Trade Areas versus Customs Unions', *Journal of Development Economics* 54/1: 169–87.

Kurzer, P. (2001), *Markets and Moral Regulation: Cultural Change in the European Union* (Cambridge and New York: Cambridge University Press).

Laffan, B. (1989), 'While You are Over There in Brussels Get Us a Grant: The Management of the Structural Funds in Ireland', *Irish Political Studies* 4/1: 43–58.

—— (1996), 'The Politics of Identity and Political Order in Europe', *Journal of Common Market Studies*, 34/1: 81–101.

—— (1997), *The Finances of the European Union* (Basingstoke and New York: Palgrave).

—— (1998), 'The European Union: A Distinctive Model of Internationalisation', *European Journal of Public Policy* 5: 2.

—— (2001), 'Financial Control: The Court of Auditors and OLAF', in Peterson and Shackleton (2001: 233–53).

—— O'Donnell, R., and Smith, M. (2000), *Europe's Experimental Union: Re-thinking Integration* (London and New York: Routledge).

Landmarks (2002), *The European Public Affairs Directory* (Brussels: Landmarks sa/nv).

Laursen, F. (ed.) (2002), *The Amsterdam Treaty: National Preference Formation, Interstate Bargaining and Outcome* (Odense: Odense University Press).

Lehning, P., and Weale, A. (1997) (eds.), Citizenship, Democracy and Justice in the New Europe (London and New York: Routledge).

Leonard, D., and Leonard, M. (eds.) (2001), *The Pro-European Reader* (Basingstoke and New York: Palgrave).

Leonard, M. (ed.) (2000), *The Future Shape of Europe* (London: The Foreign Policy Centre).

Lequesne, C. (1993), *Paris-Bruxelles: Comment se fait la Politique Européenne de la France* (Paris: Presses de la Fondations Nationale des Sciences Politiques).

—— (2000), 'The Common Fisheries Policy: Letting the Little Ones Go?', in Wallace and Wallace (2000: 345–72).

Lindberg, L. (1963), *The Political Dynamics of European Economic Integration* (Stanford, CA: Stanford University Press).

—— and Scheingold, S. A. (1970), *Europe's Would-Be Polity: Patterns of Change in the European Community* (Englewood Cliffs, NJ: Prentice-Hall).

Lipset, S. M. (1963), *Political Man* (London: Mercury Books).

Lord, C. (1998), *Democracy in the European Union* (Sheffield: Sheffield Academic Press Ltd.).

McCormick, J. (2001), *Environmental Policy in the European Union* (Basingstoke and New York: Palgrave).

McDonagh, B. (1998), *Original Sin in a Brave New World: An Account of the Negotiation of the Treaty of Amsterdam* (Dublin: IEA).

McGowan, F. (2000), 'Competition Policy: The Limits of the European Regulatory State', in Wallace and Wallace (2000: 115–47).

McKay, D. (2001), *Designing Europe: Comparative Lessons from the Federal Experience* (Oxford and New York: Oxford University Press).

McKeever, R (1995) *Raw Judicial Power? The Supreme Court and American Society*, 2nd edn. (Manchester: Manchester University Press).

McNamara, K. (2001), 'Managing the Euro: The European Central Bank', in Peterson and Shackleton (2001: 164–85).

Majone, G. (1996), *Regulating Europe* (London and New York: Routledge).

—— (1999), 'The Regulatory State and its Legitimacy Problems', *West European Politics* 22/1: 1–24.

Majone, G. (2000), 'The Credibility Crisis of Community Regulation', *Journal of Common Market Studies* 38/2: 273–302.

—— (2002), 'Functional Interests—European Agencies', in Peterson and Shackleton (2002: 299–323).

Manners, I., and Whitman, R. G. (2000), *The Foreign Policies of European Union Member States* (Manchester and New York: Manchester University Press).

Marks, G., Hooghe, L., and Blank, K. (1996), 'European Integration from the 1980s: State-Centric v. Multi-Level Governance', *Journal of Common Market Studies* 34/3: 341–78.

Marks, G., Scharpf, F., Schmitter, P., and Streeck, W. (1996), *Governance in the European Union* (London: Sage).

Mayhew, A. (2000), 'Enlargement of the European Union', *Sussex European Institute*, SEI-working paper, No 39.

Mearsheimer, J. J. (2001), *The Tragedy of Great Power Politics* (New York and London: Norton).

Metcalfe, L. (2000), 'Reforming the Commission: Will Organizational Efficiency Produce Effective Governance?', *Journal of Common Market Studies* 38/5: 817–41.

Michalski, A., and Wallace, H. (1992), *The European Community: The Challenge of Enlargement* (London: Royal Institute of International Affairs).

Milward, A. (1984), *The Reconstruction of Western Europe, 1945–51* (Berkeley: University of California Press).

—— (1992), *The European Rescue of the Nation-State* (London: Routledge).

—— (2000), *The European Rescue of the Nation-State*, 2nd edn. (London: Routledge).

Moravcsik, A. (1993), 'Preferences and Power in the European Community: A Liberal Intergovernmentalist Approach', *Journal of Common Market Studies* 31/ 4: 473–524.

—— (1998), *The Choice for Europe: Social Purpose and State Power from Messina to Maastricht* (Ithaca, NY: Cornell University Press/London: UCL Press).

—— (2001), 'Despotism in Brussels? Misreading the European Union', *Foreign Affairs* 80/3: 114–22.

Morgan, R., and Bray, C. (1986), *Partners and Rivals in Western Europe: Britain, France and Germany* (Hampshire: Gower Press).

Nelsen, B., and Stubb, A. (eds.) (1998), *The European Union: Readings on the Theory and Practice of European Integration*, 2nd edn. (Boulder, CO: Lynne Rienner, and Basingstoke and New York: Palgrave).

The Netherlands (1990), *Government White Paper on the 1990 Intergovernmental Conference*, June.

Neunreither, K., and Wiener, A. (eds.) (2000), *European Integration After Amsterdam: Institutional Dynamics and Prospects for Democracy* (Oxford: Oxford University Press).

Nicolaïdis, K., and Howse, R. (eds.) (2001), *The Federal Vision: Legitimacy and Levels of Governance in the United States and the European Union* (Oxford and New York: Oxford University Press).

Nugent, N. (1999), *The Government and Politics of the European Union*, 4th edn. (Basingstoke and New York: Palgrave).

Nuttall, S. (2000), *European Foreign Policy* (Oxford and New York: Oxford University Press).

O'Donnell, R. (2000), *Europe: The Irish Experience* (Dublin: Institute for European Affairs).

Patten, C. (2001), 'In Defence of Europe's Foreign Policy', *Financial Times*, 17 October (available from **www.ft.com**).

Pierson, P. (1996), 'The Path to European Integration: A Historical Institutionalist Analysis', *Comparative Political Studies* 29/2: 123–63.

Peterson, J. (1995), 'Decision-Making in the EU: Towards a Framework for Analysis', *Journal of European Public Policy* 2/1: 69–73.

—— (1996), *Europe and America: The Prospects for Partnership*, 2nd edn. (London and New York: Routledge).

—— (1997), 'States, Societies and the European Union', *West European Politics* 20/4: 1–24.

—— (2002*a*), 'Europe, America and 11 September', *Irish Studies in International Affairs* 12/1.

—— (2002*b*), 'The College of Commissioners', in Peterson and Shackleton (2002: 71–92).

—— and Bomberg, E. (1999), *Decision-Making in the European Union* (London and New York: Palgrave).

—— and Cowles, M. G. (1998), 'Clinton, Europe and Economic Diplomacy: What Makes the EU different?', *Governance* 11/3: 251–71.

—— and Shackleton, M. (eds.) (2002), *The Institutions of the European Union* (Oxford: Oxford University Press).

—— and Sharp, M. (1998), *Technology Policy in the European Union* (Basingstoke: Macmillan).

—— and Sjursen, H. (eds.) (1998), *A Common Foreign Policy for Europe? Competing Visions of the CFSP* (London: Routledge).

Piening, C. (1997) *Global Europe: The EU in World Affairs* (Boulder, CO: Lynne Rienner).

Pollack, M. A., and Shaffer, G. C. (eds.) (2001), *Transatlantic Governance in the Global Economy* (Boulder, Colo., and Oxford: Rowman and Littlefield).

Preston, C. (1997), *Enlargement and Integration in the European Union* (London and New York: Routledge).

Putnam, R. (1988), 'Diplomacy and the Logic of Two-level Games', *International Organization* 42/3: 427–60.

Redmond, J., and Rosenthal, G. (eds.) (1998), *The Expanding European Union. Past, Present and Future* (Boulder, CO: Lynne Rienner).

Rieger, E. (2000), 'The Common Agricultural Policy: Politics Against Markets', in Wallace and Wallace (2000: 373–99).

Rittel, H. W. J., and Weber, M. (1973), 'Dilemmas in a General Theory of Planning', *Policy Sciences* 4/1: 155–69.

Rometsch, D., and Wessels, W. (1996), *The European Union and Member States: Towards Institutional Fusion?* (Manchester: Manchester University Press).

Rosamond, B. (2000), *Theories of European Integration* (London and New York: Palgrave).

Sandholtz, W., and Stone Sweet, A. (1998), *European Integration and Supranational Governance* (Oxford: Oxford University Press).

Sbragia, A. (2001), 'Italy Pays for Europe: Political Leadership, Political Choice, and Institutional Adaptation', in Green Cowles, Caporaso, and Risse (2001: 79–96).

Scharpf, F. W. (1999), *Governing in Europe: Effective and Democratic?* (Oxford and New York: Oxford University Press).

Schimmelfennig, F. (2001), 'The Community Trap: Liberal Norms, Rhetorical Action, and Eastern Enlargement of the European Union', *International Organization* 55/1: 47–80.

Sedelmeier, U., and Wallace, H. (2000), 'Eastern Enlargement—Strategy or Second Thoughts?', in Wallace and Wallace (2000: 425–60).

Short, C. (2000), 'Aid that doesn't help', *Financial Times*, 23 June (available from **www.ft.com**).

Siedentop, L. (2000), *Democracy in Europe* (London: Penguin Press).

Smith, K. E. (1999), *The Making of EU Foreign Policy: The Case of Eastern Europe* (Basingstoke and New York: Palgrave).

Smith, M. E. (1997), 'What's Wrong with the CFSP? The Politics of Institutional Reform', in Laurent and Maresceau (1997: 149–76).

Soetendorp, B. (1999), *Foreign Policy in the European Union* (London and New York: Longman).

Stevens, A., with Stevens, H. (2001), *Brussels Bureaucrats? The Administration of the European Union* (Basingstoke and New York: Palgrave).

Straw, J. (2002), *Reforming Europe: New Era, New Questions* (London: Foreign and Commonwealth Office).

Stubb, A. (1996), 'A Categorisation of Differentiated Integration', *Journal of Common Market Studies* 34/2: 283–95.

—— (2000), 'Negotiating Flexible Integration in the Amsterdam Treaty', in K. Neunreither and A. Wiener (eds.), *European Integration After Amsterdam: Institutional Dynamics and Prospects for Democracy* (Oxford: Oxford University Press).

—— (2002), *Negotiating Flexibility in the EU: Amsterdam, Nice and Beyond* (Basingstoke and New York: Palgrave).

Telo, M. (ed.) (2001), *European Union and the New Regionalism* (Aldershot and Burlington, VT: Ashgate).

Urwin, D. (1995), *The Community of Europe: A History of European Integration Since 1945*, 2nd edn. (London: Longman).

Van der Wende, M. (2001), 'The International Dimension in National Higher Education Policies: What Has Changed in Europe in the Last Five Years?', *European Journal of Education* 36/4: 431–41.

Vibert, F. (2001), *Europe Simple Europe Strong: The Future of European Governance* (Oxford: Polity Press).

Viner, J. (1950), *The Customs Union Issue* (New York: Carnegie Endowment for International Peace).

Walby, S. (1999), 'The New Regulatory State: The Social Powers of the European Union', *British Journal of Sociology* 50/1: 118–41.

Walker, D. (2000), *The Rebirth of Federalism*, 2nd edn. (Chatham, NJ: Chatham House).

Wallace, H. (1971), 'The Impact of the European Communities on National Policy-Making', *Government and Opposition* 6/4: 520–38.

—— (1973), *National Governments and the European Communities* (London: PEP/RIIA).

—— (1996), 'The Policy Process: A Moving Pendulum', in Wallace and Wallace (1996: 39–64).

—— (1997), 'Introduction', in H. Wallace and A. Young (eds.), *Participation and Policy-Making in the European Union* (Oxford: Clarendon Press).

—— (2000*a*), 'EU Enlargement: A Neglected Subject', in M. Green Cowles and M. Smith, *The State of the European Union: Risks, Reform, Resistance and Revival* (Oxford: Oxford University Press), 149–63.

—— (2000*b*), 'The Institutional Setting: Five Variations on a Theme', in Wallace and Wallace (2000: 3–36).

—— and Wallace, W. (eds.) (1996), *Policy-Making in the European Union*, 3rd edn. (Oxford: Oxford University Press).

—— —— (eds.) (2000), *Policy-Making in the European Union*, 4th edn. (Oxford and New York: Oxford University Press).

—— and Young, A. R. (eds.) (1997), *Participation and Policy-Making in the European Union* (Oxford: Clarendon Press).

Wallace, W. (1990), *The Dynamics of European Integration* (London: Pinter).

Weale, A., and Nentwich, M. (eds.) (1998), *Political Theory and the European Union: Legitimacy, Constitutional Choice and Citizenship* (London and New York: Routledge).

Weiler, J. H. H. (1999), *The Constitution of Europe* (Cambridge: Cambridge University Press).

—— (2002), 'Reassessing the Fundamentals: Integration in an Expanding EU', *Journal of Common Market Studies* 40(4): 555–63.

Wessels, W. (1997), 'The Growth and Differentiation of Multi-Level Networks: A Corporatist Mega-Bureaucracy or an Open City?', in Wallace and Young (1997: 17–41).

—— (2001), 'Nice Results: The Millennuium IGC in the EU's Evolution', *Journal of Common Market Studies* 39/2: 197–219.

Williams, S. (1991), 'Sovereignty and Accountability in the European Community', in R. O. Keohane and S. Hoffmann (eds.), *The New European Community: Decision Making and Institutional Change* (Boulder, CO: Westview Press): 155–76.

White, B. (2001), *Understanding European Foreign Policy* (Basingstoke and New York: Palgrave).

Whitman, R. G. (1998), *From Civilian Power to Superpower? The International Identity of the European Union* (Basingstoke and New York: Palgrave).

Woolcock, S. (2000), 'European Trade Policy: Global Pressures and Domestic Constraints', in Wallace and Wallace (2000: 373–99).

Zito, A. (2000), *Creating Environmental Policy in the European Union* (Basingstoke and New York: Palgrave).

Index*

NOTE: entries in bold indicate on which page a term is defined, whether in text, a box or the glossary.

---

* Compiled by John Peterson